THERE'S AN EASTER EGG
ON YOUR SEDER PLATE

THERE'S AN EASTER EGG
ON YOUR SEDER PLATE

Surviving Your Child's Interfaith Marriage

STEVEN CARR REUBEN

Westport, Connecticut
London

Library of Congress Cataloging-in-Publication Data

Reuben, Steven Carr.
There's an Easter egg on your seder plate : surviving your child's interfaith marriage / Steven
Carr Reuben.
    p. cm.
  Includes bibliographical references and index.
  ISBN 978–0–275–99339–9 (alk. paper)
    1. Interfaith marriage–United States.   2. Interfaith families—United States.   3. Jewish
families—Religious life—United States.   4. Parenting—Religious aspects—Judaism.
I. Title.
  HQ1031.R44   2008
  306.84′3–dc22   2007030220

British Library Cataloguing in Publication Data is available.

Library of Congress Catalog Card Number: 2007030220
ISBN: 978–0–275–99339–9

First published in 2008

Praeger Publishers, 88 Post Road West, Westport, CT 06881
An imprint of Greenwood Publishing Group, Inc.
www.praeger.com

Printed in the United States of America

The paper used in this book complies with the
Permanent Paper Standard issued by the National
Information Standards Organization (Z39.48–1984).

10 9 8 7 6 5 4 3 2 1

This book is dedicated to my family for teaching me the things that matter most in life. To my parents, Betty and Jack Reuben, who have always been role models of how to be the kind of adult you want your children to grow up to be; to my sisters, Ronna and Debra, whose grace, flexibility, and openness within their own interfaith marriages have taught me more lessons than I could ever enumerate; to my sister, Carolyn, who is the best writer I know and has always been my role model; to my daughter, Gable, whose remarkable talents continue to fill me with awe and joy; and to my life partner and wife, Didi, who is my soul mate and the love of my life.

CONTENTS

ACKNOWLEDGMENTS

I am deeply grateful to all the interfaith couples and families with whom I have had the privilege of working for the past thirty years. They have been a constant source of inspiration and faith in the essential goodness and loving nature of human beings regardless of religion, race, or culture. I hope this book serves them well.

I am also grateful to my agent, Linda Konner, who never gave up and had faith in me year after year, proposal after proposal. Thanks for making this happen.

A profound thank you to Suzanne Staszak-Silva, my editor, and all the staff at Praeger and Greenwood Publishing for their professionalism and patience.

Thanks as well to Saloni Jain, Project Manager at Aptara in Delhi, for seeing the project through and giving me my first personal experience of the real meaning of globalization.

Words alone can't express my gratitude to Lisa Rojany Buccieri of Editorial Services of Los Angeles, my personal editorial savior for her love and support and for being there every time I panicked to rescue me once again.

And of course thank you to my daughter, Gable, for being the best gift in my life and to my wife, Didi, for telling me every single day how much you love me and are proud of me—I am who I am because you are the love of my life and my life partner—without you nothing else would matter.

INTRODUCTION:
"THE INTERFAITH CHALLENGE"

In the last two decades, interfaith marriage has emerged as one of the primary cultural realities of North American religious life. Catholics are marrying Protestants, Methodists are marrying Lutherans, and there are millions of men and women involved in Jewish/Christian interfaith marriages, with the numbers growing by leaps and bounds each year.

The very face of religion in America is being steadily transformed. We no longer live in a neat patchwork quilt of distinct faiths and communities with clear, well-differentiated ideological boundaries. It is obvious to all that interfaith marriage is at an all-time high and will continue as a major cultural reality far into the future.

As the numbers of interfaith marriages continue their pattern of steady growth, it has become increasingly apparent that there was a need for a practical, supportive, nonjudgmental counseling book to help ease the emotional pain and bewilderment so often experienced by the parents of interfaith couples. Without question, it is the parents of those who intermarry who are the least prepared to cope with the wide range of spiritual, emotional, psychological, and family issues that interfaith marriages inevitably provoke. This book has been written to address exactly those needs, wrestle with exactly those issues, and help the parents of interfaith couples to be able to have the very best possible relationship with both their own children and the new family configuration that is suddenly an important part of their lives.

Usually, by the time a couple reaches the point in their relationship when they decide to get married, they have already gone through months or even years of talking about and living with their religious differences. If they are conscientious and at all serious in their recognition of the potential stresses and everyday challenges that will be a part of their interfaith lives, they have available numerous articles, books, and programs that can help them along their path to marital success. The same cannot be said for the parents of interfaith couples for whom there are precious few resources of any kind. This book has been written for them.

It is these same parents whom I have seen over the years demonstrate a remarkable and uncanny ability to live in a perpetual state of "interfaith denial," no matter how long their child has been involved with a man or woman from another religious background. It constantly amazes me how often they react with complete shock upon learning that their child has "suddenly" decided to intermarry, even if the couple has been living together for years.

Above all else, parents want their children to be happy. They want their children to find loving, supportive, nurturing, sensitive, and caring marital partners who will stand by them, provide for their needs, and help them to live productive and satisfying lives. But beyond those fundamental desires, they also very often have an unspoken and unacknowledged need to see their own values and beliefs perpetuated into the next generation, passed down to their grandchildren and the generations beyond.

Thus it is often the case that confronting the stark reality of interfaith marriage raises deep-seated feelings of guilt, failure, loss, and pain for the millions of parents whose children are making those marital choices every day. Hopefully, in the pages that follow, the parents of interfaith couples will learn how to successfully sort out their own mixed emotions as they discover clear, nonjudgmental advice as to how best to cope with the various interfaith situations that will now be an ongoing part of their lives.

Couples have the best chance for marital success if their relationship is built on a strong foundation of shared values, life experiences, and culture. That is why interfaith couples often find themselves straining to forge their own unique religious lifestyles against the backdrop of individual religious beliefs and life experiences.

In the middle of this already difficult situation, facing the overt hostility and lack of support shown by so many angry and frustrated parents only adds unnecessary stumbling blocks along the road to the creation of a successful, loving marriage.

It is my hope that this book will be a valuable source of information, guidance, and support for parents of every religion, race, and cultural background.

It contains concrete, practical suggestions about how to maintain the best possible relationship with their children and be a positive influence upon their grandchildren. It addresses directly the issues of coping with prejudice (theirs and others), feelings of failure, what to say to friends and family, the proper role of an interfaith grandparent, forming positive relationships with in-laws of another faith and culture, and presents concise explanations of key differences among various major religions.

Hopefully, this book will serve as a personal guide and counselor to allow them to spend time alone or with their spouse or partner, learning how best to cope with the new and sometimes uncertain demands placed upon them by their child's interfaith relationship. In ages past when a child intermarried, it was inevitably seen as a rejection of their parents and their values, a rejection of their family and their religious traditions, or a running away from their individual religious identity. Today, the landscape of interfaith marriages is very different. This book is designed to provide parents whose children intermarry with the tools to continue creating the most loving, supportive, and emotionally fulfilling relationship they possibly can with their children and grandchildren throughout their lives.

One

WHERE IT ALL STARTS—UNDERSTANDING INTERFAITH DATING

THE "INTERFAITH DENIAL SYNDROME"

If we are lucky, romance eventually comes to us all. We breathlessly watch it unfold on television and the big screen in theaters from the time we can first walk. We dream of it as teenagers and play-act at love as brides and grooms with our girlfriends and boyfriends or read romance novels in the darkness of our bedrooms at night. We think about it, sing about it, write about it, read about it, fantasize our prince will come or we will sweep the princess off her feet and always, always live "happily ever after." It is the universal dream, the universal goal, and in many spiritual traditions and with many spiritual masters it is the ultimate fulfillment of why we are here on earth in the first place—to learn to love.

And yet for all our dreaming and all our scheming, all our hoping, and all our planning, most of us end up falling in love at the most unlikely times and often with the most unlikely partners. We meet our loves in a class or on a bus, in a club or on a blind date, through friends or on the Internet, at church or synagogue or temple or mosque, through an introduction from a mutual friend or in the next cubicle at work. Indeed, the arrows of Cupid seem to fly indiscriminately—and when we are struck, we fall.

According to the Adherents.com Web site, in the United States today there are approximately 123 million Protestants, 75 million Catholics, 6 million Jews, 5 million Muslims, 7 million Anglicans, a million Buddhists, and millions of people with a wide variety of other religious denominations and identifications.[1] Though we hardly ever speak of the "melting pot" anymore, we are a remarkably rich casserole of religions, races, ethnic backgrounds, faiths, languages, and cultures who live and work and play, and go to school side by side every day. Is it any wonder then that interfaith marriage is perhaps the primary cultural reality of our age?

Why Me? How I Became an Interfaith "Expert"

I cannot remember ever thinking about interfaith marriage until I was sixteen years old. I grew up in a non-Orthodox Jewish family in Santa Monica, California, with parents who were very involved with our local Reform synagogue (for explanations on "Orthodox" and "Reform" Judaism see Chapter 10), and my social life mostly involved Jews as well. My friends were primarily from my synagogue religious school. I even went to Jewish summer camp each year. And growing up in the 1950s none of my parents' friends (and none of my friends' parents) had interfaith marriages. So it never crossed my mind until the year in which I turned sixteen. That was the year my oldest sister suddenly announced that she was getting married to a man she had met at work who was Greek Orthodox.

Not to be overly dramatic, but around my house, from that moment on, life as I knew it was over. My parents were devastated at the news; and having no experience at all with intermarriage and not knowing anyone else who had dealt with this trauma or any place to turn for help or support, they were totally unprepared to handle the situation. Unlike today, forty-two years ago there were no books, articles, magazines, Web sites, discussion groups, or hardly anyone at all in the Jewish community willing to talk out loud about intermarriage. If they did, they considered it a betrayal of thousands of years of Jewish life. Or they accused those involved of voluntarily doing to the Jewish people what Hitler failed to do to us: wiping out the next generation of Jews through assimilation and abandonment. It all began with marrying outside the faith (for more on coping with feelings of loss, failure, and guilt see Chapter 3).

That year, it was not a pretty picture around my home. Everything related to the wedding and all talk about my sister's upcoming marriage seemed to resonate with gloom, a heaviness that portended disaster. I was not sure whether the impending doom was my parents' expectation of the fate of my sister's marriage or more a reflection of their own feelings of failure and loss at the broken image of the family and grandchildren they had always imagined having a Jewish future. Either way, as an adolescent watching my parents going through such deep anguish and emotional distress (to the point that I heard my mom crying in her room every night for weeks), it had such a powerfully negative impact on me that I made a personal vow that I would never marry someone who was not Jewish because I would never be the one to put my parents through that again.

The wedding came and went (with my own band at the time performing as the entertainment). Life went on. Soon, my sister and her husband produced first one and then a second grandson whom my parents adored; and my parents' relationship with my sister and her Greek Orthodox husband mellowed quite a bit. Over time both my parents and the Jewish world in which we lived had become much more conscious and aware of the complex dynamics of intermarriage, with all the challenges and opportunities for fulfillment and success it represented. By the time that my youngest sister (I have three) married a wonderful man who was both Catholic and Puerto Rican and moved with him to Puerto Rico to live and raise her own family, my parents' attitudes had taken a 180 degree turn; he was welcomed openly, warmly, and completely into their home as part of the family.

Yet in spite of the tremendous changes that my parents have experienced in their attitudes toward intermarriage through all these years, the early scars and pain that their powerful initial rejection of my first brother-in-law caused have really never healed. Thus, I learned early on in my experiences with intermarriage that there are things we do and words we say that no matter what happens in the future or how our attitudes personally change, we might never be able to take back.

These initial experiences of my youth where I saw how unprepared my parents were to cope with the challenges of their child's intermarriage were what first gave me the idea of creating tools to help families who were coping with the complex emotional and spiritual challenges of intermarriage.

I am certain that these early intermarriage experiences with my own family and the resulting trauma surrounding my sister's wedding were primary reasons why, from the moment I was ordained as a rabbi over thirty years ago to this very day, I have been one of the few rabbis in the country who have always been willing to officiate at interfaith marriage ceremonies. I have chosen to do whatever I can to create the most positive, loving, supportive, nurturing, spiritual matrimonial experiences for each couple and each family at every wedding.

My involvement with counseling and marrying thousands of interfaith couples throughout the decades is also what led me to write the two books *"But How Will You Raise the Children?" A Guide to Interfaith Marriage* (Pocket Books, 1987) and *Making Interfaith Marriage Work* (Prima Publishing, 1994). As a result of the books and articles I have written I have had the opportunity to travel the country speaking to couples and their parents and extended families, to appear on television and radio shows that reach out to intermarried families, and to conduct workshops and give lectures about interfaith marriage, and the challenges of transforming interfaith relationships from traumatic experiences to building blocks to a better future.

Working with interfaith couples and their families throughout the last thirty years, I have watched as resources for intermarried couples have expanded exponentially to include scores of books, Web sites, articles in magazines and newspapers, and intermarried support groups in every metropolitan city in America. Yet throughout this time, despite the fact that the resources for couples have continued to grow, the one area I have seen ignored time and time again is the complex emotional, spiritual, and social challenges that face parents whose children intermarry. That is why I have written this book—so that no parent will ever again go through what my own parents experienced so many years ago.

With interfaith marriage today an indisputable cultural reality, you would think that the true story I am about to share with you would no longer constitute the norm. But despite decades of growing numbers of interfaith relationships in North America, the experience of Tom, a Christian, and Marcy, who was Jewish (all names in the book have been changed to assure anonymity), remains all too common.

Theirs was a typical college romance. Tom and Marcy met in Spanish class in their freshman year and began their friendship by exchanging class notes and helping each other with homework. Soon they were walking to class together, eating lunch on the lawn, and filling their hours discussing the challenges of being a college student in the twenty-first century. They engaged in heated discussions about the great issues of the day; they argued passionately over campus politics; and they schemed about how to change the world they had inherited from their parents into one that was more compassionate, tolerant, and egalitarian.

Inevitably their relationship grew deeper and then naturally turned to romance, with the flush of new love and the thrill that comes from discovering another human being who shares your dreams and has a similar outlook on life.

By the time of their graduation four years later, they had accepted each other's love as their natural state of being and both knew that the inevitable next step would be marriage and a shared life. Throughout their growing relationship during the previous four years, they had often visited each other's parents and families back home together as a couple. Naturally, they assumed that their parents would not only expect the marriage, but would also be excited and happy for them as well.

Imagine their surprise when the day arrived in which they both proudly presented their respective parents with the exciting news of their formal engagement, only to discover that both Tom's and Marcy's parents suffered from what I have come to call the "Interfaith Denial Syndrome."

As any bride-to-be, Marcy was looking forward to the beaming smiles of pride and joy that she would see reflected in her mother's eyes at the announcement of her daughter's long-awaited engagement. Instead, even though her parents had always seemed to like Tom very much, with their voices choking back emotion, they announced that even though Tom was "a very nice young man" they were 100 percent against Marcy marrying him. Moreover, they were upset, disappointed, and hurt that she could seriously consider it after how she had been raised and considering how important her Jewish religious tradition was to her family.

Tom fared little better with his own parents. They, too, were unhappy that his college romance had become much more serious. They told him that "although she is a lovely girl and we have always been quite fond of her and as gracious as we could be," they certainly hoped that Tom understood the deeper implications of what he was doing and why they would naturally be upset and think it was ill-advised for him to seriously consider marriage with Marcy.

Tom and Marcy were dumbfounded. What had happened to the parents they had grown up with? The ones who had always taught them the importance of judging a person not by his color, nor religion, nor language, nor ethnic origin, but by his character and by how he acted in the world? What happened to all the egalitarian values that they thought their parents embraced and presented as the ideals to strive for in our society? What happened to the liberal political pronouncements that they had grown up hearing their parents passionately defend?

What happened was a case of the "Interfaith Denial Syndrome" rearing its ugly head. Ultimately, both sets of parents suddenly realized that when push came to shove, their professed ideals seemed to take a back seat to the prejudice, fear, and guilt that their respective religious traditions had ingrained in all of them.

Marcy and Tom's situation is so typical, in fact, that in some ways they are the reason that I have written this book. It is to help the Toms and Marcys of the world continue to have the best possible relationship with their parents by giving their parents tools. These tools will help parents unpack those prejudices, and will give them a step-by-step guide to achieving the lifetime of harmony, of mutual respect, and of affection that they seek between themselves and their adored children.

Tom and Marcy could not understand why their parents seemed to accept without judgment the years of dating, yet angrily rejected the suggestion of marriage as if it were a kind of deep, personal betrayal. For their parents, betrayal exactly described how the announcement felt and how they experienced it. How could their children reject some of their most precious and important values?

Tom and Marcy had never encountered prejudice regarding their relationship before. They had always found each other so intellectually and morally compatible that it never occurred to them that religion would ever be a problem. Suddenly they were thrust into a confrontation with their differences and the fears of their parents—and both were totally unprepared for it.

What is even more poignant is that their parents had never experienced the deeply rooted emotions *they* were feeling. Both sets of parents had espoused and lived by similar values their entire lives. They believed that one's religion did not make one a good or bad person. They believed that all religions contained many important truths about life and the world in which we live, and that people should be judged by who they are and how they act, not by the religion or group to which they belonged. They believed fervently in all these ideals and values—values that they thought they had passed on to their children. So they were even more shocked than their kids to discover that when those values were put to the test, a whole host of hidden fears, anxieties, and prejudices suddenly appeared, manifesting themselves in loud, unexpected, and ugly ways.

It is understandable why their children were so taken aback by the strength of their parents' rejection of their proposal of interfaith marriage. "After all," said Marcy, "of course I was raised to know that I was Jewish, but my family was never particularly religious. I don't understand why all of a sudden my parents feel so strongly about Judaism when they never went to temple, except perhaps once a year on the High Holy Days. They never seemed to care if I went to Jewish religious school or had a Bat Mitzvah or got a Jewish education or not."

Tom was also concerned upon hearing his parents' strong negative reaction. Was there suddenly a touch of anti-Semitic prejudice in his family, even though he had never experienced it before? Since he had not gone to church much as a child—and not at all since he was about twelve years old—he could not understand his parents' strong objections. In reality his parents' objections had absolutely nothing to do with anti-Jewish prejudice. Their objections were the result of the typical case of parents resisting the idea that their children might grow up differently than they imagined or marry someone so different from what they had pictured.

The "Interfaith Denial Syndrome" is simply that: the denial that so many parents live with that, in spite of the interfaith world in which their kids grow up, they will somehow be immune to its reality. They, often unconsciously, expect that their children will naturally choose to fall in love with and marry someone from the same religious, cultural, racial, or ethnic tradition in which they were raised. Sometimes the denial is so strong, so real for us parents, that we simply refuse to see what is right in front of our faces until it hits us like a ton of bricks.

This denial is the case for tens of thousands of parents every year. The sudden confrontation with the reality of life in America today is not easy for many parents to accept. The inevitable recognition that we live in a world of cultural diversity and that there is no going back to some fantasy about a homogenous society of yesteryear is a dramatic shock and difficult for many to accept. But accept it we must if we are to live in the real world and find ways to maintain a loving, nurturing, supportive, mutually respectful relationship with our children as they grow into adults—adults who make their own decisions about how and with whom they live their lives.

The purpose of this book is to provide help to all of us who as parents must confront the difficult reality of what it means for our children to grow into adults with minds, dreams, and lives of their own.

Confronting the "Interfaith Denial Syndrome" is a crucial first step for any parent who is suddenly facing the reality of a child's engagement to someone from another religion. Step one is to recognize our own ability to deny in our own lives what we so readily see in the lives of our friends and extended families. Given the number of interfaith marriages that take place in North America every year, I can say with total confidence that if anyone reading this book is willing to look dispassionately at the lives of their own extended families and friends, I am sure they will immediately be able to identify interfaith marriages among them. Interfaith marriage is no longer an anomaly, it is a pervasive cultural reality.

So if this is true of so many other families you know, why should it be such a shock to discover the same reality in your own life? Overcoming this denial is absolutely necessary if you have any desire in establishing or maintaining a relationship of mutual respect and love with your child.

Step one is accepting the reality of your child's impending interfaith marriage. Step two is sitting down with your child and letting him or her know that the most important thing in the world to you is their happiness and success in life, and that if this relationship is good for them, then it will be good for you as well.

Many parents will read these words and say to themselves, "Impossible!" Others might say, "Can't I just tell my child that they are making the biggest mistake of their lives?" Still others will insist, "Can't I tell him how much more difficult and complicated his life will be because of this decision?" And the ones practiced in guilt might offer up, "Can't I tell her that she is insulting all the generations of our family who have followed the precepts of our religious tradition in the past?"

Yes, of course you can tell your child all of these things if you want to. You just have to be willing to accept the consequences of *your* choices and the reactions that your children will have if you choose to continue down this path of rejecting *their* choices. You will be creating a situation whereby your child is forced to choose between you and your feelings and the feelings of the person your child loves and has made a commitment to spend his or her life with. You can do it if you want, but my experience is that nearly 100 percent of the time if you make your child choose between you and the love of his or her life, you will not be happy with the outcome of that choice.

WHEN IS IT TOO LATE TO SAY SOMETHING TO YOUR CHILD?

Parents often ask, "If I don't agree with my child's decision, isn't it my obligation as a parent to share my concerns with my child? Isn't that always my role as a parent—to do my best to protect my child from pain and sorrow and making the wrong choices in life? After all when is it too late to say something to my child?"

So when *is* it too late to say something to your child? It's already too late. Once they walk in hand in hand with someone they love to announce their engagement and upcoming marriage, it's too late. It's too late when they have been dating someone of a different faith or culture for two or three or four years. It's too late when they have already gone away to college. And it's too late when they are old enough to have already moved out of your home and into their own.

Talking with your children about how you feel about interfaith marriage needs to take place all throughout their childhood while you are raising them in whatever religious tradition you cherish. It needs to be an organic part of your daily or weekly spiritual lifestyle so that they learn the lessons of why it is important to you from their everyday experiences of living their religion each day. And the reality is that regardless of how much you talk the talk and walk the walk, your child may make choices that you may not expect or desire.

In truth, at any time in their lives there is very little you can say to guarantee that your children will grow up and marry within your own religious tradition. Studies of interfaith relationships seem to indicate that even children who grow up greatly valuing their own religious traditions are not immune to the possibility of falling in love with someone from another religious tradition. Our world is simply too diverse and our society is simply too open.

HOW TO DISCUSS YOUR BELIEFS BEFORE THERE IS AN IMPENDING MARRIAGE

Regardless of the difficulty in avoiding the reality of interfaith marriage, be assured that as a parent there are many ways that you can legitimately discuss your beliefs and feelings with your children in such a way as to often have a significant impact on the choices that they make in their lives. How do you talk with your children about your beliefs? How do you talk with your children about how you feel about your traditions and culture in a way that impresses upon them how important they are to you and how strongly you feel about your desire for them to marry someone from within your own religious or cultural group?

The first step is to realize that your children will learn these lessons more from what you do than from what you say. It was James Baldwin who once famously said, "Children have never been very good at listening to their elders, but they have never failed to imitate them."[2] You are always the number one primary role model for your children—whether you want to be or not.

From their earliest ages, your children are watching everything you do and taking it all in. Every time a parent wonders about how to deal with an issue between themselves and their children, the best advice is: Be the kind of adult you want your children to grow up to become. Behave the way you would like them to. It is not a surefire guarantee that the behavior you desire will always be reflected in your children, but it is ultimately the only measure you can take that really matters.

Everyone has heard the parenting exhortation, "Do as I say not as I do," and every one of us knows how foolish that is. But in every arena it is your own behavior that matters most—not your professed beliefs. That is why the best way to discuss your beliefs with your children is to live your life in such a way that they experience the value of your beliefs in their daily lives as well as seeing them in action in yours.

Your children need to grow up experiencing what makes your religious tradition beautiful, meaningful, and inspirational for you. You need to be telling them all throughout their childhood what matters to you most about who you are and why your religious tradition helps you to find a sense of meaning and purpose in life. Living a purposeful life is an inspirational model as much for your children as it is for adults. Heartfelt beliefs that are lived out on a daily basis can be powerful lessons for your entire family.

Of course, if you have picked up this book, chances are that you already have a child old enough to be dating, or engaged to, or married to someone from another religious tradition. In that case, how do you discuss the importance of your personal religious convictions with your child even at this late date? You do so with tact, sensitivity, respect, and love.

Even if you have a child who is already dating someone of another religion you can still broach the subject of interfaith marriage. The best approach is to be straightforward, unapologetic, and yet sensitive at the same time. You might sit with your child when he or she comes home from college for winter or summer break and simply say that you want to have an open, heart-to-heart talk for your own sake as much as for theirs.

You have a right as a parent to make sure that they know how you feel about issues that are important to you. Without being judgmental or accusing them of betraying you and your ancestors, you can tell them from your own personal perspective how you feel about your own religion, why it is important to you, and why your desire would be for them to ultimately marry someone from the same religious background, raising their own kids with the same traditions that they were raised with.

The most significant key to having a positive experience when talking with your children about the importance of your religion in your life is to keep the conversation in the first person present tense, that is, "I feel _____ about being Catholic/Lutheran/Jewish/Buddhist/Muslim/etc. And it is important to me because it gives me _____ in my life." When the conversation is about *you* and not about your child nor how upset you are or how wrong they are for what they are doing or for how they are living their life, they are more likely to actually hear what you have to say. Meet the issue head on, personalizing it to your own life, but do not be a bully about it.

You can discuss your beliefs with your child at any time and make it clear to them how important it is to you that they marry someone from a similar background and religion as long as it comes across as an explanation of how you feel and what is important to you—and not as an attack against them. No one likes to be attacked, especially by one's parents. Every child carries resentment against his or her parents for innumerable childhood hurts—both real and imagined. Attacking your child for his or her adult decisions only brings out these childhood hurts and resentments and is most likely to push them away rather than bringing them closer to you.

MAINTAINING THE BEST RELATIONSHIP YOU CAN WHILE SHARING YOUR OWN BELIEFS AND RELIGIOUS COMMITMENTS

How can you maintain the best relationship possible with your child while at the same time share your personal beliefs and religious convictions? It is important to always keep in mind what your ultimate goals are in having any conversation with your child about interfaith relationships. You will be better off if your goal is not "to change my child so that he or she will never marry someone from another faith," even if that is what you fervently desire. A better goal to have is "to make sure my child knows the values that I cherish, the importance of my religious tradition in my own life, and the greater sense of meaning in life that my religion gives me." Taking this approach assures that no matter what decision your child ultimately makes regarding who he or she marries in life and how they raise their children together, you are likely to be able to find numerous ways and opportunities to communicate lovingly the importance *to you* of *your* religious values.

After all, your children will end up making up their own minds and making their own decisions no matter what you do. If you want to maintain the best possible relationship with them you must do what you can to make sure that they always know that they are loved and accepted by you, regardless of whether or not you agree with the individual decisions that they make from one day to the next.

Your children need to know that it is *who they are* that you love and that what you are taking issue with is their individual decisions. They need to feel your parental acceptance of who they are—even when you would have made a different choice.

It is a fundamental reality of human existence that children always desire their parents' approval throughout their lives, no matter how old they might be. That is why what you say is so important to your children and why your rejection of them if they marry someone from another faith can be painful and so destructive that it has often driven apart parents and children for the rest of their lives.

What you do not want to do is react in such a way as to create an estrangement from your child that cannot be repaired. In many families, the initial reaction of the parents to the announcement of an impending engagement is all the child ever heard and all the information the fiancé needed to make a lifetime judgment about his or her in-laws. Even long after the in-laws had accepted the relationship and made peace with their own child's decision, opening up their arms to the son-or daughter-in-law and their children, the initial rejection hung like a dark cloud over every single moment together *for the rest of their lives.*

Such anger, rejection, and bad blood poison the parent–child relationship. This is both tragic and unnecessary. The most important thing to remember is it is never too late to do the right thing in life. As long as you are still alive, you have the opportunity to repair broken relationships and mend torn hearts. Your children are never too old to want their parents' acceptance of them and their decisions, and to be proud of who they are as people.

That is why the most productive way to maintain the best possible relationship with your child is to focus on the values that you *do* share rather than the values that you *seemingly* do not. When parents examine the implications of the choices that their children make, nine times out of ten they realize that the choices their children make in life are still, fundamentally, reflections of their own values as seen through their children's eyes. For example, if you have taught your children to judge people not by their color or religion but by the content of their character and how they act in the world, you can pretty much guarantee that if they have chosen someone to love from another religious tradition, it is because they see in that person a reflection of the values and ethics and morals that you have taught them in the first place.

Certainly if you have taught your children that there are many different ways to experience God's presence in our world and that there is not one religion that is "right" while all the others are wrong, you can hardly be surprised if your children have taken you at your word and fallen in love with someone whose spiritual understanding differs from your own. In such a case it seems obvious that a child might legitimately believe that you would embrace anyone from any religious tradition as yet another legitimate person through which God becomes known in the world.

Regardless of how you may differ in beliefs from your own child (and often it is more a matter of degree and style than of substance), you will best serve the long-range interests of your parent–child relationship if you act to preserve open lines of communication and continually reinforce how much you will always cherish and respect your children simply because *they are your children.*

TALKING SO THEY WILL LISTEN AND LISTENING SO THEY WILL TALK

One of the greatest parenting skills you can develop is the skill of talking so that your children will listen and listening so that your children will talk. If your children are constantly on the defensive, feeling that you do not respect them or their decisions, feeling that your love is conditional upon their willingness to accept life on your terms and not theirs, or accept God according to your theology and not theirs, it will be difficult to maintain an open, loving relationship of any kind. If you do not learn to talk in such a way as to make it easy to hear what you have to say, all the talking in the world will not matter.

Again, the best way to talk so that your children will listen is for you to talk in such a way that your children feel when you are telling them about *your own* beliefs and feelings, that you are taking them into your confidence and sharing something deeply personal and important with them. When you can tell them "I want to share with you some of the things that are really important to me about life" and not tell them in the same breath "and if these aren't important to you then I will be deeply disappointed in you as a person" they will more likely be open to hearing what you have to say.

Every child wants to know what makes their parents tick. Every child is curious about how their parents came to believe what they do, to think how they think, and to see the world the way they do. If you can let down your guard and tell your child in a quiet, private setting that although you do not usually talk about these things very often anymore, it is very important to you that your child understand the beliefs and values that you cherish, it will feel like a privilege to them to be let into your heart, mind, and soul. That is the best way to talk so that your child will listen.

The same is true of your child's desire to be heard and seen and acknowledged as a thinking, independent adult. Most parents know that the number one way to drive a young child crazy is simply to ignore him. Children would really rather be hit by a parent than ignored, because at least when they are hit (not that I am recommending it) they know that they exist and are seen by the parent. When they are ignored, it is the equivalent of a kind of spiritual and emotional death—as if they simply do not exist in the world.

It is a sad but essential reality of life that every one of us as we are growing up experiences our most powerful sense of self and place in the world as a result of the reactions that others have to what we say and what we do in our lives—especially when we are young. We judge our self-worth, we judge our relative status in relation to other peers, we judge our value as human beings, we judge our impact on others, and we judge our ability to matter at all by the feedback we get from every person, young and old, with whom we come in contact.

And if strangers can influence our sense of self-worth by their reaction to us, the role that parents play in defining our very sense of self is that much more important. Although this is most powerful and acute when we are children, on some levels it never ends. Parents continue to have a unique power to push their children's emotional buttons and cause them to feel important or insignificant by how they react to or ignore them.

That is why the way you listen to your children is one of the important keys to creating a climate in which they will be willing to share important concerns, decisions, and challenges in their lives. If you engage in what is called "active listening," where you listen without making judgmental statements in reaction to what is being said, but instead constantly do your best to repeat what your child tells you back to her so that she can let you know whether or not you are truly understanding what she is telling you, she will be more likely to continue to tell you important things that really matter.

If you are continually interrupting what your child is telling you with "How could you do that?" or "I thought I raised you better than that," or "I can't believe I am hearing this," be assured that you will discourage your child from attempting to share anything emotionally powerful or important with you again. To listen so that your child will talk requires a nonjudgmental approach to listening—and this is perhaps one of the most difficult attitudes for any parent to adopt.

Parents are constantly insisting, "It's my job to be judgmental and tell my child how to act and how to behave in society, what to believe, and how to lead a virtuous, moral life. After all I am the parent, and he or she is the child." It's certainly not that you are wrong as those jobs do fall into your parental purview; however, the time to express and teach these beliefs is when your children are little, still growing up, and living in your house. By the time they are at the end of their teen years and into their twenties, they already know what you believe, what is important to you, and how you want them to act. At that point the best thing you can do is whatever you can to understand how they have taken your values and translated them into their own unique version of how the values *you* have taught them will be expressed in their own lives.

Treating your grown children as adults means treating them with respect, truly wanting to know what they believe and why they believe it. Do you really know what your child believes is his or her purpose in life? If you are genuinely interested in who they are and what they have to say, your children will be flattered and feel valued by you because you will have reinforced this by your actions. This is the most important gift you can give your children: recognition of their inherent self-worth and value.

Two

"THE AGONY AND THE ECSTASY"—SURVIVING THE INTERFAITH WEDDING

WHEN YOUR CHILD SAYS, "WE'RE GETTING MARRIED!"

Most interfaith couples worry about their parents. They worry about how they will juggle the anticipated disapproval of their parents with their own needs for creating a fulfilling, loving relationship with someone who turned out not to be from the same religious, cultural, or ethnic background. They worry about how their parents will treat their boy/girlfriend when they are first dating and then how that will change if they get married. They worry about how their parents will feel about the numerous decisions that will be made regarding how their grandchildren will be raised. And when they have finally worked through their own relationship issues to the point where they are ready to get married, they worry *a lot* about what their parents will say when they get up the courage to announce, "We're getting married."

Some couples end up waiting for years to get married simply to avoid having to deal with the explosion of parental disapproval that they anticipate will greet what ought to be a happy announcement. The ugly scenes that they imagine they will have to endure all but haunt them.

Time and again, couples have sat down in front of their clergyperson agonizing over exactly how they were going to tell their parents that the time had finally come and that they were ready to take the plunge.

"Frankly, Rabbi," they often tell me, "although we love each other a lot and have worked hard to ensure that our relationship will work out, we are both scared to walk up to our own parents and say, 'Hi, Mom and Dad, guess what? We're getting married.'"

And yet those very parents who are the anticipated source of such worry and concern are usually quite surprised when they learn the level of anxiety that their children feel over this issue. Indeed, most parents live with the mistaken notion that their children do not really care very much *how* they feel. Especially since they believe they have made their disapproval of interfaith relationships clear to their child many times and their child chose to get involved in an interfaith relationship anyway.

Given these circumstances, it is really hard for parents to believe that their children are so profoundly affected by their parents' reaction, by what they say in response, or whether they approve or disapprove of the choices their child has made in a marriage partner.

The truth, of course, is that more often than not parents greatly underestimate their own power, influence, and importance in the lives of their children—not just on marriage, but on many other issues as well. The psychological reality most of the time is that—no matter how old a child may be, no matter how successful or independent, whether male or female, single, married, or divorced—on some level most children forever desire the approval of their parents.

This fundamental reality is probably the reason that most child-raising experts will tell you that the single most devastating punishment a parent can visit upon his or her child is withholding approval. In fact, parental *disapproval* continues to have a powerful effect on children throughout their lives. It is not something to be taken lightly, nor is it something to be withheld carelessly either, especially if you are determined to maintain a good relationship with your child throughout his or her life.

The results of this deep-seated human need for parental approval are evident throughout our society in much of the acting-out, antisocial behavior of children. What happens too often both in school and social settings is that many of the children who become known as "behavior problems," are primarily reacting to perceived disapproval or rejection by their own parents. For many children even getting a *negative* reaction from their parents is better than no reaction at all; as such, by acting out they have at least found a way to make sure that their parents pay attention to them.

This is also one of the reasons why so many couples experience fear and trepidation at the prospect of confronting their parents with the news of their decision to marry someone of another faith, race, or cultural background.

Even when a couple has been living together for quite some time and their eventual marriage would appear to be inevitable, the possibility of facing parental disapproval over one of the single most important decisions in their lives can be a powerful and upsetting experience.

One of the most important philosophical realities is that who we are and who we become in our lives in large part is determined by the choices that we make. Indeed, it is a truism that the quality of our lives is directly the result of the quality of our choices. Moreover, the act of choosing a life partner in marriage is inevitably a reflection of many of the deepest and most important aspects of our character, our sense of self-worth, and our identity.

Throughout this process and throughout their lives, parents maintain a unique position with their children. They can either reinforce in a positive way this ongoing sense of self-worth, personal value, and positive self-regard, or be a force that diminishes their child's self-esteem and causes long-lasting emotional pain and distrust. That is why how you, as a parent, react to the "We're getting married" announcement from your child (as well as the many other issues that we will discuss in this chapter) will, to a large degree, set the tone for your relationship with your child long into the future.

"YOUR" INTERFAITH FAMILY

One of the first important realizations for you to accept is that your child's decision to intermarry means that *you* are now a part (or soon will be) of an interfaith family as well. In many ways, our entire lives can be compared to a pond into which pebbles are constantly being tossed. As others around us act and make decisions, what they do sends ripples through the pond of *our* lives, affecting us whether we like it or not.

Such obvious interdependence is one of the certainties of life. Not one of us lives on a desolate island in the middle of nowhere, cut off from the rest of the world. Instead, we live our lives in ever-expanding concentric circles of influence and connectedness. Our children, parents, siblings, our extended families, in-laws, colleagues, work, social clubs, religious and political community, fraternal organizations, service clubs, and community institutions all form the matrix of our lives, connecting us in innumerable ways to the larger network of our relationships.

Each of us affects the other by what we say, how we act, and the choices that we make. When your child chooses a mate, whether you like it or not, you are thrown headfirst into a complex system of relationships and family connections that will affect your life forever. That is why the way you choose to react to the reality that is presented to you has such a profound impact on your relationship not only with your child, but with so many others as well.

So now you are about to become a part of an extended interfaith family. It is natural to have questions about how this will affect your life and the lives of your child and grandchildren, how your extended family and friends will react, what decisions you will have to make, how you will relate to your new in-laws, what you might have to learn about another religion or culture, and so on. Perhaps one of the most important actions you can take immediately is to give yourself permission to have the full range of mixed emotions that you have probably already experienced. Do your best not to judge your feelings and thoughts as "wrong" or "bad," or worry about how you "should" or "shouldn't" be feeling, thinking, or acting. At least not right away.

You have a right to those mixed emotions, and it is never healthy to deny them. Frankly, it is important for you to be as aware and conscious as you can be about what your feelings actually are, to figure out how you feel about your child, your religion, and the choices that you and your child have made in your lives. That will help you gain mastery over and give direction to your behavior so you can produce the most productive and positive results in your own parent–child relationship.

As with most aspects of family relationships, whether between parents and children, siblings or spouses, it is important that you communicate in such a way that you are not creating a win/lose situation. There is absolutely no reason why everyone cannot be a winner when it comes to negotiating the sensitive issues that are part of interfaith family life, as long as "winning" is defined as leaving each person with their dignity and sense of self-esteem intact, regardless of the specific decisions that are made or whether or not everyone involved agrees with one other.

This is especially important when it comes to issues surrounding weddings. Even under the best of circumstances, weddings, perhaps more than any other life-cycle event—except perhaps having a child—tend to be emotion factories. Weddings stir up memories from the past, longings and dreams unfulfilled, unresolved issues between parents and children, and personal notions about marriage, divorce, personal fulfillment, and loss. What is a challenge under any circumstance becomes that much more powerful when a family system is dealing with issues surrounding an interfaith or interracial marriage.

Sensitivity to each other's feelings is a hallmark of successful family life. It is even more crucial a factor when dealing with *interfaith* family experiences. Obviously, each situation requires its own form of tact and diplomacy. The same message can be communicated in two different ways and achieve totally different results.

For example, imagine a king who calls upon his two soothsayers to foretell the future. The first comes to the king and says, "Your Majesty, as I look into the future I see a great personal disaster for you and your family. You will witness the tragic deaths of both your two sons." Hearing this prophecy the king becomes outraged and immediately commands that the insolent soothsayer's head be cut off. Then he calls for the second prophet. This wise soothsayer bows low before the king and says, "Your Royal Highness, I see for you a long and prosperous life. In fact, you are so healthy and virile that you will outlive your entire family." Naturally, hearing this prophecy, the monarch becomes so pleased that he orders rewards of bags of gold and silver for the second soothsayer.

What is the moral of the story? More often than not, it is not merely the message, but how you communicate the message that really matters.

Being sensitive to the feelings of other members of your family, including those of your child, does not mean suppressing your own needs and desires. It simply means going out of your way to show others that you care about them enough to listen to what is important to them, and that you will do your best to take them into consideration when it comes time to make decisions of your own.

WHOSE WEDDING IS IT ANYWAY?

One of the most powerful of the traditional Ten Commandments of the Jewish and Christian Bible is found in the biblical book of Exodus, Chapter 20, Verse 12, where it says, "Honor your father and your mother." There are few more concrete demonstrations of that honor and respect than for your children to allow your own deeply held religious beliefs to influence and help shape the nature of their wedding. That would be a beautiful wedding gift from your children to you, and something about which you could feel proud as parents.

However, there are many ways your children can honor you, and this just might not turn out to be one of them for you. It is usually a bad idea to expect your children to feel required to run *their* wedding according to *your* needs, your feelings, or your desires. In fact, perhaps the greatest gift that *you* can give to *them* during this uniquely important moment in their lives is to constantly remind yourself that ultimately it is *their* wedding, not yours.

Yes, as much as you have fantasized about your son's or daughter's wedding for so many years, it is still the couple's day. Of course you have a right to share your feelings, your opinions, your preferences, and your desires. But if your ultimate goal is to nurture and maintain the best possible relationship with your child and his or her spouse both during and after the wedding (which it should be), then keeping a proper perspective on the limits of your influence in their wedding plans is crucial.

COOPERATION, COMPROMISE, AND FLEXIBILITY—THE KEYS TO RESOLVING CONFLICTS

Perhaps the three most important tools for maintaining a good relationship with your child throughout this emotionally challenging time are cooperation, compromise, and flexibility. In almost any situation, with almost any decision that has to be made, these three tools will go a long way toward eliminating potential conflicts and hurt feelings between you, your child, your future son- or daughter-in-law, and his or her extended family.

After all, once the decision to get married has been made, your thoughts need to turn toward the future. Now is the time to commit yourself to creating the most loving, positive, supportive, and open relationship with your child throughout his or her marriage that you can. To do that will require patience and a clear sense of your own values.

Every parent wants their child's marriage to provide them with love, support, fulfillment, and satisfaction for the rest of their lives. Yet the contemporary reality of marriage is such that we all realize how fragile marriages can be. That is why parents confronting the challenges of an interfaith relationship and wedding need to keep focused on *their own long-term relationship with their child.*

After all, no matter what happens between your child and his or her spouse, *you* will always be a constant in your child's life. What you want most of all is for *your* relationship with your child to stay strong, consistent, and good throughout all the trials and tribulations of individual relationships (whether there are one or more marriages, divorces, domestic partnerships, cohabitations, or the like).

You may still want to be the one he or she turns to later in life for counsel and advice, for a shoulder to cry on if necessary, and for approbation and congratulations for successes and triumphs in life. You can best nurture this relationship, especially when you are involved in wedding plans and decision making, by always keeping in mind the three keys: cooperation, compromise, and flexibility.

On the simplest level, it is a matter of clarifying priorities for everyone. With regards to the wedding, to the marriage, and to your extended family beyond that single wedding day, it is ultimately crucial that you set your own goals regarding the kind of ongoing relationships that will best serve you and your family.

Maintaining a clear sense of what is really important in your life, and not allowing yourself to be swept away by the emotional passion of a given moment or decision that anyone involved with the process might make, is always in your best interests. After all, when it comes to interfaith weddings, emotions are inevitably on edge. There are an endless number of choices and decisions that can potentially push your emotional buttons and make you uncomfortable or cause you pain.

The best perspective is lifelong rather than short-term. The challenge is to keep in mind that life will go on after the wedding, that your relationship with your child is much more important than who officiates, where it takes place, who is invited, or the color of the wedding gown—no matter how important these issues may seem at the moment.

WHO DECIDES? YOUR ROLE IN PLANNING THE WEDDING

One of the problems that occurs often in interfaith marriages is that parents begin to feel left out of important decisions. This is particularly true when you live far away from where the actual ceremony will take place, since it is usually someone close to the scene who is called upon to participate in the day-to-day decision-making process. Unfortunately, sometimes this happens even when you live in the same town. For it is often the case that if the wedding will primarily reflect a religious perspective that is not your own, it is very easy to quickly feel estranged from the entire process and unconsciously begin to resent those who are making the decisions.

The truth is that it is not any easier for your children to be open and honest with you about their feelings than it is for you to be totally honest about yours with them. Sometimes it takes a little probing, a little prodding, some help from another family member, relative, or close friend to uncover their true desires. Most parents can find a way to accommodate their needs and desires to those of their children, *if* they are clear about where the potential problems exist in the first place.

One of the important messages that gets communicated to your children when you take time to get involved in the planning of their wedding is how important *their* happiness and success is to you. It communicates that *they* are your priority, that you recognize that it is *their* wedding, and that it truly is *their* happiness that is most important to you at this special moment in their lives.

It is also important to realize that marrying someone of another religion does not necessarily mean your child is rejecting you or his or her religion. Most likely, he or she is simply choosing to create a loving partnership with someone he or she loves who happens to come from a different background. Recognizing this reality has often had the effect of giving parents the emotional permission to be the loving, supportive, and nurturing parent that they want to be in the first place.

So what *is* your role in planning the wedding? Although there are a plethora of "wedding protocol" books on the market that will go into great detail outlining whose responsibility it is in one tradition or another to pay for the flowers, or the clergy, or the rehearsal dinner, our focus here is quite different. Our concern is not on who pays for what, but on the *process* through which those decisions are made.

The final decision is always less important than how you arrived at the decision in the first place. Ultimately, no matter who writes the check—the bride or groom, their parents, a rich uncle, or a local charitable organization—in the end, what will most reflect the nature of your relationship with your child will be how you went about making those decisions in the first place.

As with any relationship, the key to successful decision making is to make sure that each party involved feels that his or her feelings, concerns, and integrity have been acknowledged and validated by the others. Once you feel that your child has really listened to your needs and has heard your own priorities, and he or she feels the same respect has been accorded to them and to your new in-laws, it is always easier to come to an agreement on specifics.

The greatest problems are those that fester. When anyone who is part of the decision-making process withholds information about what is really important to them or where their most important priorities lie, it is an invitation for feelings of rejection, failure, and loss to interfere in the process.

That is why families who are in the midst of planning a wedding need to sit down, all together, and give each other permission to have different dreams, different priorities, and different feelings about religion, culture, rituals, and even values. To accept that part of what makes the world such an interesting and wonderful place is that everyone is *not* exactly alike is an important place to start. After that, you can move on to the specifics of how to make individual decisions in the least conflict-producing manner.

The simplest formula for resolving potential conflict over wedding decisions is to have the bride and groom (remember, it is *their* wedding) *assign* specific responsibility for individual decisions to specific people. The more specific the better—"Mom, I'd love you to go with me to look for a wedding dress," "John (the groom) will make the decision about what the men in the wedding party will wear," "John's parents are going to take responsibility for the rehearsal dinner," etc.

In this way, if the bride and groom take responsibility for making the assignments of who is responsible for what, it reduces the number of decisions over which there will be conflict and disagreement. Of course, if *everyone* keeps in mind that the ultimate goal of the wedding is to create the most loving, joyous, supportive, and wonderful day for the couple to begin their married life together, then conflicts will be kept to a minimum.

IN-LAWS AND THE WEDDING—BLENDING FAMILIES IN HARMONY

One of the greatest challenges in any marriage revolves around the issue of how to successfully blend two often very dissimilar families into one cohesive extended family. That challenge is all the greater when the two families come from different religions, cultures, or ethnic groups. The opportunity for misunderstandings or misinterpretations of words, gestures, or associations between families seems to hang over every gathering.

The best way to diffuse these potential misunderstandings and misinterpretations is to openly acknowledge that in fact, real differences *do* exist between the two families. The more openly you can discuss your fears and anxieties about inadvertently hurting the feelings of someone in the other family, the more naturally you will create an environment of tolerance, openness, ease, and comfort. In this manner, comments that otherwise might have the potential for hurting the feelings of the other family will lose their emotional power. Instead, every encounter becomes an opportunity for self-discovery, for learning to enjoy and even celebrate differences, and for understanding that ultimately there is always more that unites us than there is that divides us in life.

After all, the United Nations was founded on this very idea. This organization has been strengthened over the years through the willingness of its members to learn in a nonjudgmental way about the political, social, and religious cultures of others. The same thing is possible on a smaller scale in your own home with your family. You, too, can create an open and safe environment in which your two families can discover both your differences and your similarities, reducing to a minimum the degree to which the differences are experienced as threats to your own beliefs or way of life.

This ability to get along well with your in-laws (or future in-laws) will be easier if you are able to openly discuss any issues potentially affecting the wedding with your child and his or her partner early in the decision-making process. The longer you wait to become involved in this discussion, the more likely it will be that feelings will get hurt and misunderstandings will occur.

Sometimes it helps to involve a third "neutral" party to help facilitate the conversations. A trusted minister or rabbi, a therapist or family counselor, or even a close family friend whom your child also trusts can all potentially serve in this role.

Ultimately, however, it is *your responsibility* to figure out how to create the best relationship with your new family. If you can succeed in meeting this challenge, it will be one of the greatest gifts you will ever give your child. Too many times pain, sadness, and sorrow interrupt otherwise loving parent–child relationships because the different in-laws will not sincerely attempt to find common ground.

It is helpful to remember that even when it does not seem like it, what you feel and think matters to your child. Have you ever met a child whose true desire is for the unhappiness and disapproval of his or her parents? It may often seem as though children go out of their way to make choices in their lives *designed* to give their parents more gray hairs than they deserve, but the reality is that it only *seems* that way. In truth, children usually are doing what they can to make the best decisions they know how for themselves, in spite of *their* parents' best advice, in spite of their parents' heartfelt desires. And just like their parents, they then must learn to live with the consequences of their choices. And by the way, it is *not* your job to point out these consequences or to furnish these negative consequences.

As parents, although you do not have it in your power to make your children's choices for them, you do have it in your power to choose how *you* will react to those choices. You can choose to react in such a way as to give support and love to your child rather than condemnation and disapproval. You can choose to react with suggestions for how you can help build greater family harmony and cooperation with your new in-laws rather than see every decision as a potential source of competition for the affection and love of your child. It can also help for you to choose *not* to issue any warnings or "I told you so's" in the hopes that you may change your child's mind. The reality is that the wedding will happen regardless of what you say or do. You can only control your own behavior.

Why not be the first to reach out to the other family? Invite them to your home if you can. Suggest opportunities to socialize and get to know each other. Assume that the other family is wrestling with the same fears, anxieties, stereotypes, and potential misunderstandings as you are, and they will welcome the opportunity to reduce that anxiety through personal contact with you and your family.

In fact, the more open you are in sharing your desire for the two families to get to know each other *because* you know they come from different backgrounds or cultures, the easier it will be for the two families to be together in the first place.

There is no magic formula for extended-family harmony. Instead, it is a slow, deliberate process of extending yourself—one invitation at a time, one gathering at a time, one step at a time. The most important key to successfully blending your families is to have the right attitude. With a positive, open attitude toward your new extended family you will find that almost anything is possible.

KEEPING THE JOY IN YOUR PARENT–CHILD RELATIONSHIP WHILE PLANNING A WEDDING

It is so easy to get caught up in these myriad challenges of wedding planning that you lose sight of exactly what you are planning for and where your priorities really belong. In the midst of choosing cakes and colors, dresses and bands, invitations and guest lists, it is easy to forget that it is all happening because your child has fallen in love and chosen to make what is probably the single most important commitment of his or her life. To keep the joy alive and thriving in your relationship with your child during the planning of the wedding, it is crucial to keep your eyes on what matters most. It is often just that simple. And what matters most when the last dance is over and all the guests have left the party will be the memories you share of this special moment in your child's life and the ongoing relationship with your child and his or her new family.

That is why it is so important to do whatever you can *before* the wedding to ensure the best relationship possible *after* the wedding. First, communicate to your child that it is important to you to have the best relationship possible both with them and with your new family. Second, let your child know that your goal is to do whatever you can to help ensure the best, most loving and joyful ceremony and celebration possible. And third, tell your son or daughter that you know it is his or her wedding, and that you are there to help, to give support, and to give your love in whatever way he or she needs most. In fact, if you invite your child to feel free to tell you what he or she needs throughout the process of decision making and planning, and then continue to communicate your love and support, you will most likely have an even better relationship when the wedding itself is over.

THE CEREMONY—CHOICES, COMPROMISES, AND CHALLENGES

Perhaps no aspect of wedding planning is more fraught with emotional dangers than the decisions around the ceremony itself. Will it be a "religious" or "secular" ceremony? Will the family priest, minister, rabbi, or clergy person officiate? If so, *whose* family clergy will it be? Will there be more than one person officiating? What rituals and customs will be incorporated into the ceremony itself? Will there be mention of a specific form of the deity? Will prayers be invoked that are specific to the bride's or groom's religion? And ultimately, who will make these decisions? The possibilities are vast, and the potential for injured feelings and sensibilities enormous. Sometimes, the ceremony decisions are so fraught with anxiety for the wedding couple that they simply hand the decision over to one set of parents or the other and then just show up at their own wedding.

When this happens, it is usually the parents who are the most passionate (or inflexible) about their religion who are given the power to make the decisions. Often, as you can imagine, this creates tremendous resentment from the other family whose religious tradition has been ignored or purposefully excluded.

Sometimes the anxieties over what the ceremony will include, who will officiate, which religious rituals will be included or left out, and which family's feelings will be most injured when it's over are so painful that the couple ultimately skips town and elopes to a wedding chapel in Las Vegas. Chances are that then no one is happy, and everyone feels like they lost out.

That is why, as with other aspects of wedding planning and nearly every other decision that must be made in the course of interfaith life, I encourage couples to remember "Reuben's Rule." It is simple, direct, and to the point: "Whatever works, works." If it works for the couple to have their parents decide, then so be it. If it works for them to have multiple clergy representing different religious and cultural traditions, then so be it. If it works for them to use an outside advisor to make all the potentially controversial decisions for them, then so be it. Whatever works, works. Period.

For example, I participated in a wedding between a white Jewish man and an African-American evangelical Christian woman. The ceremony (held in the groom's synagogue) included a rabbi, a cantor, an evangelical minister, and an African shaman, all of whom contributed rituals that were unique to their tradition. It was a long ceremony, but a remarkably beautiful one. And most importantly, it was what the bride and groom wanted, so they loved it.

The role of parents in weddings varies from family to family. It is often a combination of what the individual family members have grown up thinking is the usual and appropriate role of parents, combined with whatever each party can negotiate for themselves. Some parents desire a greater role in the wedding planning than others, and some get involved primarily because the *other* family is so demanding of the privilege that they feel emotionally bound to demand equal representation.

Want to be a really smart parent? Then give up as much control and decision making as possible to the bride and groom. Once again, if you are able to remember that it is ultimately *their* wedding, it will often reduce the heartaches and frustrations.

MONEY, POWER, AND WHO GETS TO DECIDE WHAT

Of course the reality often is that money plays a powerful role in determining who gets to decide what when it comes to planning a wedding (and a lot of other things in life as well). More often than not, the parents who are primarily footing the bill for the affair expect that along with their checkbook comes a certain amount of power both to veto and to make decisions as to what *they* would like to happen throughout the day.

The use and misuse of money as a weapon of power and control has perhaps caused more unhappiness and resentment when it comes to wedding planning than any other single issue that I have experienced.

Parents often feel caught in a bind. On the one hand they are *expected* to pay for the wedding, and indeed most of the time are delighted if they can. On the other hand, they are asked to ignore their own strongly held feelings about interfaith ceremonies, or perhaps even "other faith" ceremonies and simply grin and bear it (and, of course, keep writing checks). It can be a precarious emotional ride for many. And strong feelings of conflict and resentment, along with the expectation of having a say when you are footing the bill, are totally understandable.

Nevertheless, asserting one's "right" to make decisions based primarily on an ability to pay is usually an emotionally dangerous road to travel. Your kids resent it. Your new in-laws resent it. And mostly what you end up with is a pyrrhic victory with only the appearance of success—and lots of hurt feelings afterward.

Better to make peace with the choices that your children make, stand behind them as best you can, be prepared to help pick up the pieces if things do not work out, and cheer if they do. This can be very difficult for those with strongly held religious beliefs and cultural pride, but if your goal is to maintain a positive, loving relationship with your child, there is no other way that works better.

Sometimes there are parents who simply cannot condone the choices of their children if those choices take them outside the family's religion or cultural background. Such parents must be willing to accept the consequences of their rejection and open disapproval, or even their radical decision to break off contact and further relationship with their own children. There are few decisions in life more painful than this one, and no one can ever make it lightly.

Nonetheless, the purpose of this book is to help those parents who want to maintain the strength of their own integrity and beliefs *and* have the best relationship possible with their children. This is possible regardless of the decisions those children might make during the various twists and turns of their lives.

Money should never be used as a weapon. The temptation is often strong, especially with families where money has traditionally been used as a tool for parents to get their way with their children. Resisting such temptation, however, will greatly reduce the possibility of unexpressed resentment on the part of the bride and groom toward their parents. There is also a great possibility of creating discord between the wedding couple themselves when there is the perception of particularly heavy-handed behavior on the part of one set of parents over another. That is why using money as a weapon to get your way regardless of the desires of the bride or groom is almost a guarantee of resentment.

USING A "WEDDING COORDINATOR" TO SMOOTH RELATIONSHIPS AND PREVENT POTENTIAL DISAGREEMENTS

Sometimes the best thing that wedding couples and their families can do for the continued health of their relationship is to figure out how to *avoid* getting involved with each other during the planning of the wedding. In such cases hiring a professional "wedding coordinator" is highly recommended.

Wedding coordinators are party planners with a specialty in organizing and planning weddings. They can be found in most cities by using the yellow pages, going online on the Internet, or calling potential wedding sites and asking whom they have worked with successfully in the past.

There are several advantages to using a wedding coordinator. First, since they specialize in planning weddings, they have more information and potential choices for just about everything—right at their fingertips. Wedding sites, bands, florists, caterers, specialty service providers (such as dancing bears and jugglers, balloon artists, or organ grinders with monkeys), and anything else your imagination might conjure up—fulfilling matrimonial desires is their specialty.

Second, putting many of the simple but numerous decisions that must be made in planning a wedding into the hands of a coordinator takes them *out* of the hands of those who are most likely to argue or get upset about which *other* family member is making decisions that they would like to be making. Using a wedding coordinator is one of the simplest ways to maintain wonderful relationships between family members and among in-laws, since it places many of the decisions *outside* the family system itself.

A skilled wedding planner not only knows how to arrange for exactly what the bride and groom have in mind for their wedding, he or she also knows how to diplomatically communicate with the various members of the extended family who all have an emotional stake in the wedding. Experienced wedding planners can be the go-between among parents and children when it comes to discussing difficult decisions, and can draw upon years of personal experience and wedding "successes" to make recommendations and suggestions that none of you might have ever have considered.

Above all else, the use of a wedding coordinator can serve as a lightning rod that deflects some of the tender feelings that are inevitably part of the wedding planning experience. After all, it is much safer to show impatience or even anger with a stranger (whom you are paying for the privilege of listening to your complaints anyway) than it is to vent your frustrations or concerns with a beloved family member who will still be around (hopefully) long after the wedding is over.

PERSONAL STORIES FROM THOSE WHO HAVE BEEN THERE

There are hundreds of potential personal stories that could serve to illustrate the kind of emotional challenges that families are faced with when planning a wedding. In fact, anyone reading this book can draw upon personal experiences as well or those of friends or family members who have been involved with weddings in the past.

Of course, not all weddings end up with tears and trauma, and the purpose of this chapter is to help you *avoid* just such an experience. Still, it is often helpful to learn firsthand from the personal experiences of others so that you will be reminded of what *not* to do, as well as choosing the best course to take when called upon to make wedding decisions.

A typical example of wedding dysfunction was reflected in the approaching nuptials of Henry and Jill. Henry, twenty-five years old with no religious background, and Jill, twenty-three years old and Jewish, found themselves on the tail end of a downward spiral with his parents over pre-wedding plans. Henry told me, "We tried to shelter them, because we thought that would be in their best interests, and then they felt left out and it backfired. It got so complicated that it just seemed like we couldn't do anything right."

"The main problem was simply that we didn't know how to ask his parents what *they* wanted to do and how they felt about some of the wedding plans," Jill added. "So, what we did instead was to make decisions on their behalf that we *imagined* they would be happy with, and that got us deeper and deeper into trouble."

When Henry's parents heard about what their son was experiencing, they found themselves in agreement! "It was a nightmare for us, too," his father said. "We kept feeling like we were not very important to Henry since he didn't seem to put much effort into asking us for our input, but we didn't say anything to him about how we felt. Of course that meant that our pent up feelings of being left out and not very important just kept building and building. Fortunately, his mother is more willing to share her feelings than I am and much less willing to allow issues to remain unresolved between members of our family. So, one night she just invited Henry and Jill over for dinner and made sure that we brought everything out in the open."

"After we actually began to tell each other how we felt and to talk about the things that made us feel hurt or unimportant, the issues were quickly resolved," Henry's mother added. "It turned out that our kids were trying to protect us out of their love and regard for our feelings, but we had interpreted their silence as a lack of caring. When we all realized how easily all of our feelings could be hurt, how easy it was to misinterpret the actions of the others, we made a commitment to communicate more openly with one another. All of our decisions became easier from then on."

As this personal testimonial illustrates, when it comes to interfaith weddings, feeling "left out" is a common parental problem. Sometimes it seems as if *everyone* feels left out, no matter who they are or what decisions are being made. That is why the best strategy is always the most direct: Share your feelings with each other and ask others what they want. Then allow the wedding couple to assign tasks. In this way you and your children will not only survive their interfaith wedding, you will emerge with an even better and stronger relationship with them. You will also have established a pattern of communicating about important issues that will serve you well long into the future.

Three

FAILURE, LOSS, AND GUILT

COPING WITH FEELINGS OF FAILURE

"Somehow, somewhere I feel like I have failed as a parent." How many times have those words been uttered in a moment of self-revelation and anguish by a parent whose child has just announced that he or she is marrying someone from a different religious background? Too many.

"What did I do wrong?" a parent asks, a question which is usually followed by the self-accusatory confession, "I should have been more religious at home when my child was growing up."

The truth is that children from every conceivable background fall in love with each other and intermarry regardless of how strict or lax their parents were in their religious upbringing. Although there is some truth to the assertion that intermarriage is less prevalent among children from strict fundamentalist Christian, Jewish, or Muslim backgrounds, the undeniable reality is that even Orthodox Jews and fundamentalist Christians and Muslims have children who intermarry.

When it comes to parenting there simply are no guarantees—regardless of how you raise your children. Most of us know of families with several children where one child would not think of marrying outside the faith and another does not give it a second thought.

The reality is that every human being is an individual, a one-of-a-kind creation with a mind of his or her own. Each human has individual dreams, singular attitudes, and unique experiences that result in myriad particular choices that made each day. And it is these choices that ultimately determine the direction of our lives.

So when parents of interfaith couples lament the decisions that their children have made it is often fundamentally an expression of their own feelings of failure as parents coupled with profound feelings of guilt and loss. Though such feelings are a normal part of the range of emotions that interfaith relationships evoke in parents, they are still essentially misguided and misdirected expressions of parental frustration over the recognition that when it comes to our children we are ultimately powerless to direct their behavior as adults.

So what is an appropriate response to that nagging feeling of having failed your child, failed your family and its values (often passed down for generations), and perhaps even failed your religion or culture or ethnic group? A wise philosopher once said, "The proper response to the inevitable is relaxation." That advice works well here.

If you feel like you have failed your child it is most likely because you believe that what is in your child's best interests is to marry someone from within your own religious tradition. As a parent you know that creating and sustaining a successful relationship and a successful marriage is a difficult and demanding enterprise under the best of circumstances. And most research confirms that "the best of circumstances" is often one in which the couple have as much in common in terms of religious and cultural background, life experiences, outlook on life, economic background, and values.

Your fear as a parent is that your child will be starting off her married life with one or two strikes against her simply because of the differences in life experiences, values, and behavioral expectations that are part of different religious and cultural traditions.

While all of these cautionary statistics are true on one hand, on the other hand the world is filled with successful interfaith relationships of every kind. People from every conceivable background have met, fallen in love, gotten married, raised healthy families, and created successful lives together. Men and women, men and men, and women and women have all found ways of transcending the initial barriers that divide them *in spite* of the obvious additional challenges that such relationships must face. There is no reason *not* to believe that your child can and will be one of those who discover the ability to create and nurture a lifelong successful relationship with someone from another tradition.

So when you feel like a failure you need to step back and see the larger picture of how people (including your own children) actually function in the world. When you are willing to accept that all you can do in life is the best that you can do, and the best that you can do really is good enough, your strong feelings of failure and guilt may lessen.

Your children are not merely "your children." If they were, perhaps it might be possible to fantasize that you could somehow exercise complete control over their lives, their decisions, their choices in friends, boyfriends and girlfriends, religious devotion and observance, expression of their daily values, etc. But the simple reality is that you cannot. You cannot control them, and you cannot direct them to do and be and act as *you* want them to once they have reached adulthood.

Sometimes the best antidote to feeling like a failure as a parent is simply to take the time to identify what our true values really are that we would most want to pass on to the next generation. So here is a little exercise to do that I call "Fail Your Way to Success." It goes like this:

1. Write out exactly what your own values and ideals really are. What are the things you stand for in life? Pick the top five values that you cherish, that you most want to pass along to your children, which you would most want your children to embrace and live out in their own lives.

2. Rank these top five from one to five, with one being the most important value and five being the least important (although since these are your "most important values" in the first place, all of them will be important to you one way or another).

3. Now take them one at a time and *really* examine what you mean by each value. Make a list of as many specific behaviors that you can think of that if someone acted that way, it would be a sure sign that they were in agreement with your values.

4. When you have completed your list of values, ranked them in order of importance from one to five, and written lists of specific behaviors that would be good indications of someone having accepted these values, sit down and take a good, hard look at your own child.

This last step is the most important one. For here you are asked to hold up a mirror of this list to the behavior of your own child and come up with as many ways as possible that you can find your values in the behavior of your child. This is both the most important step to overcome these feelings of failure as a parent—and the most challenging. For many parents who have done this exercise with me, the very process of identifying the values they cherish most has immediately revealed to them that their own children, even within the interfaith relationship, actually are expressing the values that their parents have taught them, just in different ways than their parents might have conceived of.

In fact, there are many times in which the choice of falling in love with a man or woman from a different background was *itself* an expression of exactly those values that the parents cherished most.

Time and again parents tear out their hair and are wracked with feelings of failure and guilt as if the interfaith relationship of their child were an indictment of their parenting and a clear rejection of their values. Then, after a few minutes of conversation and questions, these same parents discover that *they* had taught their children that all human beings were created in the image of God, that no one religion was superior to another or had the "right" answer to the many mysteries of life, and that no race or culture was truly superior either. So what their children were doing in the creation of an interfaith or interracial relationship was to live out their parents' values but in their own unique way.

When parents recognize this phenomenon for what it is, namely a tribute to the *good job* they did as parents, they usually cease being obsessed with the notion of their own parental failure and recognize that everyone lives out his or her values in different ways—even when the values are fundamentally the same.

An additional problem that parents face when their child enters into an interfaith relationship is the disapproval of extended family members and subsequent feelings of failure and guilt such disapproval evokes. Parents often feel as if they have let down their ancestors who fought hard (somewhere, sometime) to preserve the right and privilege to celebrate their religion as they chose. It may be easy for some to feel that their child's interfaith relationship, somehow, makes them responsible for the breakup of generations of faithful adherence to the religion of their ancestors.

In truth, every religious tradition is in a constant state of evolution and none of them ever stay the same for long. If you were to look back at your great grandparents and how they lived their lives, how they celebrated their religious tradition, the rituals and customs and holidays they celebrated and acknowledged in their lives, certainly you would see many differences between how they did it and how it is generally done today within the same religious tradition. This is inevitable, the natural process of spiritual and religious evolution that every tradition experiences.

When you truly spend the time necessary to think this through, you will most likely discover that just as you created your own unique religious lifestyle based upon your upbringing, the role models you saw growing up *and* the personal, individual choices that you made in the process of living your own life, so too are your children doing *exactly the same thing you did, but in their own way.*

What that means is that you are not a failure as a parent, but rather a tremendous success. You have most likely taught your children the values that truly matter to you and all they have done is to express them differently in their generation from the way you did in yours. If the result of that unique expression is that your son chooses to marry a woman from a different religious background, that choice itself is most likely his way of living out the very values that you taught him.

Similarly, parents often feel as if they have somehow failed, not only their children and their family, but also the religious culture in which they were raised. "How could I do this to all those generations of Irish Catholics?" Catherine, a distraught mother, said during an interview. "I feel like I have let them all down, as if their hundreds of years of struggling for the rights of Irish Catholics to worship as they please and live in religious freedom has been thrown out the window by my own daughter with no regard whatsoever to any sense of obligation to the past. It makes me sad for her and what she will be losing out on in her life, and even sadder for all the Irish I feel I have let down by not being a better Catholic mother myself."

Catherine's feelings were not unique, for the same sentiments have been expressed by Lutheran mothers, Jewish mothers, and Muslim mothers—all with the identical sense of having let down their ancestors and feeling responsible for contributing in some small way to the dying out of their cherished religious tradition.

For all these mothers, the challenges are the same—regardless of religion, regardless of culture, regardless of language. First, the future of your religious tradition does not rest on your shoulders.

All religious traditions have an internal power and weight of their own, and each has survived blows of near catastrophic proportions in the past on a much grander scale than simply one individual choosing to marry out of the faith. As personally difficult as it may be in your own emotional and spiritual life, your religion will survive the intermarriage of your child.

It is important to your own emotional health to keep the trauma of your child's interfaith relationship in perspective. Doing so will help you feel less like a failure and reduce the guilt that is often a part of interfaith life.

Second, every religion will continue to exist in the world as long as it persists in providing a sense of meaning, purpose, and transcendence to the individuals who practice it. No religion, no ritual, no custom, no philosophy, no idea ought to be carried on from one generation to the next *solely* because "that's the way we have always done it." If that were reason enough then there would never be change or evolution of religious traditions and philosophies at all.

Religions will continue to exist in the world as long as they are deemed meaningful and worthy by their adherents. When that no longer is the case, it will probably be appropriate for a given religion to cease. Think of all the people in the past who defended the institution of slavery as if it were a God-given right of one people, race, or culture to enslave another. Few today would dare make the same claim.

The same is true with every idea and institution whether social, economic, governmental, or religious that we have inherited from the past. Everyone lives their lives as best they can, incorporating into them the rituals, holidays, customs, and beliefs that give them the strength to do the right thing, values upon which to base their behaviors, and ideals by which to chart their course in life. As long as religious traditions continue to matter in the life of others, they will exist. That is why regardless of whether your child marries in your own faith or lives her life in accordance with your spiritual values will have no significant effect on the continuation of any religious way of life.

Obviously your child's decision will affect the specific religious life of your own family, the holidays you celebrate, and the people with whom you share your customs and rituals. This is no small matter. For many people the religious context of their lives is one of the main organizing principles around which their very lives function. The thought of celebrating a holiday with a child not there because he might no longer feel completely comfortable with his new wife or partner in that setting can be a painful experience for a parent. But there are specific, concrete ways you might bridge whatever spiritual or religious gaps appear to be growing between you and your interfaith married children. Family harmony and shared celebrations are the goal, regardless of the individual religious choices that parents and children might make in their own lives.

Bridging such gaps is not only possible, it has happened time and again when couples are willing to accept a few simple suggestions regarding how to talk with each other and help each other to understand their own feelings, while communicating in loving, nonjudgmental ways.

COPING WITH FEELINGS OF GUILT

One of the most important challenges that both parents and children must learn to face when it comes to interfaith relationships is the challenge of coping with feelings of guilt. That is because when it comes to interfaith relationships and the dynamics between parents and children, nearly everyone seems to find something to feel guilty about.

First of all, children inevitably feel some sense of guilt in letting their parents down and disappointing them (even when they would never admit that to their parents). The reality is that every child no matter how old she gets still wants her parent approval. The loss of that approval as a result of an interfaith relationship can be a difficult and trying emotional challenge for your children. This reality is compounded by the fact that living in denial about that guilt is one of our most prevalent coping mechanisms. That means that in order to deal with our natural feelings of guilt we have to first be able to identify them.

When it comes to parents whose children intermarry, feelings of guilt are as prevalent as they are with the children themselves. "I know it's silly," Mark, a Jewish parent, said, "but I just feel so guilty and almost ashamed of the fact that my son has married someone who isn't Jewish. I think of those 6 million Jews who were killed by Hitler and the Nazis just because they were Jewish, and I feel like I have let them all down. It's as if Michael is giving Hitler a posthumous victory, destroying Judaism from within when Hitler couldn't do it from without."

For Mark and many other Jews who grew up in the shadow of the Holocaust, denying Hitler that "posthumous victory" is itself enough of a reason to continue to be Jewish, practice Judaism, and insist that his children do the same. That is why the simple act of falling in love with someone from another religion can take on the exaggerated proportions of the emotional abandonment of 6 million Holocaust victims. Now *that* is a heavy burden of guilt to bear, especially when all Michael has done is fall in love.

So how do you cope when you suffer as a parent from that post-Holocaust guilt syndrome? The first thing you do is recognize that it is enough responsibility for each generation to deal with its own challenges in its own era, and it is not your responsibility to shoulder the burdens of generations past. Intermarriage today is no more connected to Hitler's dream of wiping out Jews and Judaism than it is to the designs of Torquemada and the Spanish Inquisition, or Haman's plot in the biblical book of Esther to wipe out the Jews of Persia.

There is an ancient proverb that says it is enough to face each problem in its own time. That goes as much for you as it does for your children. They must live their lives in accordance with their own dreams, passions, and ideals just as you have done in yours. The best you can do is live each day in such a way that you would be happy if they or even their children followed your example. The only adult to whom you are ultimately responsible is the one whose face you see in your mirror each night before you go to bed.

The second thing you can do is to give your children the gift of respect and trust. Trust that you have instilled in them the values that you cherish most and that they are simply living out those values in the best way they know how, even if it looks different from the way you would do it.

To treat them with respect means to give them the right to make their own decisions and then to live with the consequences of those decisions. Guilt comes from feeling that you have let someone down, not done what you were supposed to do in life or been unfaithful to your own values. If you can see the behavior of your children as independent from you, not as a direct reflection of who *you* are, but rather give them the ability to be their own independent human beings freely making their own choices, you may be able to let go of some of the guilt as well.

Third and perhaps most important, you are not your children and they are not you. You can only do the best you can do in life. It is enough to struggle with responsibility for your own actions, let alone attempt to take on responsibility for the actions of others. Treating your children as adults is allowing them the opportunity to be responsible for their own behavior— whether good or bad, right or wrong, wise or foolish.

COPING WITH FEELINGS OF LOSS

One of the greatest challenges of parenting at every stage of your children's lives is learning how to let go. "Letting go" is a subject worthy of a book all on its own, since from the moment you give birth to a child the only way he can learn to become an independent fully functioning human being is if his parents continually let go of their own needs and desires to protect and guide every aspect of his life.

It's normal for parents to want to protect their children from pain and suffering. Parents want to create an ideal life for their children, better than the one in which they grew up, filled with love, support, encouragement, and self-esteem. And yet, one of the great paradoxes of parenting is that the greatest gift you can give your children is the ability to stand on their own, to make decisions without you, and then to feel responsible for the consequences of their decisions. That is how fully functioning adults are created. And it is perhaps the most important job you will ever have as a parent.

That challenge is the same whether it relates to their education, their ability to work and become self-sufficient as adults, the religious and spiritual choices they make, or their ability to form healthy and mutually respectful, loving relationships as adults.

If you take seriously the gift of independence that you are giving to your children, you must be willing to accept the choices that they ultimately make.

These are *their* choices, not yours. And it is they who will have to live with them.

When you feel guilty because of a decision that your child has made, it's often merely a reflection of your unwillingness to treat them as independent adults. "But what will I say to my friends?" Mark implored as he continued to agonize over his son Michael's decision to marry a Catholic girl.

"How about telling them that Michael is marrying a wonderful, supportive, loving young woman (which Mark had also told me)?" I replied. "In a world in which the intermarriage rate within the Jewish community is routinely 50 percent, your friends are undoubtedly experiencing similar challenges. And when it comes to your extended family and the rest of the community, they are *all* trying to figure out as best they can what this new fundamental cultural reality of interfaith marriage will ultimately mean for the future. And none of them have the magic answer, just as none of them are in a position to pass judgment."

Mark knew what I had said was true. There is hardly a family within the Jewish community today that has not been touched in some intimate way by the reality of interfaith marriage. Mark needed to remind himself of all that he loved, respected, and cherished about his son. He needed to embrace the ways in which he felt pride in his son's accomplishments in life and in the kind of person he turned out to be. Life is not neatly divided into discrete categories and neither are your relationships or the feelings you have about those you love.

One of the most important of "Dr. Reuben's Rules for Life" is simply this: *life is messy*. It is not simple, clean, neat, nor tidy. Every relationship that really matters is a jumble of qualities, strengths, weaknesses, successes, failures, frustrations, joys, disappointments, and celebrations. To fully be engaged in a relationship with someone, whether a spouse or partner, child or parent, colleague or friend, is to be willing to accept the entire package that they represent. You simply do not get to choose which qualities to keep and which to discard in others—it's an all or nothing proposition.

The same is true with the decisions that your children make: You can give them guidance if they ask; you can demonstrate by your own behavior what you believe is important to you. Then it is up to them *and them alone* to live their own lives. What you tell your friends, your community, and your other relatives about the life choices of your children ought to reflect those aspects of their choices which you cherish and admire, the qualities you love and respect about them—regardless of whether you agree with every decision they make or not.

It is neither your job nor your responsibility to justify the actions of your children to others. In fact, the nonjudgmental acceptance of your children just as they are is the best message you can send to others and to your children about what your most important values really are.

Of course for many parents, regardless of how they *act* in front of family, friends, or their children, they still experience a sense of loss when confronted with the reality of interfaith marriage. In one sense it is perfectly understandable and perhaps even appropriate to experience loss on several levels. There is the loss of the passing on of a tradition that may be important to you in the same way as you have experienced and celebrated it in your own life.

When a child marries under any circumstances parents often experience a sense of loss, regardless of whom he or she marries. If you picture the family as a target with a bull's-eye, then the center of the bull's-eye would represent the nuclear family of origin, the first circle would be the extended family, the next would be friends, then community, then country or civilization, then world community. When someone gets married, what was the center of the bull's-eye moves out to become the first circle and a new center is established out of the new marriage relationship.

What that means is that the new relationship (husband/wife or even same-sex partnership) is now the couple's primary family, and what used to be their primary family has now moved out to be the first circle, therefore becoming their secondary family. If they have children, the primary family gets larger, but the children are *not* what *creates* the family, the relationship alone does that.

In a sense this is what accounts for much of the traditional tension around weddings. Children are always felt to be a part of the primary family of their parents while forming their own primary family that does not include their own parents at all. That is why parents so often feel that they are "losing" their children as they get married because the emotional reality is that they *are* losing them to their new primary family.

This loss is a real one and has nothing to do with who the marriage partner is or whether or not it is a same-faith or interfaith marriage. Unfortunately, what often happens in an interfaith marriage is that even normal social or emotional phenomena are seen as filtered through the lens of the interfaith nature of the relationship and the interfaith relationship becomes mistakenly responsible for "causing" the feelings of loss or sadness that would occur regardless of who your child marries.

Certainly, when an interfaith relationship results in parents who raise their own children without the faith or in a different faith from their parents, it is understandable that parents might feel a sense of loss of "the next generation."

The best antidote for these feelings of loss is to remind yourself that what matters most is that your child is healthy, happy, and fulfilled in his relationship, and to look at religions traditions as tools to help us achieve personal and spiritual fulfillment. If your child has achieved her own level of fulfillment and peace in her own choices, then that must be more important than the mere continuation of the religious tradition for its own sake in her life.

In addition, it helps to remember that the dynamics of human beings are such that none of us can predict what the future may hold. Just as you could not have predicted all the choices your son made in his life up to this point, so you cannot predict what he will do five, ten, or fifteen years in the future. And neither can you predict what *his* children will choose. Many times the children of one generation reject the choices of their parents, only to have *their* children reject *their* choices and embrace the religious traditions of their grandparents.

Life is filled with mysteries beyond our understanding, and certainly personal relationships and spiritual decisions fall into that category for us all.

It is true that for those parents who have deep beliefs in the importance of embracing one particular religious tradition in order to experience personal salvation in the traditional Christian sense and therefore assuring participation in heaven, intermarriage and the abandonment of that tradition by their children is seen as a deep and profound loss. It can indeed be difficult for believing Christians to accept the potential loss of personal salvation in Jesus for not only their own children, but for their grandchildren as well.

Parents who are struggling with these theological issues should talk to their priests and ministers for counsel and advice. They usually find their greatest solace in the belief that God is ultimately a loving and grace-filled God who desires eternal life for all. Such parents need to place their faith not only in God's grace, but in God's ability to see the holiness within every human being and the essential goodness and faithfulness that can be found within every spiritual tradition.

If you are a parent with strong religious beliefs of this nature, what may help you to accept the choices of your child is your faith that the God who created the entire universe and all that lies within it must have the discernment and power to see within the human heart and soul as well. The Bible says that when God looked upon all creation God declared that it was good. If you are a believer in the truths of the biblical text, then it makes perfect sense to believe as well that as God looks upon all the different ways that God's creatures have created to offer praise, thanks, and celebration. This God will be moved to find a way for all of them to enter God's heart and kingdom as well. Ultimately perhaps this is one of those spiritual tests of faith in life for which there is no easy answer other than faith itself.

FEAR OF REJECTION

As if all these challenges of faith aren't enough for parents of interfaith couples to contend with, often parents lament that it feels as if by marrying out of the faith their children are rejecting *them* as well.

In an earlier era this assumption might have been true—at least truer than it is today. It is rare indeed for "parental rejection" to be the true, underlying motivation for an interfaith marriage.

Yes, it is true that at times children rebel against their parents and their parents' perceived values in a wide variety of interesting and creative ways. And yes, such rebellion may even include dating people of whom their parents clearly do not approve. But even so, it is a great distance from "dating" someone to make a statement asserting one's own independent choices, to *marrying* someone to make the same point. Very rarely is a marriage *primarily* created as an opportunity for a child to make a statement of independence from the values of his or her parents.

On the other hand, if you are a parent with a child who is dating someone from another religious tradition, often the very worst thing you can do is to take a strong, verbal stand in opposition of the relationship. Over and over again couples have felt pushed into marriage by the strong rejection that their *parents* expressed regarding their current relationship.

This is not an issue so much of rejecting parental values or rejecting the child's parents as much as it is the more mundane and everyday issue of children needing to feel that they are adult enough to make their own independent decisions and have their parents respect their ability to make decisions and take the consequences.

It's important for parents to let go of any residual feelings that the relationship choices of their children constitute a statement either of acceptance or rejection of *them*. Life is always both complex and messy, and the "reasons" for the choices your children make in their lives when it comes to relationships are many, varied, and complex. Attempting to reduce the complexity of our relationships down to something as simple as "it's about rejecting me" will inevitably fall far short of doing justice to the reality of the complex lives, emotions, feelings, history, dreams, and expectations that contribute to the decisions that your children make.

Four

UNDERSTANDING THE ROLE OF YOUR OWN VALUES AND BELIEFS

CLARIFYING YOUR OWN RELIGIOUS VALUES

One of the most important challenges confronting all parents whose children intermarry is how to create a successful relationship with them regardless of whom they marry and choose as a life partner. It is self-evident that developing the skill of communicating in a nonjudgmental, supportive way with your children is a crucial component of any long-term and positive parent–child relationship. With interfaith families over the years, it has become quite clear that before parents can effectively communicate with their children about the importance of their religious beliefs and spiritual values, it is helpful for them to first have a clear understanding of exactly what role those beliefs and values play in their *own* daily lives.

Most of us hardly give much thought at all to the impact that our beliefs have on our everyday lives. In fact, our religious beliefs and the values we hold dear do have a profound effect on myriad choices we make each day regarding how we act, how we talk, or how we conduct our lives. This is true even at work or with friends, with colleagues or even strangers we meet in the normal course of a typical day—so of course its effects on our interactions with family are profound. Our deeply held values and beliefs about life and death, the purpose of our lives, our relationship with God, our ideas about the nature of the universe and our role within it—all these form the foundation of our decisions and choices and ultimately determine both how we see ourselves and how others see us.

This chapter is designed to help you understand the impact that your beliefs and values have on your relationships with family, friends, colleagues, and everyone you meet. The ultimate value of that self-awareness and understanding is to help you more clearly identify when your own values get in the way of your ability to understand and relate to your children and the choices they are making in their lives. The more you are aware of your own values and your cultural and religious biases, the easier it will be for you to be conscious of how your beliefs about the world affect the way you talk about the issues that touch your life each day.

We are not necessarily discussing changing your ideas in any way. We are talking here about being *aware*.

Being aware of your own values will also better equip you to talk intelligently, supportively, and unemotionally to your own child and his or her spouse who has grown up with a different set of values, assumptions, and biases in their own life.

Creating the best possible relationship with your children—one that will withstand the trials and tribulations of their personal lives while being perceived by them as supportive, nurturing, encouraging, and validating of who they are—is the goal. One of the crucial components necessary to create the kind of relationship with your children that every parent ultimately wants is the ability to articulate your beliefs and values and to understand how they relate to and are expressions of your own religious tradition.

In discussion with hundreds of people from many different religious traditions over the years, I have come to realize that just as life itself is complex, so, too, are the source and breadth of our personal beliefs and values. Very often in the process of examining these questions of belief, people discover that although some of their beliefs and values grow directly from the teachings of their personal religious tradition, very often other beliefs and values they cherish are *not* direct reflections of the specific teachings of their religious tradition at all. Instead, many beliefs and cherished ideals have been forged out of the fires of our own personal lives. They emerge from years of our personal history and the process of self-reflection that grows naturally out of the struggles that we have experienced and the relationships and lessons that we have chosen to learn as a result of those experiences.

Although you may share experiences with others, this does not necessarily lead to both of you learning the same lessons or coming to the same conclusions. If that were the case, then life would be a lot more predictable than it actually is.

Consider the story of the journalist who was writing an article about alcoholism and addiction and interviewed twins whose father had suffered from alcohol addiction, leaving a family shattered, and a life filled with pain and suffering. The journalist had chosen to interview these particular twins because one had become an alcoholic and drug addict and the other had become a well-known preacher who never touched a drop of alcohol.

As the story goes, when the writer met with each of these children and asked them how they ended up the way they were in life, they both gave the exact same answer. The first son replied, "My father was a drunk, an alcoholic, and an addict, so how else would I turn out and what else could I do of course but become an alcoholic and addict as well?"

And when the journalist interviewed the second son, his answer was *exactly the same*: "My father was a drunk, an alcoholic, and an addict, so how else would I turn out and what else could I do but become someone who never touched alcohol and helped others to avoid addiction in every way possible?"

Of course this story may be apocryphal and it is not about addictions, not really. It is about how two people can go through a similar life experience and draw totally different life lessons as a result. The same is true of your own children. If you are a parent with more than one child you will know from your own experience that even children growing up in the same house with the same parents often absorb distinctly different lessons from how their parents interacted with them and what they perceive were the lessons their parents endeavored to teach them.

For example, even when two children grow up in the same household with parents who act as consistently as possible, one child may experience his or her childhood as filled with love, acceptance, and validation and another might interpret the very same parental behavior as condescending, disrespectful, and consistently negative. Every one of us is unique, and each of us creates our own personal meaning out of the experiences of our lives. We see the world through our own unparalleled inner filter, making decisions at every turn regarding the meaning of other people's words, gestures, actions, and attitudes.

Just as we each have our own singular understanding of the meaning of the external stimuli that we receive (the words and deeds of our parents, for example), the same is true with how we interpret and understand our own religion and the values, beliefs, and lessons that we are taught growing up.

One child learns the story of Jesus creating loaves and fishes for his hungry disciples in the Galilee (from Chapter 6 of the Gospel of Mark where Jesus miraculously fed five thousand of his followers who had come to hear him preach from a mere five loaves of bread and two fish) and understands the lesson to be that what Jesus wants most is for all human beings who are hungry to be fed, all human beings who are naked to be clothed, and all human beings who are homeless to be housed. A second student learns the exact same story about Jesus and the loaves and fish and understands the lesson to be that poverty and hunger in the world is nothing that we human beings can control, but only prayer and relying on the saving power of God through Jesus will ultimately heal the sick and feed the hungry.

Is one of these interpretations "right" and the other "wrong"? Or as with most of life, are two distinct individuals with their own unique life experiences simply interpreting and understanding the biblical story in light of those different experiences, biases, and prejudices about life and about people? Most likely it is the latter and not the former, and that the same applies to many, many social interactions as well as our interpretation of everyday values. People cannot help but see the world through their own eyes, hear the world through their own ears, and make choices and decisions about life and death, and the important values of life based on their own unique experiences.

One of the biggest mistakes that parents make with their children is expecting them to be carbon copies of themselves. Of course every parent on some level would love their children to embrace the values they cherish, to celebrate the holidays and important life-cycle events in the same way they do, and to profess the same faith and beliefs that have been handed down from previous generations. The reality of life suggests, however, that such direct mirroring of the lifestyles of parents by their children is rare.

Most of the time children absolutely *do* reflect the values of their parents— they just do so on their own terms, in their own language, and in their own "contemporary" way. In fact, even when the life choices of a child appear to be very different from those of their parents', when you dig just beneath the surface behavior and apparent differences, you actually find more commonality than difference.

Such misreading of a child's values and the resulting disapproval, rejection, and family disharmony that can follow is often found in relationships between parents and children who are gay or lesbian. Many times I have spoken with parents who are distraught, disheartened, and dismayed at what they consider the rejection of their values by their children who are gay or lesbian, when in fact the *children* believe that their values and the values of their parents are *the same*, just expressed in a different manner.

For example, parents often lament that their child has rejected the importance of marriage and stable family life in favor of "a gay or lesbian lifestyle of casual sex and multiple relationships." When the children in question speak out, it is often the case that they long for the exact same stable, long-term relationships that marriage has provided for their parents but simply have not yet met the right person with whom to share the rest of their lives. The observation made about "casual sex and multiple relationships" is not an accurate one, but a stereotype about homosexuality in general. Let's put it this way: Don't most heterosexuals date until they find "Mr. or Ms. Right"? Didn't you? Homosexuality was not the reason these children were not yet "married." It was because in the first place homosexuals are denied the right and privilege of marriage by most of our society, and in the second place, their ability to find and establish a loving lifetime partnership with someone they cherish and love is made even more complicated and difficult by the homophobia in our society as a whole.

The fact is that if parents are actually able to sit and have a serious conversation with their children (whether gay or straight) about the values they cherish, they often discover that their kids actually share many more of those same values than they reject. They might express them in a different way, with different language, or rituals, or style than their parents would ever have done. That is why whenever the parents voice upset or frustration over the rejection of their values by their children, I do whatever I can to bring parents and children together to have a conversation. Parents usually walk away from such encounters feeling much, much closer to their children and with an understanding that their children have not rejected them or that which they hold precious, they have merely reinterpreted those same values on their own terms and in their own ways.

What You Really Believe about Your Own Religion

So first, let's take a serious look at what you really believe about your religion. Whether you are Catholic or Protestant, Muslim or Jewish, Buddhist or Rastafarian, if you have children who are involved in an interfaith relationship it will be helpful for you to take the time to identify your core beliefs regarding your core values in order to talk intelligently and clearly with your child about these issues.

In truth, there are many paths to religious self-discovery and awareness. It is really up to each individual parent working alone or as a team to find the path that will work best for them. Often it is useful to seek out the help of a clergy person, therapist, support group, sibling, or friend as you go through this process of clarifying your values and identifying the priorities they claim on your convictions and loyalties. Many times having a conversation about your desire to clarify the beliefs and values that really matter to you with a close friend whom you believe shares your religious perspective is the quickest path to finding out what you really believe.

Here are some concrete suggestions on how to proceed: First, make a list in writing for your friend (or spouse or other helping professional) of your five most important beliefs. Begin with the following five items:

1. What you believe about life and death
2. How you understand good and evil and how they function in the world
3. Your beliefs regarding heaven and hell
4. Your beliefs about the meaning of life
5. What you think about why bad things happen to good people.

Once you have written down the answers to those key religious questions, you can then have a conversation with your child (or write a letter or email if it seems less confrontational[1]) explaining that as a result of his or her interfaith relationship you have been giving a lot of thought to *your own* religious values and wanted to share with him or her some of the insights that you have come up with regarding your own personal beliefs. You might thank your child for making religious values a much higher priority to you than ever before in your life, and then invite your child to help you as you wrestle with what you believe are very important and fundamental questions regarding *your own* ethics and beliefs.

Ask your child to share with you his or her reaction to your spoken and/or written statement of beliefs and then identify with your child those beliefs that you share in common. Tell your child that although you would guess that most parents and their grown children rarely have such conversations at all, you care deeply about the quality of your lifelong relationship with each other and have such respect for your child as an adult that you are interested in what your child thinks are his or her own core religious beliefs or values as well. Tell your child you love him or her and really want to understand him or her as best you can in order to have the very best relationship possible for the rest of your lives—no matter what religious choices your child makes in his or her life now or in the future.

Go to your local church, synagogue, mosque, or other religious institution reflecting your beliefs and to which you belong (if any) or go online to find the informational Web sites of the religious tradition, denomination, or spiritual discipline that you embrace; get copies of their "official" doctrines and statements of belief. Use these publications as a starting point for examining your own truly held beliefs about the issues outlined above and see where you agree or disagree with the "official" position of your religious tradition.

There are individuals who have read through the publications of the religious denominations that they had identified with their entire lives only to discover that they did not actually agree with the "official" articulated system of belief that their particular religious tradition taught. These adults realized that they had been carrying around throughout their entire lives an inaccurate picture of what their family religious tradition actually espoused and expected of them as a faithful adherent.

There are also adults who have discovered that they do not actually believe in what their own denomination teaches. They may even decide that the only way to maintain their personal integrity is to leave that particular church or synagogue or mosque, stop identifying with that particular religious denomination or tradition, and go in search of a church or synagogue or mosque or religious movement or tradition that *does* speak to them in a more powerful and meaningful way.

Another way to clarify how you feel about your religion is to identify the different characteristics of your religious tradition and examine them one at a time to see which ones you accept, which you reject, which you are unsure about, which you see blending into another religious tradition (i.e., which aspects are unique to this tradition and which are shared by other traditions), which are primary, and which secondary.

For example, a Lutheran church in Pacific Palisades, California, declares in its pamphlet, "We believe that, because of human rebellion and his desire to live in relationship with us, God became a man. Jesus the Christ, born of a virgin, is fully God and fully man. Through his death and resurrection, Jesus made it possible for all people to live in relationship with God. We believe that Jesus is the Way, the Truth, and the Life. Through him alone we enter into a relationship with God." What if you, who have identified yourself as a Lutheran all your life, realized that this did not express your personal beliefs at all? Or what if you were raised going to your local Presbyterian church and considered yourself Presbyterian, but recently, when you read in your local church's bulletin, "We believe that homosexual practice, like many other contemporary activities, is sinful. Regarding abortion, we believe the Bible does not distinguish between prenatal and postnatal life, and that attributing personhood to an unborn child is absolutely normative," you feel that you no longer embrace those ideas. You then have the challenge of looking at other denominations, reading their materials, talking to their ministers or clergy, and figuring out where you really fit today as an adult within the religious community.

Some religious traditions are fundamentally based on specific beliefs and others revolve more around experiencing a sense of belonging and connection to community. You owe it to yourself and to any child who is involved with an interfaith relationship to have as clear a sense of your *own* beliefs and religious commitments as possible *before* discussing them with your child. The clearer you are about what you believe the easier it will be for you to have conversations with your child about his or her beliefs and how you can be supportive as a parent to the religious and spiritual life choices that your child has made while maintaining your own religious integrity.

If you have been away from the religion of your childhood for a long time you might consider taking a class at your local place of worship like the ones offered for potential converts. Such "Introduction to . . ." classes that each denomination offers are an excellent way to remind yourself of what your own tradition teaches and to help you understand to what degree you still believe the precepts of your religious tradition are true and meaningful. Of course if you have a spouse or partner, he or she could attend such classes with you so that you have a shared religious vocabulary with which to talk about these important religious issues and a way of helping to keep your own relationship as a spiritual partnership alive. Experiencing religious education as an adult couple is different than exposure during childhood. Many adults choose to take this journey together simply so as not to end up with a totally different religious consciousness from your partner or spouse.

What You Believe about the Beliefs of Others

The next challenge is to understand what you believe about the beliefs and religious traditions of others. One cannot help growing up with a host of prejudices and preconceived ideas about other people's religious traditions, rituals, beliefs, and customs. These notions are derived from our personal experiences with friends or acquaintances that are devotees of other religious traditions, from popular culture like television and movies, from the rumors and gossip we experienced as adolescents, from books we might have read, and from myths that are part of the general culture.

"Presbyterians are cheap and loathe to spend money." "Irish Catholics drink too much." "Jews are clannish and pushy." "Mormons are secretive and feel they are superior to everyone else." We all grow up with preconceived ideas like these about each other's cultures, traditions, and customs, ideas that are based on myth and prejudice more than fact and personal experience. This is particularly important to remember when you are part of an interfaith family, when your child is involved in an interfaith marriage, and when you have inherited a group of in-laws and relatives who belong to a different religion and/or religious tradition.

It is easy for your own prejudices to color the way you see, hear, and experience the family of your new son- or daughter-in-law. As such, it is to your advantage and for the good of your lifelong relationship with your child as well as your new family to break out of these prejudices as soon as possible.

The easiest way to identify your own beliefs about the culture of others is simply to write down various questions and answers:

1. Catholics (or Jews, or Muslims, or Hindus, or Protestants, etc.) are_____.
2. Catholics (or Jews, or Muslims, or Hindus, or Protestants, etc.) believe_____.
3. Things I have heard about _____ include _____.

Whichever questions and answers will help you to get in touch with and identify the preconceived ideas you have about another religious tradition will also help you to dispel the myths and misinformation that those preconceived ideas are usually based upon.

This exercise is something that you can undertake to help clarify your own views; it is not something you have to show to anyone else. You can further clarify your own thinking if you take a few minutes by yourself and complete the following sentences:

1. When I think of my religion, I _____.
2. When I don't celebrate our holidays I feel _____.
3. As a child religion to me was _____.
4. My favorite religious experience is _____.
5. My most profound religious experience was _____.
6. The thing I like the most about my own religion is _____.
7. The thing I like the least about my own religion is _____.
8. If it were up to me everybody would believe _____.
9. If I had the nerve I would tell other people _____.
10. When I think of God (Jesus, the Holy Spirit, Allah, etc.) I know _____.

Think about how you feel when you hear someone talking about their religion and expressing beliefs that are contrary to your own. For example, think of a time when you were in a religious setting that was not your own. How did you feel? If you have never stepped into another religious setting before, now is a good time to start. Go to a local church or synagogue or mosque or temple that is different from your own. If you are allowed to sit in the sanctuary while the service is being conducted, monitor the thoughts and feelings that come up for you during that experience.

Notice if you find yourself silently wondering how all these seemingly intelligent people could possibly believe all this stuff they are saying and reading. If that is what you are thinking, be aware of the negativity of that judgment, and then ask yourself where those negative thoughts and feelings might have come from. Are they the result of negative stereotypes of other religions that you grew up hearing at home? From your own religious leaders and preachers? From kids on the playground at school? Discovering the source of your own prejudices, judgments, and expectations can help you understand that those ideas are not simply objective "facts," but ideas that were planted in your own consciousness that have actually gotten in the way of true openness and understanding of those who practice differently than you.

It is very hard to grow up involved with one particular religious tradition and not at the same time think poorly of other religions. It is often an underlying belief of every religion that their religion is the "right" one—and therefore all other religions are wrong. After all, in one way or another, *all the traditional theologies of every major religion in the world* embrace the following basic premises:

(a) There is only one true way (theirs, of course)
(b) God wants us to believe about the meaning of life and death the way they do
(c) The rewards or punishments that God metes out are outlined in the text they prefer
(d) Sin and salvation, heaven and hell are only defined the way they describe it
(e) What God has in store for the world and humanity as a whole is outlined by their tenets
(f) God's willingness to respond to prayer and to explain why the good often suffer in this world occurs in precisely the way their religion explains it.

Religious conflict often comes from the fact that these deep and important religious questions are answered differently by each religious tradition. To believe that there is only *one* right way to think, believe, and act on these religious principles is destined to lead to heartache, disappointment, and, ultimately to pushing your loved one away.

What You Believe about Sin, Salvation, Heaven, and Hell

Do you know what you believe about such universal spiritual issues as the source and nature of humanity and all creation? What about what we mean by sin and salvation, punishment and reward, heaven and hell, life after death? And what about the existence of a God who interacts with others in this universe, who responds to prayer, or who makes decisions about who shall live and who shall die?

If you do not, you might consider taking a class on theology or comparative religion at a local college or college extension program to help you to clarify your own feelings about religion—whether your feelings are deeply ingrained or whether you feel a certain ambivalence. The more you are willing to openly look at your own beliefs, examine the beliefs of others, and openly confront your own prejudices and preconceived notions, the easier it will be for you to be open to understanding the religion and religious ideas of your child's partner.

Tell your child that you are interested in understanding his or her partner's beliefs and religious convictions and commitments. Ask your son or daughter to get you one or two books that might best explain his or her partner's beliefs to someone from another religious tradition. Then read the books or materials that you are given and find someone like your own minister, pastor, rabbi, counselor, or good friend with whom you can discuss and clarify your own emotional and intellectual reactions to the material.

Often we have a much greater *intellectual* tolerance for ideals that are not our own and a much more limited *emotional* tolerance for those same ideas. It is easier to discuss on a rational or intellectual level the religious beliefs of others and much harder to reconcile the mixed emotions and negative emotional baggage stirred up by such discussions—especially if they involve your children. One such area of religious belief where people's intellectual ideas are often out of sync with their deep-seated feelings and strong emotional reactions is the issue of sin and salvation.

It seems that most religious traditions teach some notion of sin and the concomitant process of achieving salvation from that sin. Once issues of sin and salvation have been raised, it is inevitable that such discussions will lead to a further exploration of what individual religions teach about the afterlife and whether or not they have descriptions of heaven and hell or the "world to come."

We seem to be living in an age in which suicide bombers throughout the world, especially in Muslim countries, act as if they believe that achieving their own deaths by killing nonbelievers will qualify them as "holy martyrs" in the eyes of God. Martyrdom, they believe, is rewarded with God's grace and blessings in whatever form God deems appropriate. Typical western Christians and Jews who hear about such religiously motivated decisions to commit mass murder through ritual suicide simply cannot fathom how someone who is "religious" and who believes in God could make such a decision. In the twenty-first century, Western ideas of sin and salvation preclude the murdering of innocents simply because they believe differently, even though this was not always the case.

Throughout the Middle Ages, especially during the time first of the Crusades and later in the time of the Spanish and Portuguese Inquisition, thousands if not millions of men, women, and children were tortured, murdered, and burned at the stake simply because they were considered infidels who did not accept the spiritual supremacy of Jesus Christ as Lord, Savior, and the Son of God.

Today, the same religious ideology seems to have been taken up by intolerant Muslim extremists who now commit the exact same act of murder on Christians, Jews, and other "infidels" who don't accept Allah as the one God and Mohammed as his prophet. Moreover, we often see that the Islamists believe that it is not enough merely to be a Muslim; if one is not the *right* kind of Muslim, one can still be considered an infidel and nonbeliever. That is why there is such rampant sectarian violence and murder throughout the Middle East to this day.

How then do you take a serious look at what you really believe about sin, salvation, heaven, and hell? You do so by simply asking yourself questions in regard to these philosophical and theological ideas in the same manner as I suggested earlier. What if your son- or daughter-in-law were to ask you to explain your beliefs about sin today? How would you answer the following questions?

1. What would you say you believe regarding the notion of sin?
2. How would you describe your understanding of what you do and do not consider a sin?
3. Are there different degrees of sinning?
4. What is the worst kind of sin?
5. Are there sins committed against you that you would consider unforgivable? Are there things you have done which you fear will never be forgiven by others?
6. How is a sin related to the teachings of the scriptures or sacred writings of your religious tradition?
7. How do you recognize a sinful act when you see one?
8. Does everyone in your religious tradition agree on this definition of sin?
9. What is the range of belief in your religious tradition regarding sin, and where could someone read about it if so desired?
10. Finally, how does your understanding of sin affect your daily behavior, your expectations of relationships with your own family, work colleagues, or those professing another religious tradition?

After you have gone through these questions by writing down the answers or using them as a guide to engage in a dialogue with your child or his or her partner, you can do the same with the issue of salvation:

1. How does your particular religious tradition understand the idea of salvation?
2. Is there more than one legitimate way your religion allows you to think about salvation?

3. Is salvation something that happens to each individual on a personal level or is there some kind of collective or communal sense of salvation brought about by people acting in accordance with the will of God?

4. In some religious traditions the very goal of life itself is to experience the grace of God by being granted personal, individual salvation of the soul and, as a result, the gift of eternal life. Is that how you understand the idea of personal salvation? And should that be the goal of every individual?

5. Is there some other way to understand the idea of salvation so that it includes everyone or is it always a singular, solitary challenge?

6. Finally, does salvation from God inevitably lead to life everlasting in heaven?

After clarifying what you believe about sin and salvation, you can focus on what you believe about heaven and hell:

1. Do you think that both heaven and hell exist?

2. Is heaven the reward for the good and hell the punishment for the bad?

3. Are there specific, agreed-upon steps that one may or must follow in order to get into heaven?

4. Can people of other religious traditions get into heaven or is it reserved only for those who believe like you do?

5. If there is only one right way to believe and if only those believers can enter the Kingdom of God in heaven, does that mean that most of the world is condemned to go to hell?

6. How do you understand the idea of hell?

7. What does hell look like?

8. How does one merit being sent to hell rather than heaven, and are people given a chance to repent before being consigned to hell?

9. Is hell a place of eternal damnation or is it possible to be pardoned or earn your way out of hell once you have been sent there?

10. If you believe that the only way to get into heaven is by believing in one particular religious doctrine or tradition then most of the world will be condemned to hell for being nonbelievers (since there is no one religion or religious tradition in which the majority of the world believes). What do you think this says about the nature of God?

11. How would you describe your personal understanding of why God would condemn most of the people of the world to hell rather than create a system, which insures that most people end up in heaven?

After you have spent time clarifying your own particular beliefs about religion, sin, salvation, heaven, hell, and other religious ideas, it should be easier to sit with your child alone or in partnership with his or her chosen spouse and have a conversation about the role of belief in your own religious life. The purpose of such a conversation is to allow your children to understand how *you* feel about religion and belief, and for you to understand *their* beliefs, feelings, and religious commitments.

Given that your child has decided to be in a relationship with someone of another religious tradition, creating a supportive, respectful relationship with your child is probably more challenging than if he or she had married someone of his or her own faith in the first place.

LEARNING TO LIVE WITH DIFFERENCES

Ultimately, the key to success in an interfaith parent–child relationship like yours is to learn to live with differences. Learning to be tolerant and understanding of the religious, cultural, and spiritual practices of others is always a challenge. It is even a bigger challenge when you have an emotional reaction to every religious decision your child makes because his or her choices are contrary to your own.

The truth is that no two families celebrate any holiday, ritual, or custom exactly the same way *even when they are both in the same religion and practicing the same religious traditions together*. If you are Christian you probably celebrate Christmas a little differently in your own home from the way your parents had you celebrate it when you were a child. If you are Jewish you probably celebrate Passover with a Seder that is different from the ones you grew up with and different even from the Seder of the Jewish family next door or even that of your sibling. This diversity is a reflection of the wider variations of religious nuances that every religion tolerates when it comes to holidays, customs, and celebrations of all kinds.

Even when we marry someone from the same religious background as our own, inevitably the way their family celebrated a given holiday was somewhat different from the way we celebrated it in our own homes as children. This is true even with *same-faith* couples, so obviously the differences will be even more exaggerated with couples from different religious backgrounds as they blend their lives together, making myriad religious and ritual choices.

Learning Emotional Flexibility

The first key to learning to live with religious differences—whether with those of a child who has taken another path as an adult, or with the differences expressed by your child's spouse or partner—is learning emotional flexibility. Sometimes, it is just plain hard to watch your child saying prayers from another religious tradition, participating in different and unfamiliar religious rituals and customs, or professing religious beliefs that are not yours. Emotional flexibility and tolerance is absolutely crucial and can be a lifesaving skill to cultivate.

It often takes tremendous emotional flexibility and tolerance to go with the flow of the choices and decisions that your adult children make, *especially* if they seem diametrically opposed to your own religious beliefs. *Of course that is exactly when tolerance matters most.*

Your children need you most to be a tolerant, supportive, loving, and nurturing parent when you disagree with what they do, not merely when you agree and support their decisions. After all, unconditional love is just that— not conditional on your children making the choices that you might make, but simply because they are your children.

Sometimes emotional flexibility means taking a lot of deep breaths, or thinking of a particular phrase you can use as a kind of mantra to keep your emotions in check when you are confronted by your child's various decisions. You might silently repeat to yourself, "God is one, God is one, God is one" over and over again to remember that regardless of specific religious rituals or stated beliefs, there is ultimately only one creative power in the universe which we call God who is the same regardless of race, culture, language, name, or religious rituals.

God is God whether you speak of God in English, French, Hebrew, Arabic, Swahili, or Spanish. Ultimately although people may use a different name in a different language to refer to God, they are all talking about the same power that animates all life in the universe, that frees the oppressed, feeds the hungry, clothes the naked, and brings peace into the heavens and ultimately to earth as well.

The more we are able to remember all that unites us as human beings on this planet, the easier it will be for each of us to be flexible in our thinking, slow in our condemnations of others, and tolerant of the great diversity of religious ideas and convictions manifested on our planet.

The Power of Attitude

There is a famous story about a man who came upon a group of bricklayers working on a structure in the countryside.

The man asked the workers what they were doing, and the first one said, "I am standing outside in the hot sun all day sweating as I lay one brick on top of another until the day is over and I can go home." The second one said, "I am making myself useful by putting my talent to work building a building that others will be able to use as well." The third bricklayer paused from his labor, looked up to the sky and replied, "I am building a cathedral to God to bring glory and honor to the power that created all things in the universe."

That is a little morality tale about the power of attitude. Indeed, attitude is everything when it comes to how we experience our own lives and the assessments we make about the lives of others. That is why adjusting your *experience* of the world will allow you to adjust your *attitude* about the world. We learned decades ago from the wisdom of such writers as Viktor Frankl in his brilliant book *Man's Search for Meaning*,[2] where he tells of his experiences in a concentration camp during the Holocaust where he lost everything including his life's work, his wife, and his children. Frankl teaches us that what he learned from that experience was that people can take away *everything* you hold precious and dear, but they can never take away your *attitude* about life—unless you allow them to.

The same is true when it comes to your attitude about your own children and their choices in life, including their choice of spouse or life companion. You can use the power of attitude to overcome your own prejudices and to transcend your own petty upsets and feelings of loss or guilt at not raising children who mirror you. Attitude is a transcendent power that can allow you to create the kind of relationship that you desire with your child, your son- or daughter-in-law, and your new family.

How do you create the best relationship possible with your children and your new family? It is as easy and as difficult as treating your children like adults. When you can treat your children as the adults they are, you acknowledge your ability to make peace with their adult decisions. After all, they have the right to create their own lives, make their own choices, and even make their own mistakes. The road to creating a positive relationship with your children is letting them make those mistakes and knowing that once they grow up and become adults, you are no longer responsible for their choices in life. Sometimes their choices turn out to be the best ones for them after all—even if they are not the best choices for you.

PERSONAL STORIES FROM THOSE WHO HAVE BEEN THERE

Consider Sharon, the mother of a Jewish son who converted to Catholicism in the process of marrying his new bride. Sharon revealed, "The single most difficult thing I have ever done in my entire life was stand in that Catholic church by my son's side as he got down on his knees, recited the prayers that proclaimed Jesus as his savior and the son of God, and promised to raise his children in the body of Christ. I thought I would die I was so uncomfortable, but I also wanted to respect my son's decisions in his life as an adult, and be there for him, and maintain the best possible relationship with him for the future, so I bit my tongue and smiled during the mass at the wedding, and hugged everyone, and did my best to show my love and support for my son and new daughter-in-law."

In the meantime, when I spoke to her son, his version of the wedding was how uncomfortable he was having his entire Jewish family standing up on the altar of the church watching as he and his bride took communion, made their professions of faith, and got married in the name of the Father, Son, and Holy Spirit even though this was his newly embraced religion. He said, "Even though I have accepted Christ into my life and the reality of his death on the cross to cleanse us of our sins, I still am my parents' child and have a lifetime of emotional connections, feelings, and attachments to them. And yes, I had some feelings of conflict and a touch of guilt in front of my parents just because I knew how uncomfortable they were feeling. I simply wanted my wedding with Danielle to be perfect, and I felt a little torn between the two families at that moment."

On the other hand, William, the father of a Presbyterian girl who married a Muslim man from Pakistan, revealed that as soon as he got to know Omar he loved and admired him. "I was leery at first just because of all that is going on in the world and all the stereotypes about Muslims and Pakistanis and *jihad* and all the scary things you read in the papers and see on the news, but when I met Omar and got to know him as a real human being, I saw immediately what a caring, loving, devoted, sweet, and open individual he is. He is a perfect companion for and an amazingly supportive partner for my daughter, Susan, and I am just glad that she found someone wonderful to love. I am always a bit worried about them and their two sons every time there is some international incident with fundamentalist Muslims attacking something American in the world because I know how much prejudice there can be, but I also know he is a wonderful husband for Susan, and that's the most important thing for me."

Andrea, a devout Lutheran whose daughter married a Jewish man and agreed to raise her children Jewish, disclosed how difficult it was for her to accept that her daughter would not be raising her children in her own faith. "I just couldn't believe that after being raised in such a strong Lutheran faith and upbringing in our church that Angela wouldn't want her kids to know Jesus and that she was comfortable knowing that they might not be ushered into the kingdom of God through Jesus Christ. My faith is so strong and my belief in the power of Jesus is so firm that all I could do was turn to my pastor and ask his help and counsel, and he told me to trust that Jesus would work it out as it should be. I had a hard time with that because I have always believed that the only road to heaven is by professing faith in Jesus as the Savior and Son of God and if my own grandchildren weren't raised in the faith of Jesus that their souls might not get to heaven when they died."

Andrea continued, her face clearly mirroring the pain she had gone through at the time. "I spoke with Angela about this a lot in the beginning of her relationship with Dennis, and she told me that she was an adult and loved Dennis and I just had to have faith that God was loving enough to accept good people of every religion into His grace and into heaven. It took a lot for me to finally accept that point of view, but I realized one day that I didn't want to push my own daughter and grandchildren away or out of my life and that if I was a woman of faith then I had to *be* a woman of faith and have faith that God would work it all out as He saw fit. I know that Dennis is a good person and a wonderful husband and father and after all, Jews were God's chosen people, so I decided that having a good relationship with Angela and my grandchildren was the most important thing in my life and everything else would just have to take a back seat to that and I would leave the details in God's hands."

"Over My Dead Body"

Of course it does not always work out so smoothly that parents become accepting of the choices their children make. Sometimes they never do. Other times it takes a particularly powerful emotional experience to move them from rejection to acceptance.

Consider one of my congregants' sisters, who had been dating a divorced Venezuelan Catholic man fifteen years her senior who had a thirteen-year-old daughter from that previous marriage. When she announced to her family that they were going to get married in one year's time, her father, a relatively nonreligious and only marginally observant Jew, responded instantly (and loudly), "Over my dead body!" When questioned about his vociferous objection, at first all he would say is, "Because he is not good for her."

When the daughter began to probe more deeply of course, layer upon layer of upset was peeled away until the real reason was eventually uncovered. First she asked, "Is it because the man is a foreigner?" and the father answered, "Yes." When it was pointed out that he had also been an immigrant forty-five years before, he said nothing in reply. "Is it because he is so much older than I am?" "Yes," he replied once again. But when it was pointed out that he had married her mother who was twelve years his junior, again he was silent. Then she asked, "Is it because my fiancé has a child already?" "Yes," replied the father a third time. So she pointed out that his current marriage had been his second and that he had also brought a child to his second marriage. "Is it because my fiancé isn't financially successful like you are?" she asked. "Yes," he replied once again. And so she pointed out that he had come to this country with only $100 in his pocket, and of course he had no answer to that either.

Finally moment of truth arrived and she asked her father, "Is it really because he is Catholic?" "Yes!" he said. "That's the most important reason." Yet her father had himself married a convert forty-one years before. And besides, his daughter and her fiancé had chosen to raise their children in the Jewish faith and traditions. But even after all this discussion, with pointing out all the obvious contradictions in the father's intellectual objections to her upcoming marriage, her father would not budge in his assertions that the Venezuelan man was "not right" for his daughter. He started talking about having detectives check out the man and disowning his daughter, and remained emotionally committed to doing what he could to prevent the marriage.

So what did the daughter do? She appealed to him in the only way she knew he would understand: She got pregnant. When her father found out, he insisted that they get married, not in one year but in six weeks, at his own home, and proceeded to invite every single one of his friends, his colleagues, his family far and wide, and all their children. He paid for the Venezuelan relatives to come to the United States, oversaw a lavish wedding affair, later welcomed his new grandchild, and even learned to embrace the new husband's calling him "Abba" (Hebrew for "father"), which none of his other children-in-law had ever dared to do. In the end the power and emotional reality of contemplating not being part of a grandchild's life was what pushed this man to let go of his objections and refocus on what really matters most: the love of family itself.

Five

WHAT INTERMARRIED CHILDREN WANT
MOST FROM THEIR PARENTS

BEING HELPFUL WITHOUT BECOMING OVERBEARING

Every successful relationship is more art than science. This is never truer than when it comes to an interfaith relationship. Interfaith relationships require mastering not only the arts of compromise and negotiation, but also the arts of being supportive without abdicating your own needs and desires, of running interference and making peace between your partner and your parents, and often of tactful retreat and learning to let go. But as delicate and artful as one must be to successfully manage an interfaith marriage, it is equally challenging to walk the fine line as the parent of an intermarried child. How can you be helpful and not overbearing when it comes to issues of religion and the religious upbringing of your grandchildren?

It is true that for some couples it all seems to flow more easily than for others. This is true particularly when they agree together that they will use their own parents primarily as the surrogate sources of religion in their home—go to Christian grandparents to celebrate Christmas and Jewish grandparents to celebrate Passover, for example. As you might imagine, most grandparents are thrilled to be used in this manner and to be given the opportunity to be involved in the lives of their children and grandchildren in a way that allows them to teach their grandchildren their own religious heritage and customs. In fact, with most interfaith couples, this becomes one of the primary areas in which grandparents consider themselves the natural and obvious experts.

After all, no one lives disconnected from the rest of the world. Every interfaith family is made up of at least an extended family with not only parents and grandparents but also brothers and sisters, aunts and uncles, cousins, and even close family friends. All of these take an interest in the lives of your children and can have an influence on shaping the experiences of your children's different religious traditions, holidays, customs, and celebrations.

When you are lucky these various influences are in harmony, supportive of one another, and complementary in a way that provides a rich and nurturing spiritual tapestry that adds a greater sense of meaning to your children's and grandchildren's lives. But equally as often, these individual influences can be experienced as divisive, even viewed as competing with one another. When that happens your own children can end up experiencing your interest in sharing your religious traditions with your grandchildren as intrusive and overstepping of your bounds. Then even your grandchildren can end up confused about the role that religion plays in their lives or frustrated and resentful about religion altogether.

The key to successfully walking the delicate balance between the potentially conflicting religious needs and desires of your intermarried children is to learn how to be seen as helpful without being seen as overbearing. Your children need to be able to turn to you to help them explain some of the religious traditions and customs, holidays and celebrations, history and meanings behind how they were raised. At the same time, they have to trust that you will not proselytize your grandchildren behind their backs. Your children need to feel secure in letting you spend time alone with your grandchildren talking about religious and spiritual matters and trust that you will not tell them that you believe that there is really only one right religion in the world and it is yours.

For many parents of intermarried children this is not an easy challenge to face. After all, when you have strongly held religious beliefs it is normal and understandable to want to share them with those you love, especially your own grandchildren. As we all know, in some religious traditions it is actually a religious imperative to spread the "good news" of one's religious truth with others and is considered a God-given commandment to do so. If your religious tradition happens to be one of those, it may be extremely difficult for you to hold your tongue and act as if other religious traditions have as much legitimacy as your own. Whether you push your own religion on your grandchildren or not, the choice is yours. And it is you who has to clarify your priorities.

No one else can set your priorities in life for you. You are the only one who can decide how important it is for you to maintain a good, ongoing, lifelong relationship with your children and grandchildren, versus your own need to assert the primacy of your personal religious traditions and beliefs. If the relationships are your priority (and if not you probably would not be reading this book), then maintaining this balance will be your goal. You will choose to serve as a helpful source of information and teaching, while not crossing the line into becoming pushy and divisive about religion, and you will use what is best for your family relationships as the yardstick against which to constantly measure your own behavior.

"Being helpful without becoming overbearing" can be as simple as letting your kids know that you are available to drive your grandchildren to Sunday school or religious school if they need your help. You can tell them you would rather they call on you to drive your grandchildren than have them not go at all if logistics ever become a problem.

When it comes to walking that fine line, it is probably more *how* you do what you do than it is whatever you are doing itself. Ideally, for example, you should be able to read Bible stories or holiday stories or talk with your grandchildren about what a holiday means to you or to your religious tradition while openly treating any other religious traditions that are represented in your children's home with respect and even admiration. Such an attitude when communicated to your kids and grandkids will make it easier for them to call upon you more often for help with sharing your own religious tradition because your involvement will not be seen as a creating competition between one tradition and the next.

Imagine ending up with the kind of strain in your relationships like that experienced by Adam and Christy, an interfaith couple. After experiencing both sets of parents as constantly pushing their own religious traditions on their grandchildren, Adam and Christy told me that their advice to new interfaith parents would be, "Live far away from your relatives for the first part of your marriage and when you first have children so you can be together and work out your religious lifestyle independently of external pressure." Now do you want your children to purposefully move so far away that the only regular contact you get with your grandchildren occurs over the phone?

On the other hand it is important to retain your own religious integrity even when you talk with your grandchildren about religious issues. For example, there is clearly a difference between the beliefs of different religious traditions; therefore, it is appropriate when asked for you to be honest about your own deeply held beliefs. If your grandchildren are being raised with the monotheistic belief in "One God" while you believe in the Trinity and that Jesus is both the Son of God and divine in his own right, it is perfectly appropriate to be honest with your grandchildren about how your understanding of God may differ from theirs or the tradition in which they are being raised, if and when they ask. Offering a theological discussion of how your beliefs differ from theirs and the beliefs of their parents without being asked in the first place is an open invitation to having your children misinterpret your "explanation" as "proselytizing" which can easily cause them to misunderstand your intentions and ultimately feel compelled to impose rules as to what they are willing and unwilling to have you talk about with your grandchildren.

HELP WITH HOLIDAYS AND FAMILY CELEBRATIONS

The mandate of keeping an appropriate balance between your own religious desires and those of your interfaith children is true especially when it comes to holidays and family celebrations. One way to consistently lay the groundwork for an ever-stronger relationship with the ones you love is to offer the use of your home for holiday celebrations, and then go out of your way to make everyone who comes (especially your son- or daughter-in-law of another religion) feel comfortable, accepted, and at ease when they are there.

It is natural for people to feel a little uncomfortable when they step into a religious environment that is not their own. Most of the time people feel uncomfortable simply *anticipating* participation in an unfamiliar ritual or celebration. And this lack of familiarity with different religious traditions and customs does not disappear simply because someone has a single positive experience. Especially with holidays and celebrations that only come once a year, it may take many years of living with and celebrating the same holidays over and over again before your child's partner feels comfortable and at home with rituals that were not part of his or her upbringing.

Keeping this in mind from one year to the next gives you an opportunity to act in ways that are helpful, loving, and considerate of anyone else who might be in a similar situation, including the extended family and even friends of your children and their partners. One technique that has worked for many is to let everyone who will be coming know exactly what will be happening in advance. You can tell them what they can expect and what they will be expected to do, and at the same time assure them that they will not be asked to do anything that might make them uncomfortable or that will put them on the spot. If they know what to expect and if you explain the rituals in advance (you can even print up a "what this holiday/ritual/custom means" or "what exactly will happen when we celebrate this holiday" page and send it to people in advance of the celebration), they will be grateful for your thoughtfulness and more likely to want to come and participate in your religious holidays in the future.

What intermarried children want from their parents is an emotionally safe place to bring their children and their partners, where they can celebrate holidays together and provide an opportunity for their children to learn about their parents' religions in an accepting, nonjudgmental, and pressure-free environment.

They also can use your support and help in creating successful holiday celebrations and conducting the religious rituals and ceremonies of your religious tradition in their own homes. There may be times when your children choose to celebrate religious holidays without being surrounded by the larger extended family. Such a decision is often made because it helps them to work out together their own unique form of celebrating that takes into account the interfaith nature of their lives without the pressure of "performing" in front of or conforming to the standards and expectations of other relatives. New couples often make this choice to celebrate holidays in their own homes rather than putting themselves and their interfaith partner into the traditional extended familial melting pot as a way of protecting their relationship and their partner—especially if they haven't already had lots of major holidays celebration experiences together. Sometimes for new couples it just seems safer in their own homes with fewer people.

If you can create the kind of supportive relationship with your children that encourages them to use you as a resource and turn to you for suggestions, advice, recipes, recollections of different ways holidays and rituals have been celebrated in the past, it can become a great source of strengthening your relationship. Such intimate and supportive sharing of history and tradition helps to reinforce the lifetime of loving, living, and learning that is the hallmark of positive family life. It can strengthen the very foundation of your parent–child relationship and give you the opportunity to be seen as an ally for your child in the challenging undertaking of creating a successful interfaith marriage.

Many people have spent a lifetime using homemade ritualistic objects from their childhood. This can come in the form of creating special holiday foods, or using the same recipes used for generations, or making or collecting precious holiday decorations such as Christmas tree ornaments or Passover Matzah covers, etc. When children intermarry there is often a nostalgic sadness among parents who fear that all those loving memories will simply disappear or no longer be part of your family's religious life experiences. But when parents go out of their way to create an openness and provide nonjudgmental support to their children to help them in any way that they choose to celebrate religious occasions in their interfaith home, this lifetime of rich personal spiritual history can be seen in the most positive light as a deep and meaningful resource of positive memory and experience—with or without the old traditions.

Tell your children that you are available to help and give them support in any way that you can and that you would be happy to make available any of the childhood religious objects that may be meaningful to your kids in creating their own version of celebrating holidays to retain the warm and positive memories of the past. At the very least, this will communicate to your children that your primary concern is not about celebrating the holiday exactly the way you have always celebrated it, but rather about your relationship with them and how you can continue to play a positive, loving role in their lives—regardless of the religious and relationship choices they have made.

The same is true with nonreligious family celebrations. Whether Thanksgiving, civic holidays such as Independence Day or Memorial Day, special birthdays, or milestone anniversary celebrations, the best you can do for your own relationship with your children is to be as consistent as possible in projecting a loving, supportive, and nonjudgmental attitude about these events, going out of your way to create an inclusive and welcoming environment. Extend your hands and your home in welcome to the extended family of your child's spouse or partner, but also be prepared to support decisions of your children to bring those celebrations into their homes instead.

Interfaith families often find that religious holidays and celebrations carry with them a deeper emotional baggage and charge than do secular family celebrations. As such, it might be easier for interfaith couples to feel comfortable hosting those holidays or celebrations with their extended families in their homes. Families seem to naturally come up with their own divisions of how and where holidays and special recurring celebrations are handled. They might end up always celebrating the religious holidays that come each year (like Christmas, Passover, Easter, Hanukah, Kwanza, Ramadan) at one or another of their parent's homes and always celebrate the more secular national holidays (like Independence Day, Memorial Day, Labor Day, Thanksgiving) at their home or the home of a sibling. Creating a kind of regular expectation regarding where holidays are celebrated can help to create a sense of stability and "normalcy" regarding what might be otherwise emotionally loaded experiences for everyone in the family.

The same positive attitude of inclusion, welcome, and openness is often particularly meaningful when your child is in a gay or lesbian relationship, whether interfaith or not. There are sadly still so many openly expressed prejudices and fears when it comes to gay, lesbian, bisexual, or transgender relationships throughout the world, that if your child is in such a relationship the impact of your attitude and your willingness to go the extra mile to be inclusive and lovingly accepting will have a more powerful impact than you can ever imagine. Parents who create the kind of supportive, loving relationship that I am suggesting are often surprised and amazed to discover that their own influence and impact goes far, far beyond merely that of their own children. There are so many gay and lesbian couples who continue to feel an emotional distance and rejection from their own parents that you may discover that you have suddenly been given the gift of becoming a surrogate "parent" or "grandparent" for your child's friends and their children as well.

There are obviously additional challenges when couples with children get divorced, especially when there is acrimony sufficient to prevent a harmonious joining together of both sides at holiday times. In such cases, grandparents can be most helpful to their children and grandchildren by encouraging them to work out an alternating custody arrangement for holidays with their former partners so that every holiday, sacred occasion, or grandchild's birthday does not turn into a painful argument among all family members regarding who is celebrating what with whom. You would give your grandchildren a great and loving gift if you can be a source of mediation and moderation with your own children, encouraging compromise, and not providing additional pressure by insisting on your "right" as the grandparents to have your grandchildren celebrating holidays and special events with you every time.

FEELING YOUR CONTINUED PRIDE AND LOVE

It almost goes without saying that what every interfaith child needs and wants from his or her parents is to experience their continued pride and love. In fact, what most people want in life is "acceptance" in the broadest sense of the term, and an acknowledgment that we turned out OK and our parents are proud of us and continue to love us in spite of all the good and bad decisions we have made throughout our lives.

Everyone's life is filled with ups and downs. That is how we all learn about life itself. It is the natural process of growth and maturation. No one goes through life without making mistakes, and no one gets to the end of life without regrets and a host of "if only's" and "if I knew then what I know now" realizations. That is just the way it is. Whether you are the parent whose child has intermarried or the child who has picked a life partner from a different background, what it means to be an adult is to make the best choices we can and then take responsibility for living with the consequences.

What interfaith children want from their parents is understanding that whether or not they would have made the same choices as their kids given similar circumstances, they recognize that their children are simply doing their best to create the most loving, meaningful, and purposeful life they can. Those are the feelings of continued pride and love that our children seek from parents. All parents of interfaith, interracial, and gay and lesbian children need to make sure these positive feelings get communicated to their children in as many different ways and as often enough as is necessary to make sure that there is no question in their minds about how their parents feel about them.

NONJUDGMENTAL HELP WITH WEDDING PLANNING AND PARTICIPATION

One of the first opportunities we have to demonstrate our love and support for our children after they have made the decision to marry someone of another religious, cultural, or racial background is in how we approach helping them plan their wedding. In American culture it is still the case that most weddings are planned by brides and their families, and most grooms still just go with the flow of whatever makes their brides happy and simply show up on the designated day to say, "I do." Even so, it is a golden opportunity for both the bride's and groom's parents to demonstrate their love and support for their children at a particularly emotionally challenging and vulnerable time in their lives and relationships.

This is perhaps even more powerful an opportunity if your children are gay or lesbian and are planning a formal ceremony or wedding to reflect their commitment to each other as life partners. There are very few places in the world where same-sex couples can legally get married, but even in places where that is not legally possible, private commitment ceremonies can carry all the same spiritual, emotional, and personal commitments to the relationship that heterosexual ceremonies represent, without the benefit of legal status.

The role of parents in all these situations is to find ways of providing support, encouragement, help, and love that affirms the adult choices that your children have made, demonstrating by word and deed that you will always be standing by their sides (perhaps literally at the wedding) as loving parents.

In many ways the challenges that interfaith, interracial, or gay couples face in planning a wedding are exactly the same as any other couple might face. There are the same decisions to be made about the type of ceremony, the location of the wedding, the flowers, the clothing, the make up of the wedding party, the agony over the guest list, determining the size of the wedding, the time of day of the ceremony, seating charts, and on and on and on. Every wedding faces these issues and challenges, and every wedding has the potential for hurt feelings, frustration, exasperation, and the delicate challenge of balancing the often-competing interests of brides, grooms, and parents.

Obviously, there are special challenges and issues that arise when planning interfaith weddings, but these same challenges also provide special opportunities as well. When interfaith couples plan their weddings, they are more likely to anticipate resistance and one version or another of "push back" from parents, simply because these parents are ill at ease with the idea of their children being part of an interfaith marriage in the first place. That is why if you, the parent, can position yourself as a peacemaker within the two extended families, in which you are seen as offering nonjudgmental help, encouragement, and support to your children as they go through the wedding planning obstacle course, it can not only strengthen your relationships with your children, but also get you off to the very best start with your new son- or daughter-in-law—and potentially his or her extended family (who are about to become your family through marriage) as well.

This is one of those times when intention really matters. If you are a parent approaching the planning of an interfaith wedding, make a conscious, clear decision about how you want their children to experience you as a result of going through this process. If you cannot articulate this well, take a piece of paper and write down the specific qualities of personality and character that you would want your children to identify with you when it is all over.

After all, given how the human mind works, we mostly become what we think about in life. So if you can get a clear vision of the kind of person you want to be in this process, you will likely become that very picture. And ultimately isn't this what intermarried children most want from their parents-to be there with love and support during this most significant of moment in their lives?

Another important aspect of planning a wedding where your attitude can truly make a difference for your child, reducing areas of friction and potential conflict, has to do with your actual role in the wedding ceremony itself. Having officiated at hundreds and hundreds of wedding ceremonies during more than thirty years as a member of the clergy, I can attest that there is *no* one, right way to conduct a wedding. By the same token there is *no* one right role for parents to play, either.

There are weddings where parents walk up the aisle with their children, stand next to them at the altar, or behind them under the wedding canopy. Couples and their parents have participated in a Christian "unity candle" lighting ceremony and read words of blessing or prayer during the ceremony to each other. Parents have been included in a Jewish blessing over wine, in an African-American ceremony involving jumping over a broom, in a Hindu ceremony involving flowers and fruit as offerings, and more. And at some weddings, parents sit in the front row and do nothing at all.

All of these variations on the wedding ceremony with vastly different levels of parental participation had one crucial element in common: when they were over, the bride and groom were married. That is what the ceremony is really all about in the first place: the bride and groom exchanging wedding vows, making a public commitment in front of family and friends, and becoming spiritual partners as they continue to share their lives with each other. Everything else in the ceremony is secondary to the essential purpose of joining the couple in a shared-life commitment. Everything.

The best gift you can give your children when it comes to helping them plan as stress-free a wedding ceremony as possible is to tell them you are happy to participate in *whatever way will make them happy*. If as a parent you can refrain from putting the additional pressure of your own expectations and needs on your children as they undertake what is one of life's most stressful experiences, you will be not only giving them a gift beyond measure, but also establishing a relationship with them from the very beginning of their marriage that demonstrates your desire to be a loving parent. Whether they are willing to say anything about it or not, this is what your children want most from you—and what will be best for your relationship in the long run.

TRUST, RESPECT, AND BEING TREATED LIKE AN ADULT

Making a decision to adopt the supportive role in their wedding planning is just one of the many ways you can demonstrate another important quality that interfaith children desire: to be treated not as a child but as an adult with trust and respect.

Having and raising children is obviously a complex and emotionally challenging life adventure. On the one hand no matter how old they get, you are always their parent and they are always your children. It is inevitable that a lifetime of behavior patterns, emotional reactions, personal history, and relationship expectations will play a continued role in how you and your children interact whenever you are together. At the same time all of our relationships go through stages of personal growth and development even as we do the same in our individual lives. One of the fundamental challenges of parenthood is allowing our relationship with our children to grow and change, evolve and develop so that ultimately we relate not only as parent to child but as adult to adult as well.

Learning to treat your children with the respect and trust they deserve as adults is important for your own peace of mind as a parent and is a necessary part of the process of empowering them to be the best adults they can be. One of the fundamental tasks of parenting is learning to let go, one step at a time, of your control and influence over your children and the decisions and choices that they make. That is both your challenge as a parent and their challenge as children—to constantly redefine the nature of your relationship as they grow through the various stages of childhood into adulthood.

What all children want from their parents, whether they are single or married, whether or not they marry someone of their own religion, culture, or race, whether they are gay or straight, is to be trusted and treated with respect. As well, treating them with respect as adults is actually another way of acknowledging and recognizing the success of your own parenting. It is because you have helped to raise them from children into competent and capable adults that they deserve to be treated as such.

NONJUDGMENTAL LISTENING AND ACCEPTANCE

One of the many challenges faced by parents whose children intermarry is whether or not they are able to create a relationship with their children in which their mutual acceptance and support are the definitive aspects of the overall relationship. For many parents, this is one of the most difficult of all skills to master and for some it is an elusive expectation that is simply impossible to fulfill.

"How can I engage in 'nonjudgmental listening,'" parents often ask me, "when I really think my kids are making the wrong choices in their lives? Am I supposed to just sit there and say nothing when I think my kids are making a mistake? Isn't that my job as a parent to give them good advice and correct them when they are wrong and do my best to steer them in the right direction so they don't mess up their lives?" The answer is both yes and no.

It is "yes," of course, your role as parent to give the best advice you can to your children and to help them make the right choices in their lives. But "no," it is not your role when your kids are already grown to tell them how to live their lives—especially when their choices in relationships and parenting differ from your own. As a parent you need to have enough faith both in yourself—and the kind of role model that you have been for your children—and in your children and their ability to make good decisions or learn and grow from any bad ones they might make.

Making mistakes in life is the number one manner in which we humans learn to adapt and to grow wiser. It is a fundamental aspect of human nature that we fail our way to success in life much like an infant who must fall down innumerable times in the process of learning to walk. If children simply quit trying the first time they made mistakes and fell, or parents chided them about their uncoordinated attempts to walk, no one would *ever* learn to walk.

The best you can do as a parent is to give your grown children the respect and support that they deserve by giving them the space to make mistakes, fall, pick themselves up, and then more forward. The first step in creating a relationship with your children that is supportive and open is to practice the discipline of "nonjudgmental listening."

Nonjudgmental listening is the art of creating a safe relationship with your children where they feel they are able to share their own struggles with the difficult and challenging issues that are part of being in an interfaith or interracial relationship. It is a skill that often does not come naturally or easily to parents but one for which there is a very large reward if you are successful. The reward is a relationship of trust, openness, mutual respect, and closeness with your children. And that only comes when they feel emotionally safe enough to share their fears, longings, and dreams with you.

Nonjudgmental listening means being available as a sounding board, giving your advice and suggestions when asked, *but keeping them to yourself when not asked*. Sometimes, what your kids want most is a safe place to wrestle out loud with the emotionally charged choices that they must make. If you can create that kind of safe emotional environment for them, they will be grateful beyond measure. The very act of nonjudgmental listening makes them feel accepted, validated, and acknowledged, something all children crave from their parents.

PATIENCE

Patience is one of the most important qualities to cultivate if you want to be successful in supporting your children and their interfaith or same-gender relationships. The more you are able to cultivate patience regarding your expectations of your children and with your own behavior, the better your relationship with your children will be.

Your children know that life is not always perfect, and that sometimes they regret the choices they have made for themselves or their families. Not only will they appreciate your patience, they may also be able to use that very patience and supportiveness you supply to give them the time they need to see their own mistakes and make the changes necessary to be successful in their marriages or in their lives.

Similarly, cultivating the quality of patience is a personal spiritual discipline. Patience helps you not jump to conclusions and say something negative that you will later regret when your grandchildren run up to you all excited about something they learned in church or synagogue or mosque or temple that runs counter to your own religious beliefs. Patience helps you take a slow deep breath and listen nonjudgmentally when your children explain to you why they are not coming to your house this year for Christmas or Passover or Thanksgiving because of another family with an equal claim on their loyalty. Patience helps you to remain calm and reflective and give your children the respect and space they need and deserve when you see them making decisions about how they are raising their children that you are simply dying to correct. Patience is the gift you give to yourself to slow down your impulse to act on any negative judgments and give yourself the time to reaffirm your trust in your children, being as supportive, nurturing, compassionate, and sympathetic as you can. Sometimes genius really is patience, and practicing patience can be the greatest gift you can give yourself.

UNCONDITIONAL LOVE

In a sense what all these suggestions really boil down to is this: what interfaith children want from their parents is unconditional love. In nearly every parenting book ever written you hear and read about the power and importance of unconditional love when it comes to your children. But for many people "unconditional love" is confused with "uncritical acceptance of all behavior"—*they are not the same thing.*

Particularly when your children are young, as a parent you do not have to simply smile and accept anything your child does or says without judgment in order to demonstrate that you love him or her unconditionally. In fact, it is quite the opposite. One of your primary jobs as a parent when your children are still growing and learning about life is to be the primary source of right and wrong, the number one role model for what it means to be a man or a woman, a father or mother, a partner in a committed relationship, a good citizen of the community, a good friend, and a good child to their grandparents. That job is simply part of being a parent and is yours whether you want it or not.

Demonstrating unconditional love to your children often requires you to correct their behavior, to point out when they make mistakes, and to teach them the difference between being honest and taking responsibility for your actions or lying and cheating yourself and others by trying to hide what you have done and avoid responsibility altogether.

Unconditional love is one of the most important lessons that any parent can teach a child, and to truly demonstrate unconditional love is to love your child *not because of* his or her behavior, but *in spite* of it. It is to demonstrate to your children in as many ways as possible throughout their lives that you believe they have fundamental self-worth and value, not because they are following your orders and picking up the trash in their rooms or doing their homework on time, but simply because they exist.

Regardless of your personal religious beliefs or affiliations, if you can see your children as spiritual gifts, as if they were given to you from the power that created the entire universe, just imagine how lovingly you would treat them, even when they needed to be reprimanded. This is what it means to treat them with unconditional love. It is to recognize that every child is unique, a one-of-a-kind that has never existed before and will never exist again in the history of the universe. As such, every child is special, every child deserves to discover his or her own special voice and path and destiny in life. We show them unconditional love when we teach them this truth and live this truth as parents when we guide them on their own path to wholeness, fulfillment, and a purposeful life.

That is the attitude of unconditional love that all children want, need, and deserve from their parents. It is not the same as uncritical acceptance of every decision that our children make, but rather at the end of the day when they lie down at night, do they know that you love them, support them, care about them, and are proud of who they are despite their struggles to find their way in life? If you can say yes to those questions then you have given your children the greatest gift.

Six

"YOURS, MINE, & OURS"—INTERFAITH
FAMILY RELATIONSHIPS

MAINTAINING A GOOD RELATIONSHIP
WITH YOUR CHILD

Perhaps the single most powerful motivation behind each and every chapter in this book is the desire to help parents whose children intermarry find the tools and strategies necessary to insure that they will maintain the best possible relationship with their children.

Periodic stresses and strains between parents and children are normal and expected. These stresses become especially noticeable when a child gets married, whether the marriage is within the same faith or interfaith. After all, every time you welcome a new member into your family there are a host of experiences, behaviors, and emotional baggage left over from each other's childhoods that can interfere with your attempt at a smooth transition from single to partnered, and from family of origin to a new family. Sometimes the stresses arise simply from the challenges of shifting our expectations of behavior and relationships from "boyfriend and girlfriend" expectations to "husband and wife" expectations. All these normal and everyday challenges are exacerbated by the additional factor of learning to adjust to the increased emotional and social demands that interfaith issues bring to the new family dynamic.

This chapter is designed to help you identify and successfully cope with the important issues that may come up in your relationship with your own child, your new son- or daughter-in-law, or his or her extended family as the reality of your interfaith family system emerges.

Above all other considerations, maintaining good communication with your own child is paramount. Like it or not, divorce still stands at close to 50 percent for all new marriages in America today, so despite all the good will, positive attitude, and prayers in the world, there is still a serious likelihood that your child's marriage may one day end in divorce. This sobering reality helps further the point that as important as it is to nurture a positive, loving relationship with your child's life partner, it is even more important to do whatever is necessary to keep your relationship with your child strong, caring, and mutually nurturing—regardless of the ultimate fate of his or her current relationship. When all is said and done, whether life partners stay or go, your child will always remain your child.

So what *are* the keys to maintaining a good relationship with your child when he or she has entered into a committed interfaith relationship? Without question the first key is to continually demonstrate respect for your child and his or her life choices. More parent–child relationships are dashed because of perceived disrespect than from any other single relationship issue.

Children grow up with a deep and abiding need to experience the respect and approval of their parents, regardless of how old they become. This is true *forever*—no matter how many years they live and even if their parents are themselves no longer living, children still have a profound and deeply rooted emotional need to feel that their parents approve of how they act and who they are.

Parental approval is such a fundamental human need that many adults in their fifties and sixties still desperately try to please their parents, sabotaging otherwise wonderful relationships with loving partners because they cannot take the heat of parental disapproval or the lack of respect for who they have become that *their* parents somehow demonstrated to them, about them. This is true for some people even when their parents are no longer alive.

The second key to maintaining a good relationship with your children when they are involved in interfaith relationships is to demonstrate respect for their partners and their partners' extended families as well. Treating everyone involved with dignity—including them in your family celebrations and rituals, welcoming them in a loving and nonjudgmental way, participating when invited in their important rituals—is crucial to maintaining a supportive, loving relationship that allows for open and mutually respectful communication between you and your adult children.

Sometimes it is actually easier to develop a nonjudgmental and supportive relationship with your child's partner than it is with your own child. This is so because every parent–child relationship has a lifetime of emotional baggage that is not present with your child's partner. There simply is not the same emotional history to push your buttons and create the depth of feeling and associations that come with your own child.

You may use this lack of history with this new member of your family to help bridge any resentments or unexpressed communication with your own child that might be getting in the way of having the very best parent–child relationship possible. See if you can enlist your child's life partner as your own ally in nurturing the mutually loving and supportive relationship that both you and your child truly desire in the first place. Tell your child's partner that your goal is to have the best relationship possible both with him or her and your child whom he or she loves, and that you would deeply appreciate whatever help he or she can provide in facilitating a fabulous parent–child relationship. This is not designed to be meddlesome and is not intended to suggest that you surreptitiously enlist the support of your child's partner in a secret conspiracy against your own child. It is quite the opposite. It is as simple as letting your child *and* his or her partner know that your intention is to have the best relationship you can with both of them and ask both of them to help you and be open if anything you are doing or saying to either of them becomes a barrier to that shared desire.

Asking for help in this manner both demonstrates respect for the partner and sends a message to your own child that the value you place on your relationship is more important than any other petty issues or considerations of the religion, race, culture, language, or sexual orientation differences that might exist between you and your child and his or her partner.

PREJUDICE, MISINFORMATION, AND LEARNING ABOUT STRANGERS

The strategy outlined of including your child's partner in the process of maintaining the best possible relationship with your child is also designed to communicate your desire to eliminate any potential prejudices that you might openly or inadvertently hold against the religion, race, culture, or gender of this newest member of your family as well as the extended family that you have just inherited.

All of us have prejudices that are so ingrained in the fabric of who we are, such an integral part of our outlook on life, that we often are not even aware that they exist. For example, many white people have prejudices about black people that include assuming a group of young black men are inherently more likely to be dangerous than a group of young white men. Many straight people have prejudices that children raised with gay parents are more likely to be emotionally confused or inappropriately exposed to sexuality at a young age or end up gay or lesbian themselves than kids raised by heterosexual parents. Many Christians have prejudices that Jews are more likely to be devious when it comes to money than Christians. And many Jews have prejudices that most Christians are anti-Semitic whether they demonstrate it or not.

Everyone has prejudices. "Prejudice" simply means that we have "pre-judged" a situation, an individual, or a group based on either our own past experiences, or ideas we have learned from our parents, religious institutions, friends we trust, the media, or teachers we admire. Wisdom and maturity consists of recognizing the prejudices that we have and consciously suspend-ing those prejudices long enough to be able to judge situations and individuals on their own terms as they actually are.

Knowing that we all have prejudices can be a liberating realization for it helps us to recognize that we are not "bad" people for having them. It can remind us that we are human and subject to the influences of all the same misinformation and negative education that affect everyone else in our society in one way or another.

When we accept the reality of the limits of our own knowledge and infor-mation regarding the beliefs, rituals, traditions, culture, and reasons behind why other people act the way they act, we are better able to open up ourselves to learning about them from a fresh perspective. If you recognize how little you know about what really makes other people tick *and* reinforce to your-self that everyone wants to be known and respected as someone of value and worth, you can more easily reach out to expand your own understanding of who they really are and why they do what they do.

When you do not understand something that your child or his or her part-ner does, a ritual they have incorporated into their life, a holiday or sacred time that they celebrate, *the best way to learn about it is to ask.* You will be amazed at how much you can learn and how eager people are to share who they are and what is important to them if you seriously demonstrate an inter-est in them and their lives. This demonstration of sincere interest is one of the most precious gifts you can give both to your own child and to anyone who he or she has brought into your family.

In the biblical book of Leviticus, Chapter 19, Verse 34, God challenges the Children of Israel to "treat the stranger in your midst as the home born." Fear of strangers is as old as civilization itself. That is why this was such a profound and difficult challenge not only three thousand years ago when the Bible was written but today as well.

Xenophobia is well entrenched in our social consciousness. One of the lega-cies of the 9-11 World Trade Center disaster is a rising fear of strangers as represented by the passing of legislation like the Patriot Act, and the constant feeling of vulnerability plaguing us today. In light of these rising fears, demonstrating your ability to transcend those prejudices and welcome the stranger into your family, into the most intimate center of your life, is both an act of courage and an act of faith. It is also often one of the hardest things to do even as it can be one of the most powerful symbols of your love for your child and a beautiful reflection of your willingness to adapt, change, and adjust to the demands of changing times.

For example, if you are Catholic and your child marries a Buddhist, it will pay big emotional dividends if you take the time to learn about Buddhism and show an interest in the spiritual life of your child and his or her partner. This is obviously true regardless of your own specific religious background or culture or ethnicity. The more you can learn about that which makes your new family member different, about what he or she believes and the rituals and holidays that he or she celebrates or even simply what it feels like to live in this world as he or she does, the closer it will bring you to your own child and the better and more fulfilling will be all your family relationships.

Sometimes change is as easy as accepting the reality that along with your ingrained prejudices comes a healthy (or perhaps unhealthy) dose of misinformation about other people, other cultures, other religions, and other ways of living and believing other than your own. Once you face the simple truth of how often each of us relies on myths, hearsay, and gossip about each other as if the stories we hear are the "gospel," it is easier to do the work necessary to correct our mistaken ideas and discover what is actually true about others.

HOW TO EXPLAIN YOUR OWN RELIGION/CULTURE/ ETHNICITY/WAY OF LIFE TO YOUR NEW FAMILY

At the same time that it is important to accept how little you actually know about the religion, culture, or way of life of others, the same is true regarding their misinformation and prejudices about you. Most people know so little about anyone who is not like them that it is likely that your newest family members are mostly ignorant of the religious traditions, rituals, customs, and way of life that you cherish. That is why it is helpful to learn how to effectively share your religious and cultural traditions with your new family in a way that makes it easy for them to understand your traditions and what they mean to you. When they can learn about who you are in a non-threatening or non-confrontational manner, it allows them to feel respect for you and your way of life simply because it reflects an important aspect of who you are as a person.

Of course you cannot just walk up and announce to your new son-in-law, "I want you to understand our family traditions and values, so please sit down so that I can give you a lecture on why I believe that Jesus died for our sins and that the only way you can get into the Kingdom of God is through acceptance of Jesus Christ as your Lord and Savior." Obviously this approach would come across as a bit too aggressive and "in your face," making you appear to be proselytizing or trying to convert him to your ways of belief. Such a confrontational approach will not do anything positive for your family relationships regardless of the religious tradition that you are trying to share and no matter how sweetly you smile as you deliver the "truth" as you see it to your son- or daughter-in-law. Plus, it may be the case that your child's life partner is simply not interested in who you are or what you believe or your way of life. If this is accurate, you will do best for your own child by respecting this disinterest and only sharing your beliefs or religious and cultural traditions if asked.

If you do end up being asked, the best approach is to be open, honest, direct, and simple. Sharing your own culture or religion with others works best when you clearly present the ideas and traditions that matter to you while demonstrating respect for the integrity of the person to whom you are speaking. Of course, this is a good rule of thumb in just about any conversation in any relationship where you have strong feelings or beliefs that you want to communicate.

Most people sincerely respect those who have strong religious convictions as long as their actions and deeds in their daily lives appear to be consistent with the values they express. What people resent is perceived religious hypocrisy where someone "preaches" religious ethics and values and then turns around and puts others down, disparages their name, or tradition, or culture and in general acts as if God's love and compassion are not quite big enough to embrace anyone other than their own brand of religion.

Ultimately, the best way to explain your own religious and cultural values to another is by living your life in a way that you become a living example of the values and way of life that you cherish. It happens by inviting them to participate with you and your family as you celebrate together a sacred festival or moment at your place of worship (or in the privacy of your own home).

By simply inviting others to share an experience with you—without judgment or pressure from you for them to adopt your ways or convert to your religious beliefs—these shared moments can become truly wonderful opportunities to better understand you, your family, and the way that your own son or daughter (whom they presumably love and respect) grew up. In this way you aren't "preaching," and you aren't even formally "teaching," you are simply living your values as others watch and learn in the process.

"Learning by doing" is an ageless pedagogic principle that is still the very best method for integrating a new concept or way of life into your own lifestyle. Inviting someone to experience a religious or cultural event that is important to you with your family also gives you the opportunity to explain to them in advance what they can expect to experience, what the rituals, prayers, songs, or customs mean.

If they express an interest, you can always offer to provide them with additional material to read or references that explain your religious and cultural traditions in clear, simple language. Sometimes there are movies and DVDs that are even more effective tools for understanding what is important to one culture that may otherwise be totally unimaginable to anyone who has not grown up in those traditions. The best way to approach this issue is for you to offer to provide any books or other multimedia experiences to your child that your child feels might help his or her partner and family to understand your family, how your child grew up, and the values and traditions that have mattered in your lives. Of course you never simply "offer" to share books or tapes or DVDs about your religion with others unless you want to be seen as proselytizing and trying to convert them to your religion or way of life. These are just suggestions as to how best to share this information *if they ask for it* and if they let you know that it is something that *they* want to learn about.

It is important for you to make clear to your own child (and his or her new family as well) that you are merely doing your best to help your child to make his or her new family feel comfortable and at home whenever they participate with your family in traditions that might otherwise seem foreign or even incomprehensible without prior experience or education.

The key to explaining your own religion/culture/ethnicity/way of life to your new family is in your ability to assume a nonjudgmental approach to *them* and *their* religious traditions and customs as well. One of the gifts and unacknowledged blessings of interfaith life is that it provides a chance for families that might otherwise conduct their entire lives isolated from those who are different to learn to cultivate a profound understanding and potential acceptance of those differences. In learning to see differences as opportunities for enhancing your own understanding of life and the diversity of opinions, cultures, and traditions that exist in our world, interfaith marriage is a positive not a negative, a blessing not a curse. When you learn to embrace differences, your involvement with your new extended family will become easier and easier every year—and, heaven forbid, perhaps even enjoyable!

YOU AND YOUR IN-LAWS

In my many years working in spiritual communities, I have seen relationships between in-laws that have created heartache, suffering, regret, and endless sorrow among their children. But I have also seen these relationships be inspiring, loving, joyful, and mutually fulfilling. Neither extreme is a foregone conclusion when your child intermarries. But the latter is available to almost anyone who has the will, desire, and commitment to make it work.

Many relationships among in-laws seem to be fundamentally based on confrontation, mutual distrust, and competition for the affection of their children and grandchildren. It is as if the marriage of the children is taking place in the middle of a heavyweight boxing ring and in opposite corners pose the in-laws, coached by their respective religious advisors on how to get out there in the middle of the ring and knock out their cultural opponents so *their* way of life can stand victorious at the end of the round.

How sad is this picture? Terribly sad, especially for the children and grandchildren who end up caught in the middle. These children spend years and tons of energy trying to make peace between all their parents and doing their best not to be seen as "taking sides" one way or another in this classic no-win situation. This phenomenon occurs far too many times, and every time it is heartbreaking for everyone involved because *everyone* loses.

Creating a positive, open, easygoing relationship with your in-laws can be accomplished in three simple steps.

Step one: Get totally clear between *you and your own* spouse or life partner that you are both committed to having a good, positive, and easy relationship with your in-laws. This has to be an openly articulated and agreed upon goal between you, so that you can help each other to stay on track should either of you hear or see the other act or say something that is contrary to this goal.

Step two: Communicate that intention to your child and his or her partner as well. Let them know that having a good, positive, and easygoing relationship with your in-laws is a priority for you, and that you are willing to do whatever it takes to make sure that happens.

Step three: Sit down with your in-laws and have the same conversation. Begin with a conversation about what you have most in common: namely, each other's children and your mutual desire for their relationship to flourish and remain strong, fulfilling, and successful

If there are grandchildren involved, talk with your in-laws about how important those kids are to all of you, how it is your intention to do whatever you can for all of you to have the most supportive and loving relationship you possibly can so that your mutual grandchildren will grow up in a family that demonstrates love, respect, mutual harmony in spite of the fact or perhaps because of the fact that it is an interfaith family. You must act the way you would want others to act. Demonstrate that openness of spirit and nonjudgmental acceptance of others are important values that you want to pass on to the next generation.

You may be lucky and discover that your in-laws have exactly the same attitude and approach to family harmony and the value of creating a loving, supportive, and mutually respectful family life. Of course, their concordance will make creating an extended family that can be a role model to your children and grandchildren that much easier to accomplish. But even if they do not initially share your views or attitudes, you must always remember that you may not be able to control the world around you or the attitudes or behaviors of other people, but you are always the master of yourself. All you can do is the best you can do. And the best you can do is to live your life, treat your in-laws, and act with your children and grandchildren in a way that will serve as a constant example of the values that you want them to embrace. From my experience of over thirty years as a clergy person, I can promise that such behavior will have a profound and lasting effect where it matters most.

You and your in-laws are ideally a generational team. You can work together to provide stability, support, counsel, and the benefit of your collective years of experience to help your children succeed and thrive in their lives as individuals, as a couple, as parents, and as a family. That should be consistently your goal, and you can never articulate it out loud or in writing too often.

One of the inevitable laws of the universe is that we become what we think about. If we fill our minds with loving, caring, joyful, and supportive thoughts we become loving, caring, joyful, and supportive people. If we fill our minds with angry, frustrated, hostile, divisive thoughts, we become angry, frustrated, hostile, divisive people. That is just how it works. So make a commitment to fill your mind with the qualities and thoughts that will lead you into being the kind of person you want to become—the kind of parent, the kind of spouse, the kind of in-law whom you are proud to be.

If you are lucky you will become actual friends with your in-laws. Yes, it's true! There are in-laws who take vacations together, spend holidays in each other's homes, and do their best to create together one large, loving family unit. Yet even when this utopian vision does occur, there will still be moments when you will want to celebrate with your children and grandchildren your own holidays, or participate in meaningful life-cycle celebrations around births or other significant life moments, or even grieve in ways that reflect your own unique religious perspective and culture. If you are lucky, you can do so with your extended family, and even those who are not of your religion or cultural background will be there with you giving spiritual and moral support, not to mention the emotional space to fulfill your own needs.

Of course it is important to remember that this idea and these needs go both ways. Look for opportunities to be present and supportive of your in-laws and their religious celebrations, holidays, and events as well. This is the best way both to demonstrate respect for them and their particular religious or cultural background and to create the conditions where they feel comfortable or even compelled to return the favor in kind. If this is not possible for any number of reasons, then you need to learn when to do things together as an extended family and when you need to choose to follow your own particular religious path alone. It may be without your children or grandchildren and it may be with your child alone.

Even if it becomes necessary to celebrate or commemorate something in a smaller, more religiously homogeneous setting, you can still do so in a way that communicates your respect and admiration for those in your larger family who worship differently.

The more you can live your life and keep true to your own values while demonstrating respect and acceptance of the right of others to be different, the better your long-term relationship with your own children, your grandchildren, and your extended family will be.

NURTURING YOUR RELATIONSHIP WITH YOUR SON- OR DAUGHTER-IN-LAW

One of the best things that you can do for your relationship with your own child is to nurture your relationship with his or her life partner. Going out of your way to create a positive, nurturing relationship with your child's partner in life sends a powerful message of acceptance, acknowledgment, and approval to your child that is worth its weight in gold.

Begin by taking an interest in your child's partner and in what he or she is interested in. If she has hobbies or a particular passion in life—riding horses, collecting tea pots, playing an instrument, traveling on adventure vacations, or whatever it might be—you can demonstrate more support, acceptance, and love both for your child and his or her life partner by showing an interest in the things that interest him or her than in almost any other way. This is an old technique first articulated, I believe, by Dale Carnegie in 1930s, and it is as powerful and effective now as it was over seventy-five years ago. Be interested in other human beings—not only do they feel flattered and important, but they feel good whenever you are around and happy to have you in their life.

Ultimately, having your child's partner enjoy having you around and having you as a part of his or her life is about the best that you can ask for as an "in-law." The world of comedians is filled with jokes about mothers-in-law for a reason: it is easy to appear pushy, overbearing, meddlesome, and otherwise obnoxious simply by showing too keen an interest in the details of your child's relationship with his life partner. That is why it is so helpful to demonstrate an interest in your daughter-in-law's work or your son-in-law's hobbies or passions.

The more you can be seen as interested in how you can be supportive and helpful to your child and his or her needs, the more you will be accepted in their lives, and the more they will turn to you for help and advice when it really matters. Since the need for approval never goes away, the more you can demonstrate nonjudgmental acceptance of the choices your child has made, the more naturally he or she will see you as an ally.

Spend personal time with your child's partner away from your own child if possible. Although this may be intimidating to either or both of you at the beginning, do what you can to create a separate relationship of your own with her without your child's presence. When you are able to do so, it can naturally act to shift the focus of your relationship. Establishing such an independent, caring relationship with your child's partner will go a long way to breaking down any prejudices and barriers that you or your child may have been worried about in the first place.

As you endeavor to create the best possible relationship with your own child and his or her life partner, you will want to make it very clear when appropriate, that it is not your intention to compete with or take the place of their parents. You will want to do whatever you can to have the best relationship with the "in-laws." And you never want to be thought of as someone who feels in competition with another set of parents for the love of your children.

Send your child's partner birthday cards and include him in your anniversary and holiday wishes. Make sure he is a part of every family gathering to which your child is invited, and go out of your way to make him or her feel loved, accepted, and special in your eyes. Invite them over for dinner on a regular basis, demonstrate interest in where they have traveled, and continue to act toward them as if they are now part of the family. The more you go out of your way to include and acknowledge your in-laws, the more your concerns will be listened to if an issue ever arises. Credibility does not fall from trees or spring up overnight. It is the result of many years of devotion, service, and caring about other human beings. It is not always easy to keep these issues in the forefront of our minds, but the payoff in quality relationships is incalculable.

NEGOTIATING HOLIDAYS—WHO GETS THE KIDS AND GRANDKIDS?

The better your overall relationships are with your new family, the easier it is to negotiate who gets the kids and the grandkids for holidays and special times during the year. I have often heard interfaith families say that one of the few advantages of having an interfaith relationship is that it cuts down on the number of holidays that they are likely to fight over each year. When a couple come from different religious backgrounds and their families celebrate different religious holidays, it often makes it easier to figure out whose house everyone will be going to for which holiday.

When you can invite your children to your home to celebrate Christmas, Hanukah, Ramadan, Easter, Passover, or any other religious holiday and know that it will not conflict with your in-laws and their desire for those same kids and grandkids to be celebrating their particular holidays, the potential tensions between your child and his or her partner every year are tremendously reduced.

As with every other aspect of parenting adult children who are married or in committed relationships, it is usually a better strategy to approach your desire to have them spend holidays or special times with you with a light and gentle touch. There is a certain *art* to communicating the importance of their sharing a particular holiday or event with you without pushing the point so much that you are perceived as intrusive and insensitive to the pressures that your children experience when they have two families both vying for their attention at the same time.

Whether interfaith or same faith, similar pressures occur in every family—especially when there are divorced parents involved. These pressures come with the territory of having an extended family. Each family unit wants the others to accommodate their emotional needs and desires, whether they live around the corner, in different cities, states, or countries. This is especially true when there are grandchildren involved. With grandchildren everything seems to change, and the pressures on both you and your children inevitably become more pronounced.

You will have more successes in persuading your children to come and celebrate a special occasion with you the more you are perceived as providing an emotionally safe, sane, calm, and nonjudgmental haven for them and their children. It stands to reason that if it is easier and more comfortable to be with you and your family than with anyone else, your children are more likely to *want* to make your home the destination of choice.

The key is to be direct and clear about your desires without pressuring your children or grandchildren every single time they are with you. Talk with your children about whatever stresses they might be feeling in this regard, and do whatever you can to be seen as their advocates in reducing the stress of holidays and the emotional conflicts that so often are a part of extended family life. Tell your children that you imagine it is difficult for them to be in a position where they have to choose one set of parents over another (especially if there are divorces and remarriages leading to several sets of parents or grandparents), and that you do not want to be part of the problem if you can help it. Ask them how you can help them, what you can do to make it easier for them to be with you for the holidays, and offer to go with them to another family location if that will help.

It is helpful to take the attitude that you do not always have to be together with them in *your* home. It is more important *that* you spend time with them than *where* you spend time with them. Keep your priorities clear: creating a loving, nurturing, emotionally safe and positive environment in which your children and grandchildren can be together is the most important challenge. Where you do that and with whom you do that ought to be secondary to the opportunity of sharing the experience with the ones you love.

If your children see you as their ally every time this dilemma occurs, it will strengthen your relationship with them and reinforce that it is their welfare that is uppermost in your mind. Knowing that they can count on you for support, empathy, encouragement, and advice can create an ongoing relationship with your children and grandchildren in which you all feel like partners who are on the same family team.

PERSONAL STORIES FROM THOSE WHO HAVE BEEN THERE

Before Charles and Carol had kids it seemed that both their parents were fine with whichever holidays and birthdays they chose to spend with them. But the minute their first child was born, an emotional tug of war began between both sets of in-laws, and Charles and Carol were constantly feeling torn every which way by all of their parents.

"No matter which choice we made, it seemed to be the wrong one for someone. If we decided to go to Charles' parents house for Thanksgiving one year, my parents would pout, get upset, complain that we were 'always' choosing to be somewhere else on 'every' holiday," said Carol.

"And if we chose to go to Carol's parents' on vacation with our son," added Charles, "my parents would complain that they 'never got to spend any vacation time with their grandson.' It was a no-win situation for us—kind of damned if we did and damned if we didn't. We just didn't know what to do."

It was suggested to Charles and Carol that, if possible, they have a "family meeting" with all their parents in the same room at the same time and directly confront how they felt. Charles and Carol needed to sit them all down and tell them that they loved them all and wanted their son to grow up in a harmonious family where he felt loved, supported, nurtured, and accepted for *who he was, no matter where he was.* What they did not want was for him to grow up learning that "family" meant fighting and discord, and that grandparents were part of a family that you could never fully satisfy nor expect unconditional approval. They needed to tell their parents that they did not want their child to grow up thinking that he was only a good boy and worthwhile in the eyes of his grandparents if he came to *their* house and did what made *them* happy.

When they actually did have this family meeting it turned out to be a relief for everyone and much easier than anyone could have anticipated. Their fears of even greater family discord and hurt feelings (which were obviously a significant possibility) were simply unfounded and never came to pass. Instead their parents realized the untenable position they were each putting their children in and worked out a plan together where they would each share the time with their children and grandchild spread out over the year's worth of holidays and vacations in a way that made everyone feel that they were just as important as anyone else. In this way each was able to feel like they mattered and that it was clearly important in the eyes of their children that they be able to spend time with their grandson. As soon as they experienced the personal and parental validation that this implied, the tension went away, the sense of competition vanished, and together they all felt a sense of personal success at being able to work it out.

When Dennis first came to meet with me it was because he had heard that I often worked with interfaith families. He was frustrated with his relationship with his daughter and his ex-wife and did not know where else to turn for advice. It seemed that as with too many marriages that end badly, his ex-spouse was angry and vindictive toward him for his role in their divorce and seemed to do everything that she could to come between Dennis and his children. The situation was made even more complicated by the fact that Dennis was Jewish and his ex-wife was Catholic and their religious differences had been a constant source of tension and upset throughout their marriage together.

Dennis's daughter was in a committed relationship with another woman whom she loved, and his ex-wife seemed to exploit her mother–daughter relationship to position herself as lonely, needy, and emotionally crushed any time that her daughter spent a holiday with anyone else but her. His ex-wife talked about the arguments that she and Dennis had had over religion during their marriage as if they ought to be an issue between Dennis and his daughter as well, and communicated to her daughter that one of the ways that she needed to demonstrate her love for her mother was by rejecting Dennis's religion and choosing her mother and Jesus over him.

Dennis perceived all the postdivorce insistence on Catholicism and his ex-wife's attempt at pressuring their daughter into rejecting her father and his religion as a kind of emotional blackmail that preyed on his daughter's feelings of guilt toward her mother, a person who did not have a significant relationship with anyone else in her life. He felt that his daughter did not even see these machinations for, as he put it, "the manipulation that they obviously were" but merely reacted out of her desire to help her mother and prevent her from experiencing any more suffering.

Dennis was frustrated and felt excluded from many significant moments in his daughter's life. He felt like he was in a kind of catch-22 position, because if he insisted that she spend Jewish holidays with him, he feared coming across as "pushing Judaism on her" and alienating her even more. He did not want to come across as the "bad guy" who wanted to take her away from spending time with her mother, thereby in some way proving that her mother was right in blaming him for putting her in this lonely and needy situation in the first place.

I told Dennis that I believed that there was only one solution to such a problem: Dennis needed to sit down quietly with his daughter and her partner and as calmly, rationally, and lovingly as he could, share his own sense of loss and feelings of frustration over all the times he wanted to be with them but could not. I encouraged him to approach his daughter as a loving parent who empathized with her own mixed feelings and the emotional dilemma that she faced at every holiday, special occasion, and vacation time. He needed to speak to his daughter on an adult level and let her know how much he loved her and admired her. And he needed to emphasize his understanding that she undoubtedly felt caught in the middle between her parents.

Learning how to speak up for your own beliefs and share your own religious convictions without coming across as if you are on a religious crusade to convert your own children or grandchildren is an important skill to have. Sometimes you can only learn this skill by trial and error, doing the best you can with the best of intentions and constantly letting your children know that you are sincerely interested in having the very best relationship with them. Enlist their help in figuring out what you can do and how you can act so that it encourages and nurtures your relationship. The more you are able to sit down together and talk about these issues, the closer you will be to each other—and the more successful you will be in forging the kind of parent–child bond that you desire.

Seven

UNDERSTANDING THE CHALLENGES
OF INTERFAITH LIFE

THE TEN MOST TYPICAL CHALLENGES YOUR CHILD WILL FACE

Regardless of the age at which your child enters into intermarriage there are certain fundamental challenges that confront nearly every interfaith marriage. The purpose of this chapter is to help you understand what those typical challenges are so that you will not be shocked or surprised when you see your child dealing with these issues, and so that you will be in a better position to provide support, empathy, and love.

In this chapter you will read about the ten most typical challenges your child will face in the course of his or her intermarriage. Also included are suggestions as to how you can better understand your child and his or her struggles, and some of the approaches you can take to result in your child seeing you as a source of strength, comfort, and support.

Before we look at them in greater detail, here are the ten most typical challenges that interfaith couples face in the course of working out their relationship and marriage (in no particular order):

1. Learning to live with multiple beliefs, rituals, and religious expectations in one home
2. Making decisions as parents about how to raise children who come from different religious backgrounds

3. Creating a "team marriage" where each partner maintains his or her integrity without impinging upon the integrity of the other

4. Communicating effectively by learning to see the world through their partner's eyes

5. Negotiating how they will celebrate holidays and life cycle moments

6. Balancing the need for independence against the obligations they feel toward their individual parents who represent specific religious expectations

7. Overcoming the tendency to use religion and the "interfaith marriage" as the scapegoat for all relationship problems in the marriage

8. Assuming the role as "family expert" in their respective religious traditions as they are called upon to answer questions and explain what their religion teaches about many issues they may have never thought about before

9. Learning new communication skills that reflect both love and respect for their partner's religion and effectively communicate their individual religious needs at the same time

10. Learning what it means to be a husband and a wife (or an effective partner regardless of gender) and how to negotiate effectively when their expectations are the same or different from those of their partner

LIVING WITH MULTIPLE BELIEFS, RITUALS, CULTURES, AND CIVILIZATIONS

Perhaps the most obvious challenge for couples that enter into interfaith marriages is simply learning to live with multiple holidays, rituals, customs, and traditions in one household. On the one hand, people throughout the world have already been doing it for generations, so it certainly seems that if there is enough love in the home nearly anything is possible. On the other hand, the old adage that "love conquers all" is not necessarily true when it comes to successfully negotiating relationships, in-laws, and the complexity and emotionally charged issues of religious family life.

What your children will face together is the challenge of identifying the rituals, customs, and holidays (as well as how those holidays will be celebrated) that they care about most. In a sense their entire relationship with a partner from another religious tradition is a lifelong values-clarification experience in which they are constantly forced to make decisions over and over regarding what to celebrate, how to celebrate, when to celebrate, and with whom.

The good news and the bad news are identical: the same holidays keep coming back year after year. It's good news because it provides new opportunities each year for interfaith couples to creatively settle their differences or find new ways of coping with the religious challenges of their interfaith life.

The bad news is that every year they are forced to make the same decisions again with the ever-present possibility of disagreement and discord.

What your children and their partners have to do on their own is bring to the table all the religious traditions that they cherish and hold dear and then work out together which they will choose to incorporate into their lives.

In a sense, each and every interfaith couple ends up creating its own unique religious lifestyle that is in some ways unlike anyone else's. This is both the challenge *and* opportunity of interfaith life. Couples have the chance to be creative, to take a fresh look at the rituals and customs that have been handed down to them, and then make decisions about how important those rituals and customs are to *them*, both as individuals and as a partnership. Then they can make intelligent choices regarding exactly how they will incorporate those rituals and customs into their lives on a daily or yearly basis.

The best way for you to be in a position to offer support and help to your child as she enters into and works her way through the minefields of intermarriage (but only if your child *asks* for help) is to understand the challenges of interfaith life as fully as you can. It will give you insight into the choices that your child is making and certainly provide you with the tools to experience a greater sense of empathy for how difficult some of these decisions truly are.

Take for example the challenge of learning to live with multiple beliefs, rituals, and religious expectations in one home. If only one partner in the relationship has a religion that he or she cares about, or if they have gotten married with clear expectations laid out in advance of exactly what will be celebrated, in what way, with which rituals, and with whom, then the problems and challenges in this regard are likely to be minimal. But my experience with interfaith couples is that they rarely take the time in advance to thoroughly discuss their differences, let alone make clear and mutual decisions regarding the specific rituals and holidays they will celebrate, the blessings they will say in their home, or the customs they will follow as a family.

Instead, many of the decisions regarding specific religious practices end up being made without any prethought at all simply in the course of living their lives together. A holiday arrives and one person or the other in the relationship prepares without much thought to celebrate as he or she has always done— most often by recreating the way they have always celebrated the holiday in the family in which they were raised.

You can just imagine the surprise in their partner's eyes and voice as they find themselves on the defensive side of a religious discussion that they never anticipated having in the first place.

"I came home one day from work," Sean said, "and I noticed there was something nailed up on the right side of our front door that seemed to be a kind of tube with a Hebrew letter on it. I had no idea what it was, and when I asked Judy about it, she matter-of-factly responded, 'Oh, I just put up our Mezuzah[1] this afternoon. I've always had one on my door.'"

Sean continued, his face expressing the dumbfounded quality of his words. "I was so surprised by the whole thing—and not exactly sure what it meant to have it on my door, nor what the religious significance of it was—that I guess without even thinking I automatically sputtered, 'Well, take it off *my* door.'"

"As soon as I said that Judy's feelings were hurt since I had reacted so negatively to one of her religious symbols, and emotions just escalated in a rush. By the time we actually sat down calmly so she could explain to me what a 'Mezuzah' represented in the Jewish faith, what it meant to her, and why she wanted one outside our door, both of our feelings had already been hurt and we were raw and bruised by the whole thing."

Unfortunately, what Sean and Judy went through is typical. For Judy it was simply affixing a Jewish symbol from her culture that had always been part of her life and seemed a "normal" and ordinary expression of her identity. To Sean it felt like a small Jewish invasion of the sanctity of his home and a blatant statement about the religious identity of his home and family that he had never even been consulted about. What often ends up happening in such situations is that the non-Jewish member of the couple feels an urge to say "no" simply to be able to assert their own independent religious identity in their own home *regardless* of whether having a Mezuzah on the outside of their home would have bothered them had they been consulted about it in the first place.

What is helpful for you as a parent to realize is that experiences such as this happen *all the time* in interfaith families. Even though they eventually get worked out one way or another, such experiences point out how important it is for your child to be open and honest, first with *herself* about which rituals and customs are important to her, and then to *share that information* with her partner.

In the ideal relationship discussions like these take place long before there is a wedding, as a normal part of the process of making the decision to get married in the first place. The sad reality is that in most cases even what seems as obvious discussions like these *do not* take place before marriage. Instead they become part of the *sturm und drang* of interfaith life, providing constant fodder for upsets throughout the first few years of interfaith marriages.

More frequently than you might imagine the situation also arises that one partner chooses to formally convert to the religion of the other and then proceeds with the enthusiasm, seriousness, and zeal of so many converts to insist on more religious symbols, customs, celebrations, prayers, icons, and images being part of their home and daily life than their partner ever imagined—or wanted.

"I was thrilled when Lew choose to convert to Catholicism and enrolled our son in the local Catholic school," said Liz. "But I was totally unprepared for just *how* Catholic he became. Suddenly he wanted to go to mass all the time, started putting pictures of Jesus and Mary around the house, took to wearing a cross, and insisted that we wear ashes on Ash Wednesday and each give up at least five things for Lent—even though I had never grown up practicing Catholicism that way. It kind of freaked me out that all of a sudden I was supposed to be Ms. Super Catholic and I was almost sorry that he had agreed to convert."

Striking a balance within the family in juggling the differing expectations of religious observance can be a challenging and emotionally difficult task. That is why it is so important for couples to talk openly about their own religious beliefs, as well as the expected manifestation of those beliefs, before they get married and before one of them converts to the religion of the other.

"BUT HOW WILL YOU RAISE THE CHILDREN?"

When a pattern of ignoring the need to talk about important interfaith issues extends to the all-important issue of raising children, the potential for sparks flying is even greater. "But how will you raise the children?" is probably the single most frequently asked question in all of interfaith life. It is definitely the question most asked by parents whose kids are entering into an interfaith relationship and the question that creates the most upset, stirring up the deepest emotions among parents and children from every religious tradition.

Of course, precisely because the raising of children has the greatest potential to create upset and divisiveness among interfaith couples, it is the subject they are *least* eager to discuss. Thus we are confronted with the irony that the subject most in need of being discussed is the single most *avoided* subject prior to marriage.

"Everything was going along so well in our relationship," Wendell disclosed, "that I just didn't want to mess it up or get Joyce all upset by talking about things like baptizing any kids we might have, or my fantasies of seeing my daughter in her First Communion dress. I figured we loved each other and respected each other enough that we would just work out the differences in our upbringing or any differences in child raising expectations when the time for making those decisions was upon us."

In fact, coming from a Jewish background Joyce had *completely* different expectations. She was actually shocked and totally surprised to learn about Wendell's desires for baptism and communion for his children, especially since in all the time she had known him he only went to church once a year with his folks at Christmas time. In her mind Catholicism had never seemed very important to him at all.

As happens so often with interfaith couples, by the time this conversation even came up they were already married and she had just given birth to their first child—without doubt one of the *worst* possible moments to be discussing different child raising expectations.

In this all-too-typical scenario, both of them were equally to blame for avoiding one of the most important discussions that any potential parent needs to have. The reason their story is important is because it is much more common than you would expect.

As parent of a potential bride or groom, perhaps the single most helpful role you can ever play would be to encourage your child to *be brave enough to talk about the difficult issues before she gets married.*

It is not always easy to have such discussions with your own child. Almost anything you say or do can easily be misconstrued as meddling in his relationship, as signaling your disapproval of the relationship in the first place, or as serving as a smokescreen to mask your desire to break up the potential marriage before it occurs.

That is why it takes a lot of self-control to choose your words carefully, to make yourself clear with your child, and to assure her as often as is necessary that you are not trying to interfere in the relationship or put a wedge between her and her fiancé in any way. Tell her that whatever decisions she ends up making about how she will raise her children is up to her and that you love her and support her no matter what.

Tell her that your desire is not to impose or even suggest the direction her conversation with her fiancé will go, only that you feel strongly that it will be in the best interests of her relationship to have a conversation about how they will raise kids and about their individual expectations long before they get to the wedding plans.

You can couch the discussion in the positive. Tell your child that everything you have been reading about how couples create successful interfaith relationships has stressed the importance of taking the time *before* they get married to talk about each person's expectations regarding daily and weekly religious lifestyle, raising children, and celebrating holidays and rituals, so that each partner goes into the marriage knowing as best they can what is important to the other. (If it helps, you can even show her this section of this book).

If you can accomplish the goal of having your child clarify her own values and expectations and share those with the person she loves, while at the same time learning his values, dreams and expectations, you will have significantly improved her chances of creating a successful interfaith marriage.

CREATING A "TEAM MARRIAGE"

The third important interfaith issue that your child will confront has to do with the challenge of learning how to create what I call the "team marriage." The team marriage is exactly as it sounds: a marriage in which each partner feels that he or she is part of a team. As with any partnership and any team, success is based on trust, mutual respect, a sense of shared goals, and the ability to communicate effectively with one's partner to insure that common desires are being met and that both players are on track and heading in the same direction.

Every relationship has issues, challenges, disagreements, difficulties, and moments when decisions are made that are later regretted by one party or the other. The most successful marriages are those in which both partners feel that they are equal parts of the same team, both feel that they are equally involved in making important decisions that effect them as a couple, and therefore both are willing to accept responsibility for the successes and failures of that decision-making process.

This is even more important when it comes to interfaith marriages. There are so many built-in opportunities for misunderstandings and miscommunication when it involves people of different backgrounds, religions, or cultures that it becomes more necessary than ever for interfaith couples to cultivate a true sense of partnership and teamwork.

When they have a team marriage in which decisions are made together, it is practically impossible to make the "wrong" decision. Why? Because whether the decision turns out to be a good one or a bad one, if it was made as a team then one partner does not end up blaming the other partner and both can simply choose another path to follow for the future.

The only role that you have as a parent of an interfaith couple in this regard is perhaps to share this idea of a team marriage with your child if you ever find your advice on such matters being solicited. Some parents have the kind of relationship with their children whereby such conversations naturally come up, and others do not.

It is not a good idea to force your own views of marriage and relationships on your grown children, especially if they already have the impression that you are less than thrilled about their choice in a marriage partner. But if they ask, or if they share with you a tension that might exist within their relationship that appears to derive from resentment over one person making important decisions without consulting the other, *then* sharing this idea of a "team marriage" would be perfectly appropriate and perhaps provide a helpful framework within which your child might reconceptualize his marital expectations.

It is also never too late to develop your own marriage with the "team marriage" model in mind as well. In that way you can point to your marriage and the way you go about making decisions as an example of how it works. This can be especially helpful if you have experienced making decisions together with your own life partner that turned out not to be the best. If one of those decisions was the result of a true team decision-making process, then neither you nor your partner was likely to blame the other. Most likely you simply acknowledged the mistake and moved on—together.

Ideally that is how team marriages work. If you have had such experiences in your own life it will be a blessing to be able to share these mistakes with your child and the wisdom of the process of shared decision making. However, you need to be aware that even if they solicit advice on mistakes you might have made, they may not truly want to hear the details, or may not relate their own issues to yours. The best that you can do is to keep your own experiences in mind as potentially useful information to refer to should your child seeks out your suggestions.

There was a wise person who once said that the greatest strength in the world is being able to watch someone doing something that you know how to do better, and keeping your mouth shut anyway!

LEARNING TO SEE THE WORLD THROUGH HIS/HER PARTNER'S EYES

The fourth typical challenge that interfaith couples face is learning to see the world through their partner's eyes. The reason that this is such a crucial skill to master is that truly being able to understand your partner's feelings requires not just listening or waiting for your partner to take a breath so that you can jump in and add your own two cents, but really hearing from your partner's point of view. The ability to truly hear another requires the ability to slow down and imagine yourself standing in someone else's shoes, no matter how big or small they seem. Gaining and using this keen perspective allows you to be a much more effective communicator and is the key to authentic empathy.

In many ways, the success or failure of all our relationships rests largely on our ability to communicate with others effectively—from the mundane issues of life to the big whoppers. This is even more important in interfaith, intercultural, or interracial relationships.

I have seen couples argue over everything from who is writing checks and spending money, to whether they will rent or buy a house, with whose family they will celebrate a holiday, to where they will go on vacation. That is why it is often more important to learn *how* to go about making mutually agreed-upon decisions and how to treat each other in the course of making decisions in ways that support and nurture the relationship and trust in one another than it is to worry about what it is that is being decided upon.

The way people make decisions often reflects the true nature of their relationship. Whether or not they treat each other with respect and dignity, value each other's opinions, and solicit input and advice from each other, engaging in a process of cooperative decision making gives much better insight into the nature of their relationship than any other indicator.

That is why it is particularly important for couples to pay attention to how they communicate with each other and the process of their decision making when they are in an interfaith relationship. All things being equal, no matter how much in love a couple are with each other, interfaith relationships have many more built-in opportunities for miscommunication than same-faith relationships. This makes it that much harder for people within interfaith relationships to be able to see the world through their partner's eyes.

People who grow up in different cultures, or with different religions, or speaking different languages internalize from childhood a whole set of assumptions about life, expectations about the roles of men and women, what it means to be a parent or a spouse, and many other very basic and fundamental suppositions of which most of us are *totally unaware*.

Our expectations of life and how we are to live it; the difference between what constitutes appropriate and inappropriate behavior in a wide variety of social settings; proper etiquette; and what we mean by the words, expressions, and gestures that we use—all are colored by the cultural, social, and religious background in which we were raised.

Just as it is challenging to travel to a foreign country and do your best not to offend a native of that country by saying or doing something that they misconstrue as inappropriate, insensitive, or possibly even offensive, so too is it difficult to anticipate the intricacies of potential misunderstandings that can take place within interfaith relationships.

The key to successful communication seems to be developing the ability to see the world through your partner's eyes. I am reminded of the famous scene from the Woody Allen movie, *Annie Hall*, where the Jewish boy sitting at the Thanksgiving table of his non-Jewish girlfriend's family cannot understand why they are all so polite and quiet and uncommunicative and interprets that behavior as signaling a lack of interest in each other, while the non-Jewish girl sitting at the table of her Jewish boyfriend is aghast at how seemingly rude, boisterous, and argumentative everyone is around the table and interprets that behavior as not caring about each other's feelings and excessive meddling in each other's lives.

"I kept thinking to myself that Brian's mother is so unbelievably pushy, overbearing and obnoxious and I couldn't believe that Brian had put up with such a busy-body for a mother all his life," Debbie (who was not Jewish) said about her Jewish mother-in-law.

"She would call practically every day to check up on us, always asking us how we were doing, what we were doing, giving us both the third degree about everything that happened in our lives, and I was beginning to feel smothered by her—not to mention a little paranoid, like she was checking up on the job I was doing being Brian's wife. I didn't want to hurt Brian's feeling so I kept quiet about it for the longest time, but finally I just couldn't take what I saw as her constant interference anymore."

Debbie took a deep breath and continued, "When I eventually shared my feelings with Brian and told him that it felt to me like his mother didn't trust us to make good decisions or treat us like independent adults, he was shocked and mortified."

"To me it was just the way I had grown up," Brian interjected. "Maybe it's a Jewish cultural thing, but for my mother calling every day to see how we were doing and to put in her two cents about everything that was going on was simply her way of demonstrating that she loved us and was concerned about us and wanted to be involved with our lives. It had absolutely nothing to do with not trusting me to be an adult; it was simply her way of showing her love."

Debbie can laugh about it now because she eventually sat down with Brian's mother and told her how upset she had been and what she had perceived from her mother-in-law's behavior. After they talked about it openly and came to a clearer understanding about what her intentions had *really* been, Brian's mother had a better understanding of how easily messages could get miscon-strued, Debbie was able to believe Brian's assessment of his mother's behavior, and they all got along better than ever.

In Debbie's family, the way you indicated your love and respect for your children was to let them be on their own and not "interfere" with their lives or decisions unless asked. When Brian put himself in her shoes, he could see how his mother might seem meddlesome and overbearing.

After coming to understand that there are different ways that parents show love and concern and support in different cultures, Debbie grew to appreciate her mother-in-law's phone calls and reaching out for exactly what they were: expressions of her love.

Had they not been the kind of people who were willing to talk about uncomfortable subjects (and had Debbie not had the courage to broach the subject in the first place and not simply let her resentment fester and worsen), they might never have grown closer together; eventually this miscommunication, and others like it, could easily have driven them apart.

That is why the ability to see the world through your partner's eyes is such an important quality for interfaith partners to cultivate. It is just as important for parents whose children intermarry to cultivate the same open-mindedness about their new in-laws and their family traditions.

No matter how close you may live to, or how far away you may live from your new family, you will inevitably have opportunities over the years to be together both in religious and social settings. One of the first steps to wisdom in any situation is to recognize your own ignorance and be willing to expect differences and ask openly about them to facilitate understanding and open communication. It also is a wonderful way to demonstrate respect for another religion or culture by admitting your own ignorance and asking questions that let your new family know that you are genuinely interested in who they are and in having the best relationship possible with them.

Behaving in this way is a great gift to your child and his relationship and a wonderful role model both for him and your new in-laws as it opens the way to communication, understanding and closeness among you all.

"HOW DO I CELEBRATE MARDI GRAS IN THE MIDDLE OF RAMADAN?" AND OTHER INTERFAITH CHALLENGES

Another challenge that interfaith couples must face is the sometimes daunting task of negotiating with each other how and what holidays they will be celebrating in their new home.

Sometimes when a couple has already been living together for several years (which is increasingly common for most couples prior to marriage), they have already worked out by a kind of trial and error (or in some cases "trial by fire") what works for them in their relationship.

The biggest problem for parents of interfaith couples is simply to do *nothing* when their kids make choices with which they do not agree. You think that coming home for Easter is the most important religious moment of the year and your daughter decides to go to her husband's parents' home for Passover instead (which just happens to fall at the same time each year).

You wait all year to have your kids home for Christmas and recreate your most warm and loving memories from their childhood years, and your son decides to take his partner to Aspen for a ski trip instead.

Your favorite family experience is seeing everyone sitting around the Passover table while grandkids chant the traditional "Four Questions" that are part of the Passover home ritual, and your daughter says it's Spring Break for her kids and they are going on a cruise.

Life is filled with parenting disappointments such as this, and the challenges of what to celebrate, how to celebrate it and with whom, are simply compounded by the added complexity of life within an interfaith family.

When your child intermarries it is helpful to cultivate flexibility and understanding and to have realistic expectations of everyone. Obviously, life is not the same as it was when your children were growing up and you got to make all the decisions regarding their religious practices and celebrations.

Once your kids are grown and begin making their own choices, you will probably have the best possible relationship with them if you show them the respect that comes with understanding that their decisions are not necessarily the same ones you would make. If you act as if they are doing the best they can to live up to the values that you have passed down to them, you will be able to accept the decisions they make.

Learning to live with differences and make decisions about the emotionally charged issues of childrearing and ritual celebrations is a tremendous challenge for every interfaith couple. Knowing that these decisions are not always easy to make and that they often involve difficult emotional negotiations between marriage partners will hopefully give you the added ounce of empathy and understanding needed to treat your interfaith children as fairly as possible.

FEELING LIKE THEY ARE "JUGGLING" IN-LAWS

Learning not to take each decision that they make as a personal affront to you or your religion is a big leap of faith. It is one of the most common problems that parents of interfaith couples face: separating themselves and their own feelings from the actions and choices of their children.

Most of the time your kids are just doing their best to make the decisions that will best serve their own relationship while balancing their natural (and usually impossible) desires to please *all* their parents at the same time.

Three of the greatest gifts you can give them are tolerance, patience, and faith. Tolerance when they choose not to be with you; patience as you watch them work out these challenges over the years (since many of them will have to be made over and over again, year after year); and faith that they are doing the best they can, that they really do love their parents, and that they would choose never to hurt your feelings if they could figure out how to meet their own needs at the same time. Beyond that is the simple knowledge that in the end, the love you have for your child and the love your child has for you can survive all the trials and tribulations created by interfaith life.

Putting additional pressure on your child to spend holidays with you or take care of your needs at the expense of his relationship with his partner will only create resentment between you. Ultimately resentment becomes an infection that poisons the loving relationship that you desire. Leaving ones parents' home to create your own is the natural order of life and honoring and respecting that reality is part of allowing your children to grow up and be related to as adults with lives of their own.

The same is true for those emotionally powerful life-cycle moments involving religious rituals. For example, nearly every religious tradition has some kind of welcoming ritual for when a child is born. Whether it is baptism, a baby naming ceremony, or a *brit milah* (breet me-LAH, ritual circumcision), interfaith couples must make decisions about which rituals to incorporate into their own lives—and which they will ignore.

Often there is tension between generations over life-cycle moments such as these, especially since they tend to arouse deep feelings about family, history, and tradition. It is also during such life-cycle moments that you may feel most keenly a sense of loss or guilt or even betrayal of your ancestors if your child chooses not to include one of your cherished rituals in the life of her new family.

When that happens, take a few deep breaths, commiserate with a close friend or clergy person, talk to parents of interfaith couples who have had similar experiences, and above all remember that no ritual or custom is ultimately more important than the long-term health of your relationship with your own child.

No matter how strongly you feel about your religious tradition, put the welfare of your parent–child relationship higher on your priority list. Religion has been created by human beings to serve us, not to enslave us; it is there to facilitate our ability to experience holiness and blessings in our lives. It was not created to become a barrier to fulfillment and peace.

Always choose the people you love over the rituals you love. In the long run it will be your ability to accept the choices of your children even when they differ from yours that will determine the extent to which they continue to feel close to you as adults.

That is why one of the most common challenges of interfaith life is the need to balance individual choices and desires with the needs and desires of one's parents (namely, you). By marrying someone of another religion or culture, your child has chosen a demanding and often perilous path.

Not only will she forever be making choices and compromises about holidays, celebrations, rituals, and observances, but she will also have to make those choices knowing that her own parents might not be happy with her decisions. No matter how lightly those decisions may seem *to you* to have been made, I can assure you from my many years working with interfaith couples that they are painful to make, and very often made with a heavy heart.

Children always want their parents' approval, even when they don't act as if they do. At every age, each of us carries around within the child we once were and the emotional memories of childhood traumas, disappointments, and consequences. Each of us would love for our parents to pat us on the back, tell us how well we have done and that they approve of all our choices and decisions in life. Unfortunately, real life does not work that way.

Instead, we struggle to make the best decisions we can, given the reality of our lives, and we hope that our parents will ultimately understand that we are just doing the best we can. That is why as the parent of an intermarried child, you have the power to bestow a very loving gift every time you refrain from criticizing a decision, every time you acknowledge that your child is making the best choices he can and that you respect him for the person he has become and are there to support him and continue to give your love in any way you can.

It's not always an easy road to walk down, but it has the best possibility of nurturing your relationship with your child in the long run.

USING RELIGION AS A SCAPEGOAT

One of the most common problems that interfaith couples experience is the tendency to use religion and the interfaith marriage itself as a scapegoat for all relationship problems that may arise.

We all know that relationships are challenging and that every relationship has its ups and downs. When any two people create a life together, blending their unique personalities, backgrounds, and dreams, inevitably there will be areas of disagreement.

Over the years, many couples who in the normal process of a disagreement that arises simply because they are two different individuals, choose to characterize their disagreement as due to the interfaith nature of their relationship—whether that has anything to do with it or not.

In fact, there are lots of interfaith couples that end up placing an interfaith lens over every single argument, discussion, or disagreement they have. They find themselves saying things like, "If you weren't Muslim you wouldn't think like that," or "I know Presbyterians are supposed to be thrifty, but you're just downright cheap."

In your role as parent to an interfaith married child, you can help him by refusing to become an accomplice to religious stereotyping. You might even suggest to him that, based on your own experience, even same-faith couples have disagreements over lots of issues during the course of their relationship, and that it is not necessarily the interfaith nature of their relationship that is to blame. You might suggest that instead, disagreements are a normal part of every intimate engagement between two distinct individuals. After all, regardless of where a perceived problem arose, it arose, and must be dealt with in a productive and effective manner.

THE "INSTANT EXPERT" SYNDROME

The eighth challenge that interfaith couples often face is the new role they find themselves in as "family expert" on their respective religious traditions. What often happens is that they become the person their partner, their children, their in-laws, or even their friends turn to for answers to whatever questions they might have regarding Judaism, Islam, Christianity, Buddhism, or whichever religion they represent.

This is often a very uncomfortable role for interfaith couples to play, as they are usually not the most religiously committed and educated in the first place. They may find themselves called upon to justify the behavior of famous figures that happen to belong to their religion. They may find themselves put on the spot by their new family members to justify something that Israel has done if they are Jewish, something that the Pope has decreed if they are Catholic, or something that a Muslim extremist has perpetrated if they are Muslim.

Though there is little one can do to help a child in these situations, one little trick is to simply turn the question or issue right back onto the person who has brought it up. For example, if someone says, "How can you defend Muslims when they celebrate the murder of innocent people who do not share their fundamentalist values?" You can reply, "Well, how *would* one defend those actions? What do *you* think about that?" Often, the person bringing up the subject just wants to engage in a rant. Let them do it on their own time with their own friends.

THE COMMUNICATION CHALLENGE

The ninth interfaith challenge that your child will undoubtedly face is the need to learn new communication skills that reflect love and respect for her partner's religion and effectively communicate her individual religious needs at the same time.

Interfaith life is rife with opportunities for hurt feelings and misunderstandings. Most misunderstandings arise out of ignorance or ineffective communication between partners. It is rarely the case that one person sets out to hurt the feelings of the other, and yet nearly every couple suffers in one way or another because of poor communication.

One key to success for interfaith couples when it comes to effective communication is to learn how to speak in the first person and tell their partners how they feel and what their needs are in a nonaccusatory and nonjudgmental manner.

"I am uncomfortable having a Mezuzah hanging on my door because it makes me feel like I am telling anyone who walks by that only Jewish people live here," is a much better and less confrontational way of communicating than saying, "You have no right to put a Jewish symbol on *my* door."

Couples need to learn how to express their own needs and feelings without becoming threatening. Everyone is entitled to his or her own feelings. Since expressing those feelings does not necessarily imply a judgment about anyone else's feelings, using the first person "I feel . . ." provides a safer way to communicate about something with which you do not agree.

No matter how good your child's relationship may be, there will always be issues that come between her and her partner and there will always be times when she needs to be willing to tell her partner when something bothers her. You can be most helpful by being empathetic to the communication challenge that interfaith life creates and recognizing that there will often be compromises that she will make for the sake of family harmony. Finally, you must accept that you will most likely not be privy to the intimate discussions or negotiations that lead to the decisions they ultimately make.

BALANCING CONFLICTING NEEDS AND EXPECTATIONS

The last in our list of the most prevalent challenges that interfaith couples must face is exactly the same challenge that *all* couples face: learning what it means to be a husband and a wife (or partner) and whether your own expectations are the same or different from those of your partner.

Learning to live with another human being presents every couple with a wide variety of challenges no matter who they are. Couples often fail to learn what their partner's expectations are when it comes to their own role as well as their partner's role in the relationship.

Each of us grows up with a number of significant role models when it comes to being married. Beginning with the model of our own parents' union, we learn about being a man and a woman, a husband and a wife. In addition, we learn about these roles from watching television and movies, reading books, listening to songs, and absorbing the cultural norms of the society in which we live.

Often the images we have ingrained within us from childhood of the roles of husband and wife end up being very different from the actual relationships we have with our own partners. One of the important challenges of creating a healthy and successful relationship is to be self-reflective enough to know what our own expectations are of both ourselves and of our partner, to communicate those expectations, and then to find out from them what *they* expect from themselves and from us.

You can encourage your child to have this kind of discussion with his fiancé or potential life partner long before he ever gets married or makes a life commitment (whether he is in an interfaith relationship or not). It is a rare individual who takes the time to understand his own expectations let alone those of his partner—even though all it really takes is for your child to sit with a blank piece of paper and list what it means to be a husband, partner, or wife on one side and then list what they expect from a husband, partner, or wife on the other. Have his or her partner do the same after which they compare lists and discuss the expectations implied in each. They will inevitably find this simple exercise to be enlightening and eye opening for both of them.

The goal of this chapter was to make you familiar with the ten most typical challenges that nearly all interfaith couples will face in the course of making their relationship a success. It is helpful to have a perspective on interfaith relationships from the inside out, one that places the struggles, disagreements, compromises, and individual challenges that your children may be facing in the context of the larger picture of what is normal to expect.

In many instances there is a large gap between "knowing" and "doing." Hopefully, having this information will help you have more empathy for what your child is experiencing.

Eight

WHEN YOUR CHILD CONVERTS TO ANOTHER RELIGION

WHEN YOUR CHILD ANNOUNCES, "I'M CONVERTING!"

One of the most difficult emotional experiences that a parent can face is the moment when a child announces, "I'm converting to another religion." Whether your child has been traveling the world and meets someone while on vacation and the announcement comes absolutely out of the blue or she has been living with someone of another religion or culture for the past ten years, the implications seem so significant and wide-reaching that they inevitably arouse a sense of emotional loss and confusion that catches most parents by surprise. Even for those parents who have already been living with the reality of the different kind of life that their child has been creating with his or her spouse or life partner, there is just something so final and definitive about the word "conversion" that more often than not it arouses many emotions and fears.

"It's not that my wife and I actually practice our religion very seriously, or even that I particularly believe in the dogma I was taught as a child at all," said Garth. "It's just that hearing our daughter say the words *I'm converting to Islam* conjured up such deep feelings of rejection that it felt in a way like a total invalidation of who I am and what I have stood for my whole life. I must say I was completely caught off guard by the depth of my feelings and the profound sense of sadness and loss that suddenly came over me."

This comment is typical of many parents whose children convert from the religion of their childhood upbringing to the religion of the partner with whom they have fallen in love. It is often very difficult for parents to reconcile that by their child choosing another religion and faith it is not because they are rejecting their parents, it is rather because they are choosing something they find to be a positive force in their lives.

Garth continued: "What was strange was that Caryn had been dating this Muslim young man for the previous two years and obviously was becoming more and more serious about their relationship. He is a very good guy, bright, caring, modern, successful, and cosmopolitan in his outlook on life. He has a wonderful extended family that lives nearby in one of the suburbs of Detroit, all of whom we have met and liked and spent time with a number of times over the past two years. So it shouldn't have come as a shock at all. And yet in spite of how much I like the boy and his family, in spite of all this time getting used to them being together and knowing that Caryn is really happy and flourishing in this relationship, just hearing those words 'I'm converting to Islam' caused my stomach to drop. I couldn't seem to find what should have been the loving, supportive words that I really did want to say to her. I found myself a bit overwhelmed with the reality of it all and all the rather dark places that my mind instantly went."

Sometimes the shock of hearing that your child has chosen to convert to another religion feels even more dramatic if the religion itself is something that is totally foreign to you and out of the realm of your personal experience. In the case of Garth and his daughter Caryn, the fact that her religion of choice was Islam made it feel even more unsettling than if she had chosen another form of Christianity different from her Methodist upbringing.

"I know that some of it is specifically because the religion she has chosen is Islam," Garth said, "I realize that with all the constant press about fundamentalist Islamic terrorism around the world, the craziness of the very few has unfairly tarnished an entire religion of over a billion people. But it's also not just that it's Islam as much as it felt in my gut like some kind of personal rejection of me, of who I am, of what I stand (or at least stood) for, of the values of our family in which we raised Caryn .... I don't know how to say it, it made me feel almost like there was something fundamentally *wrong* with us and who we are."

It is helpful for parents to have counselors and clergy to talk with when their children choose to convert to another religion because it is important to be able to remember what growing up is supposed to be all about—namely separating from your parents and creating your own adult identity. Ultimately Garth was able to realize this as well: "When I think rationally about it all,

I am happy for her that she is happy, in love with a great guy, creating her own life for herself as an adult, making her own choices in a thoughtful and responsible way and to a large extent doing exactly what you are supposed to do when you grow up: move away from your family of origin and go off and create your own new family. That really is the natural way of the world, and I do understand it *intellectually.* It's just that *emotionally* it was still painful."

When parents and children have a good relationship, it is easier for the parents to realize that what they ultimately want for their children is for them to be happy, safe, and productive in their lives. If converting to another faith is the road their children take to achieve these goals, then in the end most parents are able to accept that this is the price they must pay for the personal fulfillment and happiness of their children.

"As you might imagine, my wife and I have had lots of conversations about all of this ever since the conversion bombshell dropped a couple of years ago," Garth continued. "Although at first I admit we both found ourselves crying, it's different now. Especially seeing how wonderful Caryn and Sayud are together as a couple and how much she has flourished as a person within this loving relationship."

"We aren't merely tolerating the relationship because we have no choice in it. We are actually, sincerely happy for her and the life she has created even though it is clearly a departure from how she was raised and on some level inevitably in part a rejection of our values as well."

Garth's well-articulated, detailed reaction is in many ways typical of the inner struggle that parents experience whenever their children choose as adults to follow a different spiritual path. It is understandable that most parents feel some level of personal rejection upon hearing such news. These feelings are often accompanied by anger, frustration, confusion, and fear of the unknown, not to mention concerns about what this will mean for them personally and their extended family—and all this is regardless of how open minded and accepting such parents have been in the past.

That is why one of the most important things to you can do in advance is to prepare yourself emotionally for the possibility that someday this might happen to you. If you are a parent whose child is involved with someone who practices another religion or is from another culture, there is always the chance that what happened to Garth can happen to you. This chapter is designed to help you think though some of the key issues in advance so that you will be able to choose how you will want to respond should the time ever come when a response is necessary. The more openly you think about this possibility in advance, the less of a shock it will be should your child choose to convert and the better prepared you will be to support your child in this significant life decision and to react appropriately to the news.

When your child is willing to tell you, "I'm converting," it is a statement not only about her personal *religious* faith, but about her faith in you as well. No matter how old you become and how much of an adult you are, it still takes courage to stand in front of the person who has raised you and declare that you have chosen a different direction for your own life. It is not a question of the "road less traveled," but often a different road altogether with the potential to create discord throughout the family. Initiating such a conversation takes both courage and faith—courage on the part of your child who is willing to face the emotional consequences of announcing such a dramatic change (including the possibility of outright rejection and loss of love from you or any other parents, siblings, or extended family), and faith *in you* and in the kind of person you are.

Your child's announcement is also an expression of faith in the values you represent and have lived and taught, regardless of the specific label that you have attached to those values in the past. *That is why the best response to the moment when your child tells you, "I'm converting," is whatever you can say to communicate your love and faith in your child and your child's values, essential goodness, and judgment.*

What Caryn wanted to hear from her father was some version of the following: "I love you and trust you and know that this is something you don't do lightly, but with a lot of thought, self-examination, and commitment. I admire your courage to create your own unique path in life. And I want you to know that whatever you choose in life and wherever you go, I will be there supporting you and loving you." Along with the emotional support for such a decision, it is probably a good idea for any parent who finds himself or herself in such a situation to take the time to learn as much as possible about the new religion that his or her child has chosen. This will be yet another way to bring parents and children closer to each other and reinforce the love they share while creating more opportunities for understanding and meaningful discussions and shared experiences in the future.

WHEN YOUR BELIEFS ARE NO LONGER SHARED WITH YOUR CHILD

For many parents one of the most disturbing aspects of discovering that your child is converting to another religion is the realization that your beliefs are no longer shared with your own child. In fact, many parents find it impossible to accept such a reality as true, no matter what their children say.

"How could he suddenly reject everything that we have stood for his entire life?" one parent asked. "I mean, you don't just wake up one day and say, 'Everything I have ever learned and everything I have ever stood for and believed in is now wrong, and instead I am going to simply believe something totally different.' I don't understand how that happens. Where do all your previous beliefs go? What happens to them? What makes you suddenly decide that the way you grew up is wrong, and someone else's religion is right? It just doesn't make sense to me. And the truth is that I find it pretty much impossible to accept. Of course I haven't actually told this to my son in these words. I've always tried to be the best father I can be, and even now when I truly don't understand what happened. I still do my best to be loving and supportive and tell him that if it makes him happy and he has found something that makes sense to him and makes his life work then I am happy for him and will support any decisions he makes. After all, other than a little hurt feelings on my part and his mother's (and I know his sister doesn't exactly understand it either), still it isn't really hurting anyone else. Besides, I really do believe that there are good and decent people of every religion, so I just have to keep thinking that my son is now one of *them*—a good and decent person with another religion. It's just a bit strange for me because I see him as the same kid he has always been no matter what he says about what he believes today or tomorrow or the next day."

This reaction is a common one: the sense of disbelief that a child of yours could suddenly become someone you do not know who believes something that is fundamentally different from how he was raised and from what *you* believe. It is easy to see how parents could interpret this rejection of their beliefs as a rejection of them as well. This sense of rejection in turn can evoke profound feelings of loss, as if some fundamental connection to their child that they always simply assumed would be there has suddenly vanished.

As is true with much of interfaith life, discovering that your beliefs are no longer shared with your child presents you with both challenges and opportunities. The challenges include how to maintain the most loving, supportive, and openly communicative relationship you can in spite of your new differences. You have to find ways of strengthening the bonds of your love that do not depend on a foundation of shared religious beliefs.

On the other hand, the opportunities that this moment creates are also numerous. You now have an opportunity to learn or practice treating your child as the adult he is, one who can express his own beliefs and engage in a dialogue about significant religious and spiritual issues as an equal. This is often a new world for parents and children to explore together, and in many cases helps to establish a new, deeper, and more meaningful relationship than they have ever had before.

Discovering that their beliefs are no longer shared with their child often creates the very first opportunity that parents and children have ever taken to sit down as adults and discuss some of the most important ideas and issues in life. It often prompts them to have the first real conversation they have ever had about the values that they each cherish and hold dear.

When such a moment arrives, it's time to face the big questions, step by step.

The first step is to ask yourself: "What are the underlying principles that guide my life?"

The second step is to share your answers with your children and then ask your children to articulate the underlying principles that guide their lives as well.

Step three is to list your beliefs about God and what you think God's relationship is to human beings.

Step four would be to ask the same question to your children and have a "God talk" discussion with them in an open, nonjudgmental way designed to clarify both for yourself and for your children what your beliefs about God really are.

Step five might consist of having a conversation about how you would explain to another human being what makes life meaningful and where the meaning of life comes from.

And step six can lead you into a discussion about what you believe about the afterlife and whether you think there is a heaven and hell, a reward and punishment after death for the way we live our lives while here on the earth and to find out what your children think about the very same issues.

These are the big ideas: fundamental underlying philosophies that guide our lives and give direction to decisions we make every day, even when we are not totally conscious of their impact on our decision making. Having a belief that what you do in this life affects the state of your soul forever or holding a karmic notion that what goes around in this life comes around in the next and determines who you will be in the next life, or seeing this existence right now as all there is and all there ever will be—all these ideas can have very different implications for how we see ourselves and others and for what drives our everyday life choices.

One of the potential gifts that your child can give you by converting to another religious tradition is the opportunity to have deep, serious conversations with him about these important religious issues that most people simply take for granted. The result of engaging in this kind of serious dialogue with your child can lead to a greater appreciation for the seriousness and depth of his own thinking, not to mention and an opportunity for you to update and clarify your own ideas. Most parents discover that when entered into with an open heart and a true desire to understand each other, these conversations only strengthen the parent–child bond, ultimately forging deeper respect for each other.

The important key to remember when you realize that your beliefs are no longer shared with your child is that your beliefs are not you and you are not your beliefs. Your beliefs are simply that—beliefs. They do not define your relationship or your love, nor do they form the basis of your acceptance of each other as independent human beings. They are simply the beliefs that you hold, and are totally independent of the essence of the relationship that defines you as parent and child.

FINDING AND REMEMBERING COMMON VALUES

One of the most common discoveries of parents and children who do engage in this kind of serious conversation about religious values and beliefs is that in spite of their child's conversion to another religion, there are still more values that unite them than there are that divide them. In part, this is because human beings are fundamentally the same all over the world. We have the same hopes and dreams, the same fears and doubts, the same questions about the nature of the universe and our role in it—all generally regardless of race, religion, language, country, or culture.

What often happens to parents and children as they engage in these serious conversations about life and its meaning is that children realize more and more how important their parents' values and beliefs have been in creating the foundation of their own thinking, regardless of where that thinking ultimately led them. The same is true for parents. Most of the time when they are willing to seriously look at the values that underlie the choices that their children have made, they realize that they are simply different expressions of the fundamental values that *they* have taught their children throughout their lives.

Time and again parents have shared how upset they are over an impending interfaith marriage between their child and someone of another religious tradition. Most of the time they simply cannot understand how *their* child could marry out of their own faith and reject the fundamental values in which they have so faithfully been raised.

When those same parents actually examine the real values that they taught their children, not just through sending them to a religious school or church training, but more importantly by living those values in their daily lives, they inevitably realize that it is, in fact, *exactly their own values that their children are now living out*—just in a different manner.

When parents whose children are in the process of intermarrying are asked about how they actually lived their own lives, most often they will admit that they had friends and acquaintances from many different backgrounds,: that they taught their children that all human beings (not just people of their own religion) are made in God's image, that they spoke about the basic dignity of all people, and that they stood up for issues of personal freedom. It is clear that their children have obviously learned those very lessons to their core. These parents have not been "wrong" in teaching tolerance of all human beings regardless of race or religion or national origin or culture, but absolutely in the right just as these are values that they actually do believe in, so too do their children. The particular *expression* of those values may vary from person to person and generation to generation, but the fundamental values themselves most often remain the same. Parents can feel proud of the lessons that they have taught their own children about right and wrong. They can consider themselves successful and validated by their children's actions, for at the core, their children have mirrored the fundamental values they were taught.

HOW TO ASK QUESTIONS WITHOUT BEING OFFENSIVE

One of the best ways for you to gain an understanding of both the commonalities and differences between what you believe and the beliefs of your children is simply to take the time to ask your children questions. When accomplished with respect, an open mind, and a true curiosity about understanding and learning as much about your child's new world as you can, the very process of asking the questions can help create a deeper connection between you and your child.

When a child converts to a religion that is different from that in which she was raised, it certainly appears that "parental approval" is the last thing on her mind. But the truth is much more complicated because every child's need for parental approval is both deep-seated and often unconscious. When we are young, we seek that approval by being "good" boys or girls in a hundred different ways. We may help our parents by being polite or following directions, by doing homework or getting good grades, by mowing the lawn or taking out the trash, washing dishes or cleaning our rooms. To feel that we are worthy not only as their child but as a human being, most of us need our parents' approval on the most fundamental level—and there are almost no limits to the ways we seek that validation. Sometimes it manifests in the friends we choose or reject, the activities we embrace, sports we choose to play, competitions we enter, instruments we master, dances we learn, or religious rituals and customs we embrace.

Regardless of the form it takes, almost all of these choices are, on some level, designed to reinforce the sense of self-worth we derived as children from parental approval—or perceived disapproval. When such parental approval is lacking for any number of reasons, including an inability on the part of our parents to express approval regardless of what we do or accomplish, we often seek to substitute that same feeling of personal value and self-worth denied by our parents from someone or something else that serves as a parental surrogate. For some, this surrogate figure whose approval we seek is a teacher or mentor, a priest, minister, or rabbi, a big brother or sister (biological or otherwise), a close friend and confidant, the parents of a friend, an older relative with whom we are close, even a religious figure or spiritual guide whom we never actually meet face to face.

When the religious influence comes from someone from another religious background or tradition, the sense of emotional acceptance that often results can be one of the most powerful reasons for a child to convert to another religion later in life. Obviously this isn't always the underlying rationale for a religious conversion, but there is often an emotional component to the conversion process that is undeniable. Time and time again, people who have converted from one religion to another have indicated that there was something undeniably powerful and deeply comforting that connected to their souls on a profound level that they had not felt before, which in turn gave them a wonderful sense of acceptance, approval, and belonging that felt "like coming home." That is why conversion is often *much more* than a mere intellectual choice of one set of religious principles over another, one set of beliefs over another.

We human beings are marvelously complex. At times we are not even aware of the depth of what motivates us. We do what *feels* right to us even when we are not sure *why* it feels right. This is especially true when it comes to issues of acceptance, belonging, and self-worth. Since each of us has a profound need to feel loved, accepted, and worthwhile, there are times when the solution to that need comes in the form of a new religious tradition, a new set of religious beliefs, and/or a new spiritual community where we feel welcomed, validated, and important.

This is why as a parent seeking to understand your own child and the process whereby he has chosen to embrace another religious tradition, it is often as enlightening to ask questions about how the new religion and new set of beliefs makes your child *feel* as it is to ask questions about the beliefs themselves. It is not the case that the beliefs are unimportant, for they usually do form the intellectual basis for the choices your child has made. It's just that his choices are usually more complicated and emotionally complex than simply selecting between two sets of dogma.

Tell your child that you love him now as you always have, and because of that love are seriously interested in learning about whatever it is that he finds meaningful and fulfilling in his life. You do not need to pretend (nor should you) that you are considering converting to his new religion yourself, but merely that what is important to him is important to you. You want to reassure him that your goal in asking is not to challenge his choices but to gain knowledge and foster understanding to bring you closer.

Tell him you see this as an opportunity for your own personal growth and as a way to grow closer to him and not let the conversion in any way come between you and your relationship. The best way to ask questions about his new religion without being offensive is to state that very fear out loud from the beginning. "I really want to learn about what it means to you to be a Catholic since it's not something I really know anything about and if it's important to you I at least want to have a good sense of the things that matter in your life. I am afraid that if I ask questions about it, my ignorance might end up offending you or somehow accidentally drive us apart instead of bringing us closer together. Since that is the last thing I want to do, will you please help me and tell me how I can do this in a way that won't offend you but will communicate my true desire to learn about something that is making you happy and fulfilled?"

If you approach your questions in an open, honest, and vulnerable manner like this, you will lessen the risk of offending your child or inadvertently pushing her farther away from you. Simply express your honest desire to learn and understand for the sake of loving your child and creating the best relationship you possibly can. You can also tell her that if there are (or will be) children involved, you will want help from her to make sure that you do not upset her where they are concerned, and in fact find ways together to create as close a relationship with your grandchildren as you can.

Asking questions of your child regarding the new religion that he has embraced is obviously not the same as challenging his choices, attacking what you think are "ridiculous" supernatural claims of his new faith, sharing stories about people you have known in the past who shared his new religion whom you thought were stupid or ignorant, or telling jokes you heard at your local church or club where someone from his new religion or spiritual tradition was the butt of the joke.

Expressing those caveats may seem obvious, but when parents are very uncomfortable with the religious choices that their children have made, they often do not know any other way to talk to them about their new religion except through negative examples. The negativity grows out of an awkward awareness of one's own ignorance; you may come to realize that you know so little about most other religions and traditions that you do not have a clue as how to begin an intelligent conversation about them.

Of course doing research about your child's new religion is always a good idea. With the Internet so accessible and easy to use, anyone can use major search engines like Google or Yahoo! to find more information in an instant than you could absorb in a lifetime.

One of the suggestions often made to parents who are intimidated by their own lack of knowledge about their child's new religion is to spend an evening perusing various Web sites that are sponsored by their child's religion *before* they have their first serious conversation with their child. At the end of this book are number of Internet resources that you might find helpful.

When you sit down to talk with your child and ask questions about her new religion and what it now means in her life, if you have some initial information about the basic beliefs and tenets of this new tradition, it will give a starting point to your conversation while establishing your seriousness about learning as much as you can about ideas that matter to her.

Tell her, "We spent some time last night on the Internet reading about your new religious tradition, looking at the official Web sites and trying to figure out the differences and similarities between what we believe and the beliefs of _____." Then simply ask whatever serious questions came to your mind as you were doing the Internet research, or ask your child to explain it in more detail or in a way that makes it easier for you to understand. Tell him that since he grew up understanding beliefs that he knows you have, it will be easier for him to explain his new religious tradition to you in a language you can absorb.

Asking your child to help you understand is yet another way of communicating nonjudgmental acceptance and support for him while reinforcing the family connection. If he is willing to take the time to explain his beliefs in a language that you can understand, it will automatically emphasize the ideals that you have shared, the history that binds you together, and the common language underlying the values through which your family has experienced the world. This process can be a helpful and healing approach to mutual understanding. At the very least, it is an excellent way of demonstrating the sincerity of your desire for true understanding regardless of the specific religious choices that your child makes.

Another way of asking questions without being offensive is to ask your child for suggestions as to what books or magazines you might read. This, too, will demonstrate a seriousness of purpose on your part. Once your child does make some recommendations regarding reading materials (or movies, Web sites, etc.), you can use the information contained in those sources as the basis of more detailed questions. When you enter into conversations about her new religion based on information that you have read from sources that she provided, it automatically helps reduce any potential tension, discomfort, or feeling she might otherwise have of being attacked or having her newfound religion disparaged.

Every child wants to feel that her parents respect her as an adult and the decisions she makes for herself. The more you can demonstrate your respect and admiration of her strength of character in choosing her own religious path—even if you don't agree with her new religious beliefs and would never be willing to accept the "truth" of any religion but your own—the better and stronger your relationship with her will be. You certainly do not have to agree with everything that your other adult friends believe in to be able to acknowledge and even admire the strength of their commitment or the authenticity of their passion.

Most of us recognize that there are good, decent, loving, caring, ethical people in every religion, in every country, of every race, and in every culture. Look upon your own child in exactly the same way as you would anyone else you might meet who comes from a different race, religion, country, or culture; recognize that person as a person of integrity and then learn more about who they are. If you treat your own child with the same graciousness and respect as you would anyone else, you have a better chance of continuing to have a loving and mutually respectful relationship with your child.

SEPARATING FEELINGS OF SELF FROM FEELINGS ABOUT YOUR RELIGION OR CULTURE

The purpose of this section is to encourage you to learn how to separate your feelings of personal hurt and rejection from your feelings about having your religion or culture rejected when your child converts.

In a sense it is as simple as reminding you that most of the time, regardless of how it feels as a parent, your child's conversion to another religion is not about you at all. Yes, of course there are the rare examples of children who convert to another religion specifically to announce their rejection of their parents, to cause them pain and suffering in a public way. But in reality, the numbers of individuals who convert primarily for this reason or because they have been "brainwashed" or sucked into a cult is minuscule. The vast majority of those who convert from one religion to another do so out of sincere convictions, deeply felt beliefs, and a true sense of having found something that fits more perfectly who they are and what they believe, providing them with a sense of purpose and meaning that they simply did not feel in the religion in which they were raised.

When you recognize that these are the reasons why most people convert, you realize as well that it makes little sense for parents to take these decisions personally. Hey! It's not about you! In fact, taking such a decision personally is one of the most insulting responses you could have, since it signals to your child that you do not really believe that he is making decisions about what is best for him based on what he truly believes, but instead only as a reaction against you. Such an attitude from one's parent is a powerful statement that your parent continues to see you primarily as a child.

Obviously it is natural when your child converts to another religion for you to feel some sense of personal rejection. It is normal for any parent to have similar feelings on one level or another. What I am encouraging you to do in this chapter is to realize that *you are not your religion*. Your relationship with your child is much deeper, much more complex, and much more profound than any tradition—no matter how deeply you may embrace your particular religion and believe its teachings.

This is what is meant by the challenge of separating feelings of self from feelings about your religion or culture. The more you can see the choice that your child has made to convert as just that: a choice to convert *to* something and not a rejection *of* something (including you), the easier it will be accept that decision from an adult who is creating his own lifestyle. Since most parents want their children to be happy and content above all, forging their own paths in life, this moment provides you an opportunity to demonstrate to your child that you really do care more about his happiness and fulfillment then you do about your church or religion or culture. It is a challenge to be sure. The challenge is to demonstrate that you have faith that your religion will continue to thrive and teach its wisdom to the world whether your own child embraces it or not.

COPING WITH FEELINGS OF LOSS AND FAILURE (AGAIN)

We have already talked about the natural feelings of loss and failure that many parents experience when their child chooses to marry someone of another religion or culture or race (or someone of the same gender). Chapter 3 was all about the challenge of confronting feelings of failure, loss and grief, rejection and guilt. When your child chooses conversion, often these same feelings are stirred up all over again, sometimes years after you believe you have already successfully dealt with them.

So how do you cope when those same emotions begin to surface once again? In much the same way as you did when you first experienced them, only with more personal history under your belt and often many years of personal and family experiences to help guide you through your sense of loss and grief. Having already been there once before when the idea of an interfaith relationship or marriage first presented itself to you, you can draw upon your personal experiences of the past to guide you through the same emotional mine field once again.

As with the first time these feelings surfaced, it is always helpful to find someone you trust to talk with about your feelings of loss and sadness. Everyone reacts differently to what are otherwise similar experiences; no two people respond exactly the same. Husbands and wives, fathers and mothers, life partners, siblings—all react in their own way with their own unique set of emotions regardless of how similar they have always thought they were to each other.

The best that you can do for yourself and your other family members is to give each other permission to feel whatever it is that you feel from moment to moment and then give yourself the luxury of allowing yourself to express those feelings. On the other hand, you are not *required* to feel guilty, you are not required to feel like a failure, and you are not even required to feel bad about the choices your children make regarding their spouses and partners or their religion and beliefs. If you do not feel particularly bad or guilty then give yourself permission to be *happy* for your children, to celebrate their adult choices with them, and their ability to think on their own and fashion lives of meaning and purpose and joy.

KEEPING YOUR INTEGRITY WHILE CELEBRATING THEIR HOLIDAYS

Some parents worry that if their child chooses another religion and then wants to share their new religious holidays or celebrations with them that to do so is somehow a betrayal of their own religious tradition.

This is simply not so.

Just imagine that you are a student who goes to college and has a roommate who is of another religion or culture and has his or her own unique and different holidays, customs, and traditions. If your roommate asks you to join her as she celebrates a holiday about which you know nothing, and offers to show you what it means and teach you what the symbols represent or what the specific rituals mean, would you see it as a betrayal of your own religion? No one would see you learning about and sharing a new ritual with your roommate as in any way indicating that you are suddenly converting to another religion or demonstrating disrespect for your own. It would be seen as exactly what it is: an opportunity to expand your knowledge and experience something new.

I remember very clearly how excited I was in my first year of college when, as someone raised in the Jewish tradition, I had an opportunity for the first time to help my Christian roommate trim the Christmas tree which he brought into our dorm room. It was not my tree, but I had a chance to do something that I had never done before: find out how his family celebrated Christmas and what the ornaments that he brought to school for his tree represented to him in his life, as well as experience some of the excitement and joy that he felt in celebrating his holiday. There was certainly never confusion between us or anyone else. We both knew that by helping him trim his tree (which happened to be in our shared dorm space) I was not suddenly pretending to be Christian rather than Jewish, nor betraying thousands of years of Jewish history, nor pretending that I was something I was not, nor suggesting that I believed in the tenets of a different religion. I was enjoying the new experience of celebrating someone else's holiday with them and learning about the holiday.

The same is true in your own family when you have the opportunity to learn about holidays or customs with which you are unfamiliar. Just because it is your own child who now can teach you something religious does not make it inappropriate, hypocritical, or blasphemous. It is what it is: a wonderful opportunity to grow your own religious experience and to share an event of meaning with your child that has the potential of bringing you even closer together.

What is most important is for you to feel that you are keeping your own integrity even as you choose to celebrate a holiday or custom or ritual or life-cycle moment with your child and her new religion. There will likely be ceremonies that accompany the birth of a child that are different from your own; coming of age ceremonies that differ; unique ceremonies that accompany weddings, illness, or death—and you may find yourself involved with any or all of the above during your life with your child and her new religion. Keeping your integrity through it all merely means knowing who you are and making choices each time a new life cycle moment arises as to which you are comfortable with and which, if any, you find too uncomfortable to participate in. It is always *your* option to choose to sit one out if it doesn't feel right to you. And any time you have doubts or questions as you go through life together with your child and her new religious commitments, you can ask your priest, minister, rabbi, imam, or religious authority how he or she feels about it; you can make sure to ask your child what the specific rituals and customs mean; and then you can make your own decisions based on your own level of comfort.

To most of these questions, there is not one "right" answer as to what is appropriate and what is not. As you probably know, within any given religious tradition, there are often wildly different answers regarding religious questions—sometimes even diametrically opposed interpretations. That is why it is ultimately *your* personal integrity that matters most in these decisions. If you choose what feels right for you and follow your heart and your instincts, you will undoubtedly do the right thing.

LEARNING TO ACCEPT YOURSELF AND OTHERS

For some people, learning to live at peace with a child's decision to convert is a lifelong process. It begins with the recognition that your child is an independent adult whom you have raised to think for herself, to make her own independent decisions, and to choose the paths that will bring her the most personal fulfillment and peace of mind.

Acceptance of your child's decision to live her life in a way that is different from yours is also a statement of your trust in her and her judgment. It lets her know that you have faith that you have raised her with the values that matter and have given her the spiritual and emotional tools to make thoughtful, appropriate choices for herself. This trust and faith is one of the most important gifts you can give to your child and is a crucial step along the path to reconciling yourself with the new beliefs and religious lifestyle that your child has chosen.

The key to your peace of mind will be found in learning to accept that there is more than one right way to be, think, live, and give in this world. To truly accept that your child has chosen a different religious path from that in which she was raised will require that you learn to accept both yourself and others all as children of God. They are part of the same, universal, spiritual whole, loved by the same God who loves all creatures and has created all human beings in God's own image. Your child remains a reflection of that same divine image, regardless of the specific religious label that is attached to her particular form of religious practice and belief.

I am a rabbi and my spiritual home and practice is found within Judaism. Yet I take seriously the idea found in my own sacred scriptures that the entire universe was created by one God and that every human being is therefore equally a child of and creation of that same God—regardless of the language used to describe God, the rituals and customs created by human beings to celebrate the wonder and creative power of God, or the names which human beings have created to separate ourselves and our particular forms of religious practice from each other.

That is what learning to accept yourself *and* others is really all about. It is taking a giant leap of faith, acknowledging that there are "truths" to be found in many different religious traditions, and that if God walked on earth today what God would want above all else is for human beings to recognize the holiness and divinity in each other. The more you are able to embrace the idea of a universal spiritual whole, the easier it will be for you to accept the specific form of that universal spirit that your own child has chosen to embrace.

SOMETIMES THE MORE YOU KNOW THE BETTER YOU FEEL

Most of us are afraid of the unknown. As children we often feared the dark—not simply because it was dark, but because the darkness hid from our sight unknown, fearful things that lurked within our fertile imaginations. Fear of the unknown is an almost universal human condition. That is why we have so many metaphors and expressions that connect "light" to understanding and the elimination of fear.

We speak of "enlightenment" as the melting of our fears and of fears being driven out by the very light of the day. The same is true of fears that arise from ignorance and lack of knowledge. When it comes to your child and his choice to convert to another religion, many of your worst fears of what that will mean not only for him but also for you and your relationship will melt away under the bright light of knowledge and information.

That is why one of the best things you can do to strengthen your relationship with your newly converted child and the rest of his extended family is to find out as much as you can about his new religion. The more you know; the more you learn; the more you try to understand his new beliefs and the reasons for the rituals, customs, holidays, ceremonies, and celebrations that are a part of his new religious tradition, the better you will be able to relate to his new life. Plus, you will start to see similarities between the essential values of his new religion and the values that you have always cherished.

Knowledge is not only power, it is a great eraser. It helps make fears disappear—particularly irrational ones. By taking the time to learn about his new religious beliefs instead of simply rejecting them and him for the "apostasy" of his choices, you not only communicate your respect for him and his intelligence, but also help create a closer bond between you and his other family. It is almost a truism that the more you know about others, the better you feel, because usually the more you know about other people and what they believe, the more you realize how fundamentally similar they are to you.

Take the time to learn what you can. The time will be well spent. In fact, every hour spent learning more about your child's new religion is another hour spent bringing yourself closer to understanding him better, being able to relate to his new life better, and making it easier to feel welcome in his new life.

PERSONAL STORIES FROM THOSE WHO HAVE BEEN THERE

George and Bob are a success story. They are a father and son team who were able to strengthen the common bonds of their relationship, regardless of Bob's choice to convert to another religion.

"The first time my wife and I visited our son after he converted to Greek Orthodoxy, we had no idea what to expect," said George, who, with his wife and the rest of his family, practices Judaism. "We imagined all kinds of things: that his home would be filled with Greek icons, that we would feel like outsiders in our own son's home, that he might dress differently, talk differently—I can't even remember all the fears we had. I just remember how nervous we were about seeing him for the first time post conversion and about whether or not we would feel out of place and uncomfortable the entire time we were there.

"Of course, exactly the opposite happened. Both Bob, our son, and Gloria, his wife, couldn't have been sweeter, more excited to see us, more welcoming and graceful and inclusive. They clearly went out of their way to make sure that everything went well, and it did."

Bob concurred: "I think I was more nervous than my father was. Gloria and I kept looking around our house to see if there was anything that might make my parents feel uncomfortable or out of place, and even though we knew there wasn't, I really wanted them to know that I was still the same son they had raised.

"I love my parents and respect them greatly and am who I am today because of them. To me that was the most important thing I always wanted to make sure *they knew that I knew*. I am always grateful for how I was raised, for the values they instilled in me, for the ethical role models that I always saw in them, and for the strength and confidence they gave me to make my own path in life. That was a tremendous gift on their parts and I really wanted to acknowledge that gift and thank them for their constant trust in me.

"In the end everything seemed to work out great, and I feel closer to them now then I ever have. Feeling their approval for how I am living my life and the direction in which I have taken my life was more important to me than I realized. I can't tell you how relieved and grateful I am that they were willing to tell me that they are proud of me and the person that I have become."

Not all family relationships work out as smoothly as Bob and George's did. With Marsha and Lorie the family reconciliation and peace never happened at all.

"When Lorie became an evangelical Christian I didn't really get upset at first," said Marsha, Lorie's mother. "After all, Russell and I had raised her in the same Presbyterian Church in which we had both grown up, in a small town in upstate New York, and both were active in the church and good Christians ourselves. I figured her choice of an evangelical Church was just another expression of the same beliefs we had in Jesus and the good news of Christianity anyway. Boy was I in for a surprise the first time we visited her in her new home in Virginia and went with her to her new church. We felt so incredibly out of place that I was in shock. It was like we were heathens who had lost God's favor and there was only one shining road back into God's good graces and that was through the one true path of this particular church and this particular preacher. I have never felt so put on the spot in my life, as if I was suddenly a sinner in the eyes of God—and I'm a practicing *Christian!*"

Lorie admitted that she mostly agreed with her mother's assessment. "I had such high hopes for my parents and was so excited when they agreed to come visit me and attend church with me on Sunday," she said. "I just knew that once they heard Reverend Billingsly speak it would all become clear to them and they would step forward to receive his blessing and come into Christ in the way that I have been saved. The Presbyterian Church in which I was raised was so formal and stuffy and passionless. Reverend Billingsly opened my eyes to who God really is in my life, what God wants from me, and the power I have to bring others under God's protective wing. I just wanted my parents to feel the same power and passion and love that I have felt. Instead it seemed to frighten them, and just like Pharaoh they hardened their hearts and refused to see the glory of God that was right in front of them. It's sad really because I had such high hopes for their visit and really wanted them to see how happy and content and fulfilled I am with my new relationship with Jesus."

Lorie's father Russell was also clearly upset. "The whole thing was a bit confusing for us," he admitted. "We were proud of Lorie and the fact that she had found a community of her own and made her own life for herself there in Virginia, but the church she had fallen in with felt almost like a cult of personality to us and was so different from how we have both been raised and the Christianity we follow. I guess God is still God and Jesus is still Jesus, and as long as I look at it that way I will just have to keep telling myself that at least she is still a Christian so it could be worse. I really just want her to be happy in life, but I'd prefer she do it by finding a husband, getting married, having kids, and settling down to a normal life. Now she's talking about becoming a missionary of some kind for that church she has joined, and it all just makes me nervous."

Clearly there is no one, magic formula to making life work when your child chooses a religious or spiritual path that is different from your own. The best you can do is continue to be the most supportive parent you can. You need to let your child know that you will always be there for him or her regardless of where life takes them. Be open to learning about new religions, new rituals, new ways of celebrating life itself, and the wonder and mystery of the universe. And have faith that in the end the values you have taught and the role model you continue to be will serve as the consistent link between the past you shared together and the future that you are both creating today.

Nine

BEING AN INTERFAITH GRANDPARENT

UNDERSTANDING YOUR ROLE IN YOUR GRANDCHILDREN'S LIVES

One of the most important challenges of being an "interfaith grandparent" is understanding that you have the opportunity to play many roles in the lives of your grandchildren. Some of these roles may be the traditional ones that grandparents have always played: the safe harbor for your grandchildren in the midst of the normal daily storms of growing up with their parents and siblings; a loving, supportive ear to turn to when they want some place to share their doubts or dreams about life; a calm voice that can compare what life was like "way back when" you were a young person their age (to the degree that they actually believe you were *ever* young and their age!); or simply a ready-made babysitting service for exasperated parents with no where else to turn for a break from the relentlessness of parenting.

At the same time, interfaith grandparenting provides you with an entirely new and different set of opportunities to play roles in the lives of your grandchildren that were not part of the traditional grandparenting roles in ages past where religious and cultural homogeneity was the norm. Today, being part of an extended interfaith family often means that the grandparents are the only ones comfortable talking about their own religion or culture and providing insights to their grandchildren from their own unique life perspective. This is especially true in those families where parents have chosen not to teach or celebrate any specific religion in their own home, but rather to make their home a kind of "religion neutral" zone in an attempt at preventing the issue of religion from causing friction or disharmony within their home.

This choice is not one that I personally ever recommend to parents from among the various choices that interfaith parents can make regarding how to raise their children, but it is a choice that many interfaith parents do make—especially when neither parent feels strongly enough about their own religious tradition to insist that it be shared or taught to their children. It also happens when couples get married without doing the relationship homework of talking through the various interfaith options so that they can choose a path that will honor and respect the religious traditions of both, while still providing their own children with a religious identity.

In my previous books, especially in *A Nonjudgmental Guide to Interfaith Marriage* (Xlibris, 2002) I go into great detail about the various choices available to interfaith parents regarding how to raise their children, and the implications of each of those choices both for the family dynamic and the emotional and spiritual lives of their children, so I will not repeat all that information here. I will, however, reiterate my strong belief that religious consistency encourages emotional stability in children. My recommendation is always for parents to choose a particular religious identity for their children (and I do not lobby for one over another) knowing that in any case all children have the right and option when they grow into adulthood to ultimately make that decision for themselves.

Children are quite flexible and comfortable knowing that one parent practices one religion, their other parent practices another religion, and that their parents have chosen to raise them in one or the other of their parent's religious traditions. They are generally most *uncomfortable* and ill at ease when revealing, "I know what my dad is and I know what my mom is but I don't know what I am" because their parents have avoided giving them any specific religious identity, either out of fear of confusing their children or fear of creating friction and discord within their own marriage. For such parents, the idea of avoiding decision making seems like the lesser of all interfaith parenting evils, and so they choose do to essentially nothing (other than perhaps nominally celebrating Christmas with a tree and presents if one parent was raised with any kind of Christian upbringing).

That is why grandparents in such families often find themselves serving as *the* source of grounding in any religion or spiritual discipline that does take place within the interfaith family. This of course also carries the possibility of creating tension and discord between the grandparents and their son- or daughter-in-law (or child's life partner) who was raised in a different religious tradition. We will address more of this challenge later in this chapter.

In the meantime, it is enough to draw your attention to the various opportunities you have as interfaith grandparents to play several different roles both for your grandchildren and their parents. First, grandparents often represent a primary source of religious or cultural information and education for the entire family. When children ask their parents questions about how they were raised or what it "means" to be Christian, Jewish, Muslim, Buddhist, or whatever religious tradition it is, their parents often reply, "Go ask Grandma or Grandpa and they will tell you what it means."

"Go ask Grandma or Grandpa" becomes a code between parents and children sometimes simply for "I don't want to talk about it myself," or "I'm not comfortable talking about this," and sometimes for "We don't bring up questions about religion in this family at all," and sometimes for "Bringing up questions about religion can cause a fight between Mommy and Daddy." In any of these cases the message is clear: talking about religion in their home is not a safe activity for these children, and the only safe place to go with any questions or issues relating to the various religious traditions that they know are part of their own parents' backgrounds is to their grandparents.

As you might imagine, this particular reality provides grandparents with situations that are fraught both with opportunities when it comes to their grandchildren and potential dangers regarding their own children and in-laws. That is why understanding what your specific role is in the life of your grandchildren is not always a cut-and-dried proposition. Often it is dependent upon the family dynamic present in your children's home, the decisions (or lack of them) that they have made in regard to the role religion will play within their own family life, and the role in which *they* would like to place you—whether you are interested in playing such a role or not.

The complexity of interfaith life and of interpersonal and family dynamics is such that there is no "one-size-fits-all" role that interfaith grandparents play. You may be called upon to become the expert source of religious information and knowledge, or you may be asked to stay out of religious discussions with your grandchildren altogether. You may become the safe place where holidays and lifecycle events are celebrated and taught, or you may be constantly cast in the role of "problem maker" simply because you continue to live your personal religious lifestyle, celebrate your holidays openly, and invite your kids and grandkids to be part of your religious life and practice.

One thing for sure is that there is no one, perfect, "right" answer to any of these issues regarding how best to act as an interfaith grandparent. Many different people make many different choices appropriate for them and their families and their specific lives and relationships. Hopefully, the rest of this chapter will provide some helpful guidelines and suggestions culled from the experiences of many who have faced similar challenges as to the various options from which you can choose the interfaith grandparenting lifestyle that works best.

WHAT TO DO, WHAT NOT TO DO

How Much to Share and Teach?

Of course there is no exact science when it comes to answering the question of how much of your own beliefs and convictions are appropriate to share with your grandchildren when they are being raised in an interfaith family. Much has to do with the specific choices that their parents have made regarding their religious upbringing, and the degree to which they have chosen to raise them with one or another specific religious identity. Even more important than the decision to raise them in one religious tradition or another, however, is to know what their specific desires are regarding what they do or don't want *you* to share with their children when it comes to your own religious background, tradition, and beliefs.

As with every other chapter in this book, the goal here is to help you create the best, most supportive, mutually fulfilling lifelong relationship with your entire family—your own children, the life partners they have chosen, the new extended family that their choices have brought into being, and any grandchildren that are a result of their relationships. That is why it is crucial to take your lead from their parents. The last thing you want is to become a source of contention, discord, and religious disagreement between your child and his or her partner.

How much of your own beliefs are appropriate to share with your grandchildren is best determined by having a face to face, honest, and direct conversation with your child about exactly this issue. Tell her you want to make sure to be supportive of her in her life and with the difficult decisions you know she has had to make regarding the role of religion in her family, and that you need her help in doing the right thing, being supportive without overstepping your bounds or creating friction in her marriage or family life.

Most of the time children are grateful to have a conversation in which this subject is so honestly and openly addressed. First of all, if they think you have strong feelings about your own religious traditions, they are often hesitant to do or say anything that may seem as if they are trying to censor you, who you are, or the integrity of your beliefs. This is especially true when there remains any residual guilt on their part for not marrying someone of the same faith, racial, or cultural background, which is quite often the case in interfaith marriages.

Secondly, your willingness to initiate a conversation with your children about the role they would like you to play in the religious life of their kids opens the door for them to ask for your help in providing the kind of "surrogate religion" that is a crucial role so often played by interfaith grandparents (more on this below).

Thirdly, the fact that you are the one to initiate such a conversation with them gives them one of the most important emotional gifts that any parent can give to a child, namely that you respect him or her and the choices they have made for their own lives.

Then, of course, having initiated such a conversation, you must follow through by listening to their desires and doing your best to follow their wishes when it comes to the spiritual or religious or cultural role that they would like you to play. Sometimes this is a difficult pill to swallow for it involves restraining yourself from your natural enthusiasm to teach your grandchildren all that you hold precious and dear about your own background, religion, culture, and way of life.

It is often frustrating for grandparents to find themselves in such a situation where their children have asked them not to talk about or teach their religious beliefs to their own grandchildren, or have given them guidelines regarding subjects that are permitted and subjects that are not. Given this natural frustration, grandparents in similar situations can partially satisfy their own need to pass on their particular tradition while following the requests of their children: create your own personal "spiritual journal" for your grandchildren to read someday in the future.

Creating a personal spiritual journal is a powerful way for you to take the time to clarify for yourself what you really do believe about life and its meaning, and to impart the lessons that you have learned from your own life and your own religious or cultural tradition that you want preserved for future generations. It is also a beautiful spiritual legacy to leave for your grandchildren, and one which you can give them whenever it becomes appropriate— even if it has to wait until your own life is over and your spiritual journal becomes part of their inheritance. Sometimes the most precious inheritance anyone can receive is not money, real estate, or physical possessions, but the ethical wills, writings, and spiritual inheritances that are left behind by loving grandparents.

Hopefully, your own children know how important your beliefs, religious traditions, and way of life are to you, and recognize that much of who they have become in their own lives is a result of those very beliefs which you passed on to them. Sometimes initiating conversations about your role in the religious life of your grandchildren results in your children inviting you to share whatever you desire with your grandchildren as long as you do so in a way that does not drive a wedge between them and the other side of their family.

When your children give you permission to share your own beliefs and religious lifestyle with your grandchildren, then that permission ought to come with a certain sense of responsibility, and an obligation to respect the diversity of your grandchildren's spiritual family. This means that it is one thing to share your personal beliefs about life and death, God, and the universe and quite another thing to insist that your beliefs are the only "right" and "true" beliefs and that any other beliefs are somehow blasphemous and therefore would be rejected by God.

There are families where one side is constantly telling their children and grandchildren that the other side (including, therefore, at least one of the grandchildren's parents) is going to hell because they do not believe the way God wants them to believe. The emotional trauma that this can cause to children should be obvious; it can also destroy any possibility of harmonious family relationships. And yet, people do it anyway. Some folks simply feel that spreading their version of "the word of God" is more important than family harmony, more important than supporting the difficult choices that their own children have made, and even more important than their long-term relationship with their children. The simple truth is that they have chosen dogma and religious beliefs over relationships. The results are predictable. And in most cases the destruction to the family relationships is irreversible. Ultimately it comes down to whether ideas are more important than people or vice versa—and ultimately that choice is yours.

Obviously there is no magic formula as to how much is too much to share about your own beliefs. Sometimes you have to play it by ear, do the best you can, keep the lines of communication open with your children and their partners, check in from time to time to see how they are feeling about the degree to which you share your religious life, and then be willing to adjust accordingly. Patience is always a virtue, especially when you think about being a part of your grandchildren's lives for many years to come.

In the end, the best way to teach the values that matter most to you is by being a living example. Be the kind of person you would like your children and grandchildren to become. Be the kind of role model that inspires them to think "I want to grow up to be like Grandpa or Grandma." In that way you become in your grandchildren's eyes the living embodiment of the wisdom that you profess. This is how you can have the most profound impact on those you love without having to consciously "teach" anything at all.

Giving Religious Gifts or Not?

Grandparents love to give gifts to their grandchildren. That's just part of the fun of being a grandparent. And most of us have wonderful, sweet memories of the special gifts our own grandparents gave us when we were children. For some of us, every time we came to visit our grandparents there would be a gift of some kind waiting. For others, it was every time our grandparents came to visit us, we just knew they would bring something special that reflected their love and affection. It's not that we loved our grandparents because of their gifts; it's just that both we and our grandparents derived so much joy from these exchanges. And this is especially true when it comes to holidays, celebrations, and life-cycle events that are often considered gift-giving moments. Christmas, Hanukah, Kwanza, Ramadan—there are an endless number of holidays, times, and seasons in which gift-giving is the norm in nearly every culture and family.

So the question that arises for all these moments is the degree to which grandparents use them as opportunities for passing on their personal religious values through books, music, movies, and symbols that tell their particular religious story or signify the traditional story behind a particular religious holiday or celebration. Such moments can be seen as natural opportunities for informal religious education, exposing interfaith children to the basic religious ideas, stories, holidays, and literature of one side of their family's spiritual heritage. On the other hand, they are often seen as intrusive, pushy, perhaps even devious attempts at subtly proselytizing the grandchildren in opposition to the other religious side of the family.

The same act—sharing books, music, movies, and stories from one religious tradition or another—is perceived by some as positive and loving and by others as negative and underhanded. It clearly is not the act alone of giving the gifts that determines how they are received, but rather the larger family context in which they are given, the conversations that have taken place between parents and grandparents regarding the parents' desires regarding childrearing, and the ways they are choosing to expose them to the different religious traditions represented in their home.

These are often deeply emotional issues for everyone involved and need to be approached carefully, lovingly, gently, and with an open heart and a sense of trust and faith in the love and respect you share with your children. It's not always easy to sit back and let your children raise their own children without exposing them to some of the sacred stories that you treasure. But as difficult as it is, if you are reading this book in the first place, my guess is that you are trying to figure out how to maintain the best relationship you can with your children, grandchildren and extended family, while maintaining your own spiritual and religious integrity. If that is your goal, then remember that *respect for the decisions and choices that your own children have made* and continue to make at each stage of their lives *must be the foundation of your relationship.* If you can maintain a relationship with them in which they constantly feel respected and accepted regarding their religious choices, they will be much more open to allowing you to give holiday gifts that reflect your religious beliefs and spiritual culture as these gestures will be perceived as a natural part of the larger religious spectrum of family beliefs and not as an attack on them or their own religious life choices.

Of course, the easiest way to know if a potential gift will be seen in a positive or negative light by your children is simply to ask them in the first place. Tell them what you have in mind to give and ask them for their nod of approval. If they say yes, bring the gift, and if they say no, do not. Then if they do say no, take the time to delve deeper into why they do not want you to give that particular item to their children. Use their expression of concern as a teachable moment, helping you understand their fears and concerns, their thought processes regarding the religious upbringing of their children, and their ultimate spiritual goals for their children as well. They may even find in the process of explaining their decisions and the rationale behind those decisions that they are not as clear about why they are doing, what they are doing as they had originally thought.

The more you know and understand the thought processes of your children, the easier it will be for you to be supportive of them in the future, and to know which gifts will be appropriate.

Sometimes conversations about the child raising choices that parents have made inadvertently helps them rethink their own rationales for the religious upbringing of their children and remind themselves of the values that they really do want to pass on to the next generation. Of course such a conversation is just as likely to reinforce their original choices and help them to articulate those decisions more clearly and forcefully both to themselves and to you. In either case, you will have clarified for yourself and for your children the values that are important to them.

IT IS OK TO HAVE YOUR OWN STRONG BELIEFS

No one is suggesting that you are to stifle your own strongly held religious beliefs simply because your children have married or are living with someone of another religious tradition. The same is true for the fact that your own children have chosen to raise their kids in a religious manner that is different from how you raised them or from how you would raise them if you had the opportunity to do so today. Their choices should in no way be seen as a reflection of your own religious convictions. Nor should they be interpreted as implying that having your own strong religious beliefs is wrong or that you should in any way be prevented from living your personal religious life as fully and with as much integrity as you can.

The opposite is true. As a religious person myself, I believe in the power of religious traditions in bringing meaning, purpose, and holiness into people's lives. There are many legitimate sacred traditions and not just one "right" religion, and each of us has an opportunity to find the spiritual path that best allows us to experience God's presence in our own lives and in the world. The fact that you may have your own strongly held religious beliefs, or that there are religious rituals, customs, traditions, holidays, and celebrations that you feel are sacred expressions of holiness and God's purpose is both a blessing and a gift.

Having such strongly held religious beliefs is often what makes wrestling with the right way to interact with your own children and grandchildren within the context of an interfaith relationship so challenging. If it were easy and if all the answers were obvious, you probably would not be reading this book. My own contribution to this conversation has only evolved because I have spent decades of my life interacting with and counseling interfaith families as they have struggled with how to create the most loving, meaningful, and fulfilling life for themselves and their children.

The fact is that there are not always easy answers to every challenge. Sometimes not only are the choices difficult to make, but the alternatives seem to carry as much potential for danger and family upset as they do for reconciliation and family harmony. This is especially true when grandparents have very strongly held religious beliefs. For many in this position every decision seems to be fraught with danger, as if they are gingerly walking through an emotional mine field that could blow up in their faces at any moment.

Still, it is important for people who have their own strongly held religious beliefs to find ways of relating to their children and grandchildren in ways that allow both parties to feel that their integrity remains intact as do the bonds between them.

One of the best ways I have found to do this is to separate and define the foundation of your religious values, that is the underlying religious beliefs that you have about the nature of God and human beings and the universe in which we live and the specific rituals that your particular religious tradition has adopted in order to express those values and beliefs.

For example, most religious traditions teach that God created the universe and all that is within it. Traditions that are biblically based also teach that human beings are created in the image of God. Thus you can see yourself as the embodiment of God's compassion, love, and even forgiveness every time you reach out to embrace and accept the spiritual life of your children or grandchildren—knowing that those are the divine qualities that your own religious tradition has associated with God. These qualities are not dependent on a specific form of celebrating a holiday or ritual, but are the values that fundamentally support your religious tradition's understanding of God independent of the all the rituals, customs, and holidays.

The more you can focus on these underlying values and ways in which you can express those sacred values in your relationships with your children and grandchildren, the more you will feel that your own religious integrity remains intact—even if you hold yourself back out of respect for the wishes of your children.

There is often a fine line between the two. As such, it might take a significant amount of personal prayer and meditation to continually focus both on your own spiritual needs as well as the behaviors that will best create the kind of lifelong relationships that you desire.

Sharing Your Beliefs in an Inoffensive Way

The biggest challenge for those who have strong religious beliefs is learning how to share those beliefs with those you love in inoffensive ways. It does no good to blast in to a family gathering determined to save the souls of your beloved children or their life partners or your grandchildren if you know that the end result will be a profound alienation from you or the possibility that you will be forever banned from speaking about religion or religious issues in their presence.

Sharing your beliefs in an inoffensive way is not a difficult challenge; it just takes some thought, planning, and personal discipline. The most important key is to share your beliefs in a way that lets others know that you recognize that other people think and believe differently and that these beliefs are simply *yours*. Even if you fervently believe that there is only one, right way to believe; and only one, right way to worship God; or only one, right way to pray; or only one, right way to understand issues of sin and salvation, heaven and hell; and that if someone does not believe in the right way that they are condemned to eternal life in hell, if you want an ongoing relationship with your children and grandchildren, you will have to find the discipline *not* to preach those convictions to them.

It is not that these ideas are wrong, for they certainly may be right for you. It is just that living with an interfaith family requires more tact, diplomacy, and interpersonal communication skills than simply acting as if you are the designated evangelical soul-saver in your family. If your beliefs compel you to talk that way and to act that way then you will also have to accept the likely consequences that your family will find those words and behaviors offensive and upsetting.

The best way to share your own strongly held religious beliefs is to clearly identify them as *your* beliefs, not as "the truth." Most people are willing to let others have strong beliefs, even if they passionately believe something different, as long as those beliefs are not forced on them or others.

Recognize that in a world of over 6 billion people, there are literally billions of people who believe differently than you and who are presumably living ethical, productive, loving lives. That is why the key is to keep it personal— what it means to *you*, what it has done for *you*, how your beliefs have helped *you* to be the best person that you can be. Then if others see that you live what you preach, that you live in accordance with those beliefs and are a person they feel worthy of emulation, they are more likely to explore what your particular beliefs might mean to them as well.

In my experience, this is the only way that someone with strongly held religious beliefs can share them with others and not be seen as offensive or divisive. Since most people resent being told that they are wrong and that their own beliefs are wrong, it is always better to be the kind of person that will attract others to your beliefs rather than preach those beliefs in the abstract.

GRANDPARENTS AS SURROGATE SOURCES OF RELIGION

We touched earlier upon the fact that one of the most common roles that grandparents play in the lives of interfaith families is as sources of "surrogate religion."

This phenomenon occurs naturally in many families, especially when the problems inherent in making choices between different religions become more than the interfaith couple cares to deal with. In such cases, they often turn to their own parents as religious celebration facilitators. In this way they feel that they can eliminate the necessity to choose for themselves or their children at all.

In most instances, as you can imagine, grandparents are more than delighted to be involved in the lives of their children and grandchildren in any way they can. Particularly when it comes to teaching grandchildren their own religious heritage and customs, grandparents have a tendency to see this as their natural area of expertise anyway.

When grandparents step up to fill the religious vacuum created by lack of parental involvement, it often creates a smooth, tension-free way of resolving potential conflicts over what to celebrate, where to celebrate, and with whom. Couples simply divide the religious celebrations neatly into "your side" and "my side," and since these sides often represent different religious traditions, there are rarely conflicts. In fact, many interfaith couples consider themselves lucky to be able to attend celebrations of both faiths, never having to have to choose between extended families or in-laws.

In fact, providing surrogate religion has become one of the most important roles that grandparents can play in an interfaith family structure. After all, every interfaith family is made up of an extended family including brothers, sisters, cousins, parents, and grandparents that all represent different ways of living a religion or culture. When grandparents are willing to serve as religious role models for their grandchildren without placing undue religious demands or expectations on the parents themselves, the gesture is often greeted with a great sense of relief and gratitude.

Many interfaith couples have made an overt agreement not to bring any particular religion or religious ritual into their home. At the same time, they are delighted that their children have the benefit of grandparents who will celebrate, teach, tell stories, sing songs, and demonstrate particular religious holidays, celebrations, and rituals in *their* home.

As grandparents become surrogate religious role models, they take on the task of passing down religious values, symbols, rituals, and history that the parents feel constrained from doing themselves. At times this occurs openly with the clear assent and blessing of the parents. At other times it comes across subterfuge on the part of one parent, an unacknowledged attempt to subtly expose the children to more of their particular religion than they had agreed upon in the first place with their spouse or life partner.

When either person in a relationship acts in such an indirect and manipulative way, they are asking for trouble. Anytime there is secrecy, manipulation, subterfuge, or deceit in a relationship, you are undermining the very foundation of your lives together. As if that were not bad enough, you are also teaching your children by your example that the proper way to behave within a loving relationship is to lie or subtly deceive your partner. This is anything but a positive role model.

As with every aspect of a loving marriage or partnership, it is the openness, honesty, and integrity of the communication between partners that is of utmost importance. Being open with your needs and desires is not always easy to accomplish, but it is always the best choice, and the same goes for loving life partners, and for parents and children. You want to be the kind of parent whose children can trust your integrity no matter how old they become or what life challenges they or you have to face.

Parents and grandparents might sit together and openly talk about the religious child raising decisions that the interfaith couple has chosen for their children. One interfaith couple, Gail and Gene, actually invited their parents over and told them something like, "We need your help in making the fact that we are an interfaith family work as a positive in your grandchildren's lives. We have been thinking very hard about how we can best give our children the greatest sense of family security, love, and integrity in a unified manner, while at the same time giving them the benefit of the two different religious and cultural heritages that are their inheritance.

"We have decided that the best way to do both things at the same time, while remaining consistent in the celebrations and rituals that we have agreed to have (and not have) in our own home, is to ask all of *you* to help us by being sources of surrogate religious training for them."

Surrogate religious training is often one of the most constructive uses that interfaith couples can make of their parents, and as grandparents you might find it helpful to make this suggestion to our own children when it is appropriate. It will certainly help you to feel that you have a specific, valuable role as a partner with your children in the spiritual upbringing of their children. Providing surrogate religion to your grandchildren can be a source of great joy, satisfaction, and fulfillment for those grandparents who are fortunate to be invited to assume that role. The key word in that last sentence is "invited," since forcing religious training and the like on grandchildren without the consent of their parents is a sure road to disaster in your relationship with your children.

RELIGIOUS DO'S AND DON'TS—THE "SECRET BAPTISM" AND OTHER GRANDPARENT FANTASIES

It's one thing to work in tandem with your children to provide support for them as a source of surrogate religious training, experience, and role modeling for your grandchildren. It's another thing to take on the religious upbringing of your grandchildren by doing things behind the backs of their parents merely because you believe it is "the right thing to do" or to fulfill your own religious desires.

There have been families in which even though the parents agreed not to raise their children with any specific religious identity and not to have them participate in any religious rituals that would suggest one religious identity over another, the grandparents decided, while babysitting their grandchild, to take the child to church and have the child baptized into their particular Christian denomination.

Many grandparents have had fantasies of doing the same thing with their own grandchildren, whether the fantasy involves baptism, circumcision, or any other welcoming ritual that is specific to their particular religious tradition. It should be obvious to anyone reading this book, however, that such stealthy religious intervention can only result in creating a rift between you and your children, not to mention between you and your child's life partner. Once you destroy the trust and integrity of your word, once you have demonstrated that your children cannot trust you to respect their own child raising decisions, it is all but impossible to win that trust back.

The list of religious do's and don'ts should be fairly self-evident by now—the "do's" involve listening to the desires of your children and acting in such a way that they see you as an ally in the difficult challenges of raising children in an interfaith, interracial, or intercultural family. The "do's" are about becoming a partner with them in the raising of your grandchildren, a partner they can trust and who they believe will act in accordance with their own desires and decisions. It is about accepting that there is more than one "right way" to raise children, even if your children's choices are different from the ones you would make if it were up to you. There is not only one right way to raise children and there is not only one right way to expose them to religious values and traditions, nor one right way to celebrate holidays. They can be as diverse as having an Easter egg on a Passover Seder plate or pizza to break the fast of Ramadan.

The "don'ts" of being an interfaith grandparent are equally as obvious. They include anything that will harm the integrity of your relationship with your children and their extended families. From time to time in our lives we feel the need to act according to the principle, "Better to seek forgiveness then ask permission"; but when it comes to the long-term health and welfare of your relationship with your children and your grandchildren, that plan of action is practically guaranteed to create lifelong problems instead.

If you want to take your grandchildren to a church, or synagogue, or mosque, or temple, or any other religious service, *get permission from their parents first.* If you want to introduce them to the beautiful religious rituals which have meant so much to you throughout your life, do not simply act first and ask for forgiveness later, ask for permission in advance and discuss with your children what you would like to do and exactly what their children will be experiencing if they allow them to participate in your religious rituals. A good rule to follow is this—do not assume anything when it comes to sharing your religion or culture with your grandchildren. The more you ask, the more your communicate, the more you engage your children in nonjudgmental, open conversations about how you can include your grandchildren in your religious life, the better your relationships will be with everyone.

HOLIDAYS AND FAMILY CELEBRATIONS

The same is true regarding the best way to approach celebrating holidays and family celebrations with your extended interfaith or intercultural family. The key is always to act in a way that respects the religious decisions your children have made while making sure to maintain the integrity of your own beliefs and commitments.

The easiest way to navigate celebrating holidays is to communicate your intentions in advance. If you are celebrating "religious" holidays like Christmas or Hanukah, or a secular holiday like Thanksgiving or the Fourth of July, the safest way to proceed is to let your children know in advance that you are planning to bring gifts of holiday books and music, or to share a special holiday dessert that has been passed down through the generations of your family, or to bring over a special decoration that is meaningful to you. If you let them know in advance whatever it is that you intend to contribute to the celebration, it will give them an opportunity to ask any questions they might have or simply know what to expect when the celebration arrives.

Family celebrations ought to be great moments of collective bonding, of creating loving memories together that can last a lifetime. Whatever it takes to accomplish that goal will be worth it. The role of parents and grandparents alike is primarily to create memories for our children that they can turn to whenever they need the warmth and glow of a loving family experience to get them through a difficult or challenging moment in life. In a sense, we are all in the business of creating life memories that sustain us in this important way. Your goal ought to be creating as many loving-grandparent memories as you can with your grandchildren, being the person they look to for support and wisdom, giving them the kind of memories that they will want to make sure are passed down to their children as well. This is one of the great opportunities that holidays and family celebrations present to all of us.

Tell your grandchildren stories of your own childhood. Share with them memories that you have of your grandparents and the role they played in your life. Talk to them about where you grew up, how you celebrated the same holiday or tradition you are now celebrating with them and in the very telling of the stories you will be enriching the life experiences of your grandchildren. Telling stories about your own life is one of the best ways to indirectly elucidate your own traditions and customs without negatively affecting the religious decisions of your own children. When you share stories of your own childhood it is not the same as telling your grandchildren how they should be acting or what they should be learning. It is simply sharing stories from your childhood that are important to you and that can in turn become part of the overall spiritual and family experience for your grandchildren.

HOW TO GIVE CHILD-RAISING ADVICE WITHOUT ALIENATING YOUR CHILD

Most grandparents find themselves from time to time watching their children as they make child raising decisions and fighting the urge to give them advice or at least share the benefit of their own lifetime parenting experience. Someone once said that the hardest thing to do in the world is to watch someone do something you know how to do better without jumping in to tell them how to do it right. That is certainly true when it comes to raising a child—every parent feels that they are an expert.

Letting your children make their own parenting choices without constantly feeling the need to give them the benefit of your wise counsel may not be easy, but it is usually an essential component of any good adult parent–child relationship. The way you will know when the right time is to give advice to your children is simply to wait until they *ask* for your advice. Obviously, if they directly ask for help, jump in with all the help you can give. But you are asking for trouble if you become one of those parents who is constantly giving gratuitous advice to your children about how they raise their own kids, because no matter how well intentioned your advice may be, that advice will inevitably be seen as a criticism of them and their competence as parents.

The best way to give advice without alienating your own children is to offer your help, advice, counsel, and a nonjudgmental ear to listen to their own parenting challenges, and then leave it up to them to avail themselves of your advice and counsel when the choose. Nothing quite compares with a parent's pat on the back for a job well done. All the community awards and professional certificates of achievement (even Academy Awards) in the world cannot take the place of parental approval. Nothing will ever feel as good as the simple words of a parent telling his or her child how proud they are of the adult that child has grown up to become. That is why your approval can be a powerful tool in strengthening your relationship with your children.

Giving child-raising advice is an art. The best method for communicating child raising suggestions to your own child is one in which you are constantly reinforcing your faith in them and their ability to be good parents, at the same time that you are sharing your personal experiences of dealing with similar questions and issues. The more you can communicate to your children your own vulnerability and fallibility, the more likely your children will be to seek your advice and let you in on the parenting process.

After all, there are no magic answers to parenting challenges. As an author of parenting books and having read scores of these tomes over the years, I know that every parenting issue has at least half a dozen different possible responses, any one of which might in fact be exactly the "right" answer for that particular child and that child's particular problem at that particular time. However, there never is any guarantee that the response you pick with all the best advice and intentions in the world will end up being the best choice for your child or their children. Every child is different, and even when the issues are similar, the way one child will react to a child raising decision may be the opposite of how another child will react to the exact same circumstance. That is part of the art and unpredictability of parenting. And by acknowledging that unpredictability and simply making yourself available to your own children as a supportive, nurturing presence willing to share your perspective but only in a nonjudgmental manner, you create the possibility that your children will turn to you for help and advice now and in the future.

WHEN YOUR GRANDCHILDREN'S RELIGION DIFFERS FROM YOURS

Inevitably, within interfaith families there will be children and grandchildren who have different religious identities and who see themselves as belonging to different faith communities than yours. This can be a difficult emotional experience for many grandparents, especially if they feel strongly about their own religion, religious culture, and sense of belonging to a specific religious community. For some it may even seem like the very worst thing that could possibly happen to them and their family is to have their grandchildren being raised with a different religious identity from the one that they so dearly cherish.

For some grandparents it is a matter of deep religious faith. They have a profound belief that their religion is the "right" religion, that God has shared God's truth with the world, and the rejection of that truth by their own children and the decision to raise their grandchildren in a different religion (or no religion at all) not only feels like blasphemy, but as if they are putting the future of their grandchildren's eternal souls in jeopardy. Obviously this can be extremely distressing to anyone who believes deeply that the fundamental truth of their religion was given by God to the world only to be summarily rejected by their children and now grandchildren as well.

This is perhaps the most difficult of all interfaith situations in which grandparents find themselves. In such situations, anything that grandparents might say about their beliefs and the emotional pain that this decision has caused them runs the greatest risk of alienating their children. What happens most often is that their children forbid the grandparents from engaging in any conversations at all about religion with their grandchildren. In such situations, the best thing to do is to seek spiritual counsel and advice from your own religious counselor and seek out other members of your own church or religious group who find themselves in similar situations so that you will have emotional and spiritual support as you struggle to come to terms with this difficult spiritual challenge.

For some grandparents it is not as much a belief that their grandchildren's immortal souls are in jeopardy as it is a more general feeling of loss of religious or cultural continuity from one generation to the next. Many people grow up with a very strong sense of loyalty and commitment to their religious community, culture, or people. They feel a sense of obligation to insure that their particular religious civilization continues from one generation to the next and they pass on that religious tradition to their own children with the expectation that they, too, will feel a similar sense of obligation to the community as a whole. When their children convert to another religion or choose to raise their children in a different religious tradition from that of their parents (or even no religious tradition at all), it often feels like a betrayal of all the generations past that have lived—perhaps even fought and died for—the privilege of keeping this particular religious tradition alive.

Although the sense of loss may come from an entirely different place and mindset, it is loss nonetheless. And the pain of feeling that one's tradition will not be carried on to future generations can be a source of great personal suffering and deep regret. Here, too, it is helpful to turn to your own clergy for advice and support and to find a supportive group of other grandparents who are experiencing a similar sense of loss.

No matter where you are on the spectrum of belief and commitment to the religious tradition of your childhood, having your grandchildren raised in a different religion can be a traumatic emotional challenge, fraught with all the possibilities for feelings of guilt, remorse, frustration, and failure that are addressed throughout this book, especially in Chapter 3. The best advice is still to remember that all you can do is the best you can do. Give your children a solid emotional and spiritual footing with which to face life. Ultimately the choices and decisions that they make in their own lives are theirs to make and are beyond your control.

Be the best grandparents you can, regardless of the religious label that your grandchildren wear. You will love them the same no matter what customs and holidays they celebrate, whether they fast for Ramadan or take communion or celebrate Hanukah. You will love them whether they grow up with parents who are of different genders or parents who are of the same gender. You will love them regardless of the individual choices that your own children make from year to year, and quite simply *that is the best that you can do.* Be someone they can rely on. Be a consistent, loving, and supportive force in their lives and know that in doing so you are giving them a priceless gift that they will cherish for as long as you are in their lives.

PERSONAL STORIES FROM THOSE WHO HAVE BEEN THERE

"I was devastated when my daughter, Kristen, announced that she was getting married to Michael and would be raising her children in the Jewish faith," Patricia said. "I have been a faithful, practicing Catholic my entire life, and I could not for a moment imagine my own grandchildren not celebrating their First Communion, going through Confirmation, or believing that Jesus gave his life for us. It seemed like I cried for days until my beloved and wise husband, Gordon, finally sat me down and said, 'Pat, you have got to pull yourself together. This is not the end of the world. Kristen loves Michael and he loves her and they will make a life for themselves together that will bring even more love into the world. Isn't that what Jesus is always teaching us? That he is love and we are to love each other and bring love into the world? Besides, Jesus was Jewish himself so if it was good enough for him it will have to be good enough for our grandchildren, too.'

"I realized that my crying wasn't helping me or Kristen or going to make any difference in how she chose to live her life. The best thing I could do was to keep my own faith strong, stay involved with my church and the people there I love, and be the best Catholic role model I could be for my grandchildren.

"Now it's ten years later and my faith is as strong as ever, and because I have always showed respect and support for the kids and their decisions about their girls, they are comfortable with me being who I am around them and even sending them Christmas and Easter presents because they know these are 'Grandma and Grandpa's' holidays. So ultimately I have made the best out of a situation over which I had no control anyway. I haven't sacrificed my own integrity and I have demonstrated respect for them and their lifestyle."

For Bernie and Lois it has not gone as smoothly as it has for Patricia and Gordon. "When my son, Larry, joined the Presbyterian Church and married Margaret in a Christian ceremony, it broke my heart," said Bernie. "My parents are Holocaust survivors. They were both in the camps in Europe and survived the atrocities of the Nazis, met in an internment camp, and came to America together to start a new life. Thank God neither of them were alive to see this today—it would have killed them to see Larry just give up what so many of their own families died for—like giving Hitler some kind of victory in the end. I can't even tell you how upset I was and still am to this today.

"I know there isn't anything I can do about it and that he's an adult who can obviously make up his own mind about how he will live his life. But I don't have to like it. It feels like a betrayal not only of our own family who suffered simply because they were Jewish, but of 4,000 years of Jewish history and culture and tradition as well. I just will never understand it and whether Lois has learned to live with it or not, I don't know how to make peace with it."

"It's not that I am happy about it," said Lois. "It's just that what is, is, and I can't do anything about it. I can either continue to be angry like Bernie and my son- and daughter-in-law will be uncomfortable having me around like they feel when Bernie is there, or I can do whatever I can to at least have a relationship with my grandchildren and be in their lives. I keep telling Bernie that he is cutting off his nose to spite his face, because the longer he stays angry and shows it, the less Larry will want him to be around his own grandchildren. So what good is that doing for anyone? Being angry doesn't change the situation; it just keeps making it worse."

These are just two snapshots of interfaith grandparents and their different reactions to similar situations. Although there is no one right answer for everyone, the best response is one that allows you to have the best relationship you can create with your own children—regardless of whether or not you approve of how they are living their lives and raising their children.

Ten

THE MORE WE KNOW THE LESS WE FEAR

UNDERSTANDING DIFFERENCES IN BELIEFS AND CULTURES

When it comes to issues of interfaith and interracial relationships it is definitely not the case that "ignorance is bliss." On the contrary, the more we know about others the less we fear them and their differences.

It is natural for parents to be concerned when they first discover that their child is getting seriously involved with someone who comes from a background that is significantly different from their own. Their minds may unwittingly begin filling with every stereotype and prejudice they have ever heard about this new and different religious or cultural tradition. That is why it is not altogether surprising to discover that many parents of interfaith and interracial couples allow their own ignorance of other traditions to blow the significance of those perceived differences way out of proportion. It is just this same ignorance that exacerbates whatever negative feelings that parents may already be experiencing, thereby making their relationship both with their own child and their child's new partner worse than it otherwise might be.

Instead of sitting in the darkness created by ignorance of others, we are always better off subjecting our prejudices and stereotypes to the light of day so that the enlightenment that comes with knowledge and information can better inform our attitudes and understanding. In some significant way, I believe that the dispelling of our ignorance and fear of "the other" through our willingness to open our minds to learning about and understanding their customs, traditions, and ways of life is one of the very hallmarks of civilization.

DISCOVERING COMMON VALUES AND IDEALS

This chapter exists to help you in that process of discovery and the dispelling of myths and stereotypes about various religious traditions. In these pages, you can learn, in a clear and simple form, the basic tenets of the most common religious traditions with which your children are most likely to interact. Exploring these various religious traditions will lead us to discovering the common values and ideals that link us together as part of one spiritual human family. There is always more that unites us than there is that divides us. It is clearly my hope that through understanding the fundamental principles of these religious traditions and their core beliefs, you will gain a greater appreciation for the universal ideals that underlie all human life.

There are essentially only two ways of understanding any religious tradition. The first is to believe that God is a supernatural being who resides in heaven and hands down to human beings a "truth" or divine scripture or sacred text through a particular individual or individuals. For traditional Jews it is the Torah (Five Books of Moses, or in some understandings the entire Hebrew Bible and all subsequent sacred Jewish literature) given to Moses on Mount Sinai; for Muslims it is the Koran given to Mohammad in a dream; for Christians it is the Gospel of Jesus. Similarly, one might say that for Buddhism it was the divine enlightenment of Siddhartha Gautama and for Hinduism it is found in the teachings of the Vedas and Upanishads and the Bhagavad Gita.

The second way of looking at religion is to see all religious traditions as essentially the spiritual discovery of human beings as they have wrestled with the same fundamental questions of life throughout the ages. From this religious perspective, every religious tradition has produced its own sacred texts as the concrete result of its search for meaning and purpose just as it has discovered its own understanding of spiritual truth and enlightenment. These spiritual discoveries have taken place at specific moments in history and in different geographic locations around the world as part of the universal search for the meaning of life itself by different cultures and traditions.

No matter what you believe about the ultimate source of your personal religious tradition, it is clear that among the 6 billion people on our planet, there are many different and seemingly competing religions. No one religion is accepted and believed by the majority of human beings, no one religious tradition has swept the world with its own interpretation of divine "truth."

Since no one religion is accepted and believed by a majority of humanity, it follows that if any one religion is *the* divine "truth," then most people in the world must be wrong in their religious convictions. Since I personally believe that spiritual truths come in many forms and are found in many diverse religious traditions, I believe that within each religion we can find common roots, common values, and a common spiritual core that unites us all. So let's take a brief look at several of the most common religious traditions, and perhaps you, too, will discover the unifying principles of human life that unite us as part of a common spiritual universe.

A Crash Course in Judaism

Judaism is the evolving religious civilization of the Jewish people. Like any civilization, it contains the multiple attributes of language and literature, rituals and customs, art, music, history, ethics, holy days, and a common spiritual homeland. Although Jews were originally Semites from a small segment of the Caucasian race, today Jews are found among nearly all races throughout the world, including black, white and Asian.

Above all else, what gives Jews their identity is not primarily belief, but rather the identification with belonging to the Jewish people. It defies narrow definition because Judaism has evolved over the past four thousand years into the totality of the religious strivings, national aspirations, cultural artifacts and rituals, spiritual celebrations, and philosophical ideals that are given expression in myriad ways in the daily lives of Jews.

Judaism is the living context within which individual Jews and the Jewish people as a whole work to create meaning and purpose in life. The one constant anchor throughout Jewish history has been the strong sense of identification with the *community* of the Jewish people. Religious "beliefs" have varied, theological concepts have undergone transformation and evolution, and practices differ in different communities, but the commitment to peoplehood and community has continued as the common thread that binds all Jews into a single religious cloth.

In many ways, *community* is the essence of Judaism. Jews experience themselves not only as the descendants of the biblical Abraham and Sarah, Moses, Miriam and King David, but as part of an enormous extended family that stretches to every continent of the globe.

Jews pray as a community within synagogues. The word *synagogue* is Greek, meaning "assembly" or "congregation." Synagogues first appeared as the result of the Jewish exile from Israel to Babylonia around 586 B.C.E. (Before the Common Era, what Christians often refer to as B.C.), when Jews were taken far away from their religious center in Jerusalem. Synagogues became the place of assembly and gathering of the exiled community, and were the place where personal and communal prayer was first established as a spiritual substitute for the physical offerings and sacrifices of the priests in the temple.

The idea of communal worship increasingly took the place of offerings and sacrifices by the priests in a central shrine, so that by the time the Romans destroyed "The Temple" in Jerusalem in the year 70 C.E. (Common Era, what Christians normally refer to as A.D.) and drove the majority of Jews into an exile that would last some two thousand years, the synagogue as an institution was already established.

Today, synagogues are created by their own members as independent institutions to serve the needs of its members. Most are affiliated with one of the major organized streams of Jewish life—either Reform, Reconstructionist, Conservative, or Orthodox, although some synagogues are unaffiliated with any specific movement. Each synagogue is empowered to adopt the prayer book of its choice, establish its own bylaws, rules, standards, and curriculum of religious instruction, and to hire its own professionals (like the rabbi and cantor who are the Jewish clergy who lead services, and sing the liturgy, teach, preach, and serve as the spiritual leaders of the Jewish community) at its sole discretion. The Jewish Sabbath (called "Shabbat" in Hebrew) begins Friday night at sundown and continues until sundown Saturday night. Orthodox Jews conduct services every day of the week, while Conservative, Reconstructionist, and Reform Jews generally only attend services on Friday night and/or Saturday morning.

Orthodox Jews are generally the most traditional in practice. According to Orthodox Judaism, God literally dictated the sacred scriptures of Jewish tradition to Moses on Mount Sinai. Because the Torah (understood narrowly to be the five books of Moses and broadly to include all of subsequent Jewish sacred literature) was divinely revealed by God, Orthodox Jews are obligated to follow every word and understand the Torah literally, as if God were speaking those words to us today.

For Orthodox Jews, life centers around the performance of 613 commandments or *mitzvot* (Hebrew, meets-VOTE) that God revealed through the Torah. By performing the *mitzvot* faithfully, and through strict adherence to all the Jewish laws that govern daily life, we are fulfilling God's plan for the universe and keeping our part of the divine covenant first made between God and Abraham the first Jew.

Reform Judaism began in Germany at the beginning of the nineteenth century as a reaction against Orthodoxy and a desire by Jews to bring Judaism and Jewish practice into the modern world and aid in the acceptance of Jews into contemporary society. It rejected the divine authorship of the Torah, relegated ritual laws to a matter of personal choice, and declared that every Jew is entitled to decide for himself or herself which rituals, customs, and Jewish laws he or she will follow. Reform Judaism sees the Jewish religion as constantly open to change and adaptation, and has traditionally placed great emphasis on ethics over ritual.

Conservative Judaism began as a reaction to what were perceived as the excesses of Reform Judaism. Its founders sought to find a middle path between the old world and the new world, between Orthodox and Reform. Conservative Jews hold that Jewish law is still binding, but invest the authority to make decisions regarding proper Jewish behavior with a committee of rabbis who deliberate on questions of Jewish practice and set policy for the movement.

Much more traditional in its approach to Jewish custom, ritual, law, and practice than Reform, Conservative Judaism uses more Hebrew in the service, expects observance of the laws of the Sabbath and Jewish dietary laws, and purposely makes changes slowly and with great deliberation.

Reconstructionist Judaism is the newest of the four major branches of modern Jewish life and the only movement that began in the United States. It sees Judaism as the evolving religious civilization of the Jewish people, emphasizes community and peoplehood, rejects the idea of Jewish people exclusively as "The Chosen Ones," and vests authority for decisions regarding standards and guidelines for Jewish ritual behavior with the community itself. Reconstructionism is perhaps the most aggressive champion of equality between men and women within Judaism and is consciously inclusive of gay and lesbian Jews and other nontraditional families.

Reconstructionism understands God not as an external "being" that acts upon us but as a power that works through us and is discovered in the everyday miracles of life. God is the power or process through which we achieve individual fulfillment and represents the highest ideals and values to which we devote our lives. It understands sacred Jewish texts as written by human beings as the record of the Jewish people's spiritual history and search for meaning in life.

The best estimate is that there are only around 14 million Jews living throughout the world today.[1] Jews of all denominations are painfully aware that 6 million Jews were murdered in the Holocaust of World War II, and had they not been murdered there would be some 20 million Jews in the world today. Consciousness of thousands of years of persecutions, from the Crusades of the eleventh century to the Inquisition in Spain in the fifteenth century through the Holocaust of the twentieth century has had a lasting impact on the psyche of the Jewish people and in many ways colors their attitudes and sensitivity to persecutions throughout the world. It also accounts for deep passions about defending the state of Israel and championing its right to exist as a Jewish homeland by virtually all Jews of every religious and political persuasion.

The Jewish annual cycle of holy days begins in the fall with the Jewish New Year ("*Rosh Hashana*," ROSH ha-shaw-NAH) and Day of Atonement ("*Yom Kippur*," YOME kee-POOR) and the ten days of awe and repentance that connect them, followed by the Festival of Booths ("*Sukkot*," soo-KOTE), which is a thanksgiving celebration for the fall harvest and *Simhat Torah* (SIM-hat TOE-ruh) that celebrates the end and beginning of the annual cycle of reading from the Torah scroll which contains the Five Books of Moses (and is read each week in synagogue in a continuous annual cycle).

In December, Jews celebrate the Festival of Lights called *Hanukah* (HAW-noo-kuh, which literally means "dedication") to commemorate the first recorded fight for religious freedom in 165 B.C.E. when the Jewish people defeated the Syrian Greek army after its emperor, Antiochus, had declared that Jews must give up Judaism and adopt the Greek worship of Zeus.

Purim (POO-reem, meaning "lots" in Hebrew) falls in February or in the beginning of March (the traditional Jewish calendar is primarily lunar and so dates shift each year against the solar or Gregorian calendar of the modern world). It is a holiday of costumes and carnivals and celebrates the victory in ancient Persia of the Jews over the villain Haman who schemed to murder the entire Jewish community.

A month later is the festival of Passover ("*Pesah*," PEH-sah) which celebrates the Jews' Exodus from slavery in Egypt after God, through Moses, brought ten plagues upon the Egyptian Pharaoh and led the Jewish people into the Sinai Desert on the way to receive the Ten Commandments, and then to the Promised Land of Israel. It is a weeklong holiday that is celebrated by more Jews than any other Jewish holiday of the year, primarily at a ceremonial ritual dinner called a *Seder* (SAY-der, which literally means "order" in Hebrew).

Seven weeks after Passover is the Feast of Weeks ("*Shavuot*," shaw-voo-OTE), which celebrates the giving of the Torah to Moses and the Jewish people at Mount Sinai.

The most important Jewish holiday of all is the Sabbath ("*Shabbat*," shaw-BAWT), which traditionally is observed on the seventh day of the week, following the biblical commandment, "Six days you shall labor and do all your work, but the seventh day is a Sabbath" (Exodus 20:9–10). It is traditionally a day of rest, study, and worship and includes special home rituals and prayers on Friday night (blessings over bread, wine, candles, and children) as well as communal worship at the synagogue.

If you go into a synagogue for a service on Shabbat, you will most likely see the men (and sometimes women as well) wearing a skullcap called a *Kipah* (kee-PAW) in Hebrew or *Yarmulke* (YAR-mul-kuh) in Yiddish. It is a symbol of reverence and respect for God. If the service is in the morning, most men and some women will also wear a prayer shawl called a *Tallit* (taw-LEET) in Hebrew which is a way of fulfilling the commandment in the Bible to wear fringes on our garments as a reminder of the commandments of God.

A Crash Course in Christianity

Christianity is the world's largest religion, with about 2.1 billion adherents throughout the world.[2] Its fundamental belief is that Jesus was the messiah promised in the Hebrew Bible (what Christians call the "Old Testament"), that he was the Son of God who came into the world two thousand years ago in Israel to redeem humanity from sin through the sacrifice of his death by crucifixion on the cross.

Christians believe that three days after Jesus was crucified, he rose from the dead to life everlasting and one day will return to earth to complete the promise of eternal redemption for all believers. Although they believe in only one God, Christianity also teaches that there are three essential elements to God called the Father, the Son, and the Holy Ghost or Holy Spirit.

Christianity is a religion based on the belief in Jesus and his power of personal salvation and redemption, which is practiced by communal worship at church on Sunday, where passages from both the Old Testament (the traditional Hebrew Bible) and New Testament, which contains the story of Jesus and the beginnings of Christianity, are read and taught. The New Testament is a collection of twenty-seven books written originally in Greek, by a variety of people, primarily about the life of Jesus and his teachings. The New Testament was mostly written in the century following the death of Jesus; and early Christians viewed these writings of as the fulfillment of the prophesies of the Old Testament. The first four books of the New Testament are called the "Gospels" (literally meaning "good news") of Matthew, Mark, Luke, and John, and tell the tale of the life, teachings, death, and resurrection of Jesus of Nazareth.

The New Testament is usually understood to contain three sections: the Gospels, the Epistles, and the Book of Revelation. Following the four books of the Gospels, the next twenty-one books are "epistles" or letters written by church leaders to churches that existed in various parts of the world beginning with the Epistles of Paul which purport to have been written by St. Paul who died around the year 70 C.E.

St. Paul the Apostle did not know Jesus personally but had a famous experience of conversion according to the New Testament when he beheld the resurrected Jesus on the road to Damascus. His writings are the first theological treatise of Christianity and set forth the basic principles of belief and missionary fervor through which Christians have understood their religious obligation to preach and teach "the Good News" of Jesus' life and death to non-Christians throughout the world ever since. Saint Paul is considered the primary architect of Christianity and is the single most influential of all the writers of the New Testament.

Basic beliefs of Christianity include the belief in an afterlife where believers will dwell forever in heaven with God and other believers and be free from sin and suffering. Christianity also teaches that nonbelievers will be sent to hell where sinners are punished with eternal damnation. Some forms of Christianity teach as well the existence of purgatory as a temporary place of cleansing for Christians who have died with sins for which they have failed to repent.

Most forms of Christianity also teach that human beings were created pure, but through the original sin of Adam and Eve, all subsequent human beings are born in a state of sinfulness from which they can only be cleansed through acceptance of the divinity of Jesus.

Holy days have been a central aspect of Christian worship from the beginning of Christianity, with the first holy days being "The Lord's Day" and "Easter." The Lord's Day has its roots in the Jewish Sabbath but was established as Sunday primarily because that was the day in which Jesus was resurrected.

The beginning of the church year is marked by Advent (from the Latin *Adventus* meaning "coming") and in the Western churches consists of the four Sundays leading up to Christmas. Historically, Advent was a period of fasting, repentance, and preparation for the Second Coming of Jesus. In the modern world it is no longer primarily accompanied by fasting, but rather marks the period of anticipation leading up to the celebration of Christmas as the birth of Jesus and the gift of his life to humanity.

Christmas is the most celebrated of all Christian holidays and has become a national holiday in many Western countries where it is observed as the birth of Jesus. December 25 has been celebrated as the spiritual birth of Jesus for the past two thousand years as Christians began observing it as an alternative Christian holiday to pagan winter holidays. The modern celebration of Christmas includes decorating a Christmas tree with lights and ornaments and often with an angel or star at the top. The tree is an evergreen variety to symbolize the eternal life that Jesus brought into the world, although today many people use artificial trees as a conscious statement of environmental awareness.

Other Christmas traditions include the visitation of "Father Christmas" (otherwise known as Santa Claus) and the giving of gifts, special prayers, and liturgical hymns at church services, the display of nativity scenes depicting the birth of Jesus, hanging of Christmas wreaths and lights on the outside of Christian homes, and the encouragement of peace on earth and goodwill toward all. It is traditionally a time when more people volunteer to help the poor and needy and find ways to express the best qualities of humanity than at any other during the year.

The Epiphany is a traditional Christian celebration of the revelation of God to the world in the human form of Jesus that takes place on January 6 of each year. It had its origin in the Eastern churches and was marked as the day of the baptism of Jesus and is why Christmas has often come to be seen as a twelve-day holiday (December 25–January 6).

Lent (or the Lenten Season) is the traditional name given to the forty-day period leading up to the holy day of Easter. In traditional Christianity it is a time of fasting, reflection, repentance, and abstinence. Although most Christians no longer observe Lent as a time of fasting (other than Ash Wednesday and Good Friday among Catholics), many abstain from one specific food or indulgence throughout the Lenten Season.

Ash Wednesday is the first day of Lent and in some churches (notably Catholic, Anglican, and Lutheran) worshippers place a mark of ash on their foreheads (usually in the form of a cross) to symbolize repentance and "carrying the cross into the world."

Easter is perhaps the holiest day of the Christian calendar and celebrates the central event in Christian theology, namely the resurrection of Jesus three days after his crucifixion. This is the oldest Christian holiday and the most important day of the year. In fact, the entire liturgical year of Christianity revolves around and leads up to the celebration of Easter. Its original dating was tied to the Jewish festival of Passover and became celebrated by most Christian denominations on the first Sunday after Passover, which corresponds to the first full moon after the spring equinox. It is celebrated with baptisms, the lighting of special candles, announcement that "Christ has risen," special prophetic lessons, an Easter mass, and the Eucharist (a sacrament that commemorates the Last Supper of Jesus with bread and wine and is embraced by all branches of Christianity).

A Crash Course in Catholicism

The word "Catholic" means "universal" and was a term used by early Christians to represent the "universal Christian faith." In 1054 C.E., the Eastern Church split from the Western and the West kept the name and became known as "Roman Catholic" while churches in the East became known as Greek, Eastern, or Russian Orthodox. When people speak of the "Catholic Church" they are most often referring to the Roman Catholic Church that, with nearly a billion and a half members, is arguably the single largest religious denomination in the world.

The Catholic Church is a worldwide organization with the Holy See of Rome as its spiritual and political headquarters. The Pope is the single highest authority in the Catholic Church and is considered infallible and absolute in his authority. The Church is divided into 2,782 dioceses throughout the world, each led by a bishop. The Church traces its history to Jesus and the twelve apostles and sees the bishops of today as direct successors of the apostles and the Pope as the direct successor of St. Peter. Therefore, the Catholic Church sees itself as part of an unbroken line of spiritual succession from Jesus and his apostles to today. For the purpose of statistics, Catholics comprise the world's largest religious body, and are the majority of the 2.1 billion Christians living in the world today.[3]

Some of the key theological ideas of Catholicism are given concrete expression in the rituals of Absolution, in which a priest acts on God's behalf to release someone from their sin (or sins) and the seven sacraments, which are outward signs theoretically instituted by Jesus in order to connect with the grace of God. The seven sacraments are baptism (in which a baby is sprinkled with holy water and thereby spiritually cleansed from the taint of original sin); Eucharist (the moment of consecration during a mass when God, through the priests, changes wine and bread into the body and blood of Jesus); reconciliation (the act of confession, forgiveness, and reconciliation with God); confirmation (a rite of Christian initiation); marriage; holy orders (through which priests are ordained to speak and preach and serve as spiritual leaders of the community); and anointing the sick (a ritual of healing and forgiveness of sins at one's death).

A Crash Course in Protestantism

Protestantism is generally dated from 1517 c.e. when Martin Luther, a German monk and professor at the University of Wittenberg, posted a series of theses that challenged Roman Catholic teaching. The name "Protestantism" came as a description of the protests that were issued in a document in 1529 entitled "Protestatio" issued by reformers who were rejecting the idea that divine authority can only be channeled through one particular person or institution, namely the Roman Catholic Pope.

Protestants looked to the Bible, specifically the Hebrew Scriptures and the New Testament as the ultimate source of religious authority—not religious institutions. Their movement to make religious authority more universally available to the people and take it away from the sole province of the Pope and the Holy See in Rome became known as the "Reformation."

Within two decades the Reformation had spread throughout Europe, including England (with the establishment of the Church of England or Anglican Church), France, Germany, Scotland, Switzerland, and the Netherlands. Ultimately, varying forms of Protestant Christianity have taken root throughout the world wherever Christian missionaries have gone, from North and South America to China and the Far East, from the continent of Africa to the former Soviet Union. Protestants are simply part of the world's 2.1 billion Christians.[4]

One of the key theological ideas of the early Reformation was that human beings are not saved by their individual merit or acts, but rather solely by faith itself and the grace of God. Although belief in the divine nature of the Bible is central to Protestant thought, there is an enormous range of belief and interpretation of the Bible from one Protestant denomination to the next ranging from accepting that every word of the Bible is literally the word of God to interpreting the biblical text as a spiritual allegory and metaphor for how God wants us to act in the world.

Most Protestants continue to teach that Jesus was both human and divine, the living Son of God who came into the world in order to sacrifice himself so that human beings could achieve salvation and eternal life in the world to come. Most but not all Protestant sects believe in the Holy Trinity of the Father, the Son, and the Holy Spirit; and most teach that at least two sacraments were given by Jesus: baptism and the Lord's Supper or Eucharist. But many more liberal Protestant denominations have eliminated the Eucharist and teach the Christianity is fundamentally about love and living a life in consonance with the ethical role model and teachings of Jesus rather than the rituals and elaborate rites that the church created after Jesus' death.

Protestant churches place an emphasis on teaching and preaching and not doctrinal authority nor the formal rites that the Catholic Church uses in its worship mass. Protestant churches introduced services in the vernacular of each community, congregational singing of hymns, a much simpler and less elaborate liturgy than in the Catholic Church, and a focus on the message and lessons of the preachers. Most are not centrally governed and allow individual churches to assume their own local authority and church rules and customs.

In a sense, Protestantism refers to the entire range of Christian religious expressions that began in the sixteenth century by rejecting the divine authority of Rome; it has evolved into hundreds of different denominations and thousands of individual sects throughout the world. The one common denominator of them all is a belief in Jesus and the teaching of the gospels and sacred wisdom of the New Testament as a guide for contemporary living and a key to personal spiritual salvation. There are currently over 400 million Protestants of all denominations throughout the world who assert a belief in Jesus and his teachings and the importance of personal faith as the primary road to salvation, redemption from sin, and eternal life.

A Crash Course in the Eastern Orthodox Church

Eastern Orthodox is the form of Christianity that emerged in the Eastern geographical lands of the Roman Empire—primarily Greece, Turkey, and the Middle East, and then into the Slavic lands of Eastern Europe. Like the Roman Catholic Church, Eastern Orthodoxy sees itself as the authentic spiritual heirs of Jesus and his teachings and believes it represents the direct line of succession and spiritual authority from the beginnings of Christianity until the present day.

There are about 210 million adherents of the Orthodox Church (sometimes called the "Greek Orthodox Church" although only about 15 million are Greek speaking) throughout the world today, and they are also considered part of the world's 2.1 billion Christians.[5] They live primarily in Russia, Eastern Europe, the Balkan Peninsula, North and South America, and Australia, with some Greek Orthodox believers living in Africa, Asia, and Western Europe.

The division between the East and West grew over time beginning in the fourth and fifth centuries simply as a result of natural cultural differences and physical distance from Rome in the West, to Constantinople (the Eastern center of Christianity) in the East. By the eleventh century there was a formal split when both the Roman Catholic leaders in the West and the Eastern Orthodox leadership in the East accused each other of heresies because of liturgical innovations and differences between the churches.

The word "orthodoxy" comes from the Greek word meaning "right belief," and the Eastern Orthodox Church believes that it is the legitimate heir of Jesus and his teachings stretching back the entire two thousand years of Christian history. It teaches that the entire "people of God" and not just the bishops and priests are responsible for keeping the word of God authentic through each age. They hold that the ultimate goal for every human being within the church is to participate in the life of God through worship, acts of loving kindness, and oneness with God obtained through the beliefs and practices uniting the individual with the divine through the presence of Jesus walking the earth as a God incarnate in human flesh.

The heart of Greek Orthodox practice revolves around the same seven sacraments as that of the Catholic Church, which in Orthodoxy are called the "mysteries," and the Last Supper of Jesus is known as the "Mystical Supper." The number of sacraments has never been officially agreed upon among the bishops of the Orthodox Church, so some teach that in addition to the traditional seven sacraments, there are other sacraments such as burial.

Some of the specific religious practices of the sacraments also vary from the Roman Catholic Church to the Eastern Orthodox Church. For example, in Catholicism a baptism involves sprinkling holy water upon the head of an infant by the priest, while in Orthodoxy a child or adult is fully immersed three times in water in honor of the three parts of the Holy Trinity. Confirmation, which takes place usually around age twelve in the Catholic Church, is called *chrismation* and takes place immediately after baptism among the Orthodox. While divorce is not allowed in the Roman Catholic Church, second and third marriages are allowed to take place within Orthodox Churches throughout the world. In addition, Orthodox priests are allowed to get married as long as the marriage takes place before their official ordination as priests. Only bishops are required to be celibate, refraining from any sexual activity.

One of the most notable differences between the Eastern Orthodox Church and all other forms of Christianity is the flourishing of religious icons that grew up in the East. The Orthodox Church taught that because God had chosen to become incarnate in the human form of Jesus, contrary to the commandment in the Hebrew Scriptures that forbade making images of God, the very humanness of Jesus was worthy and desirous of description. The church taught that through the inspiration and beauty of art God could be worshipped all the more passionately, and as a result an entire form of art depicting Jesus and his life grew up among the Eastern Orthodox community of believers. Their churches are filled with icons of Jesus and form a kind of pictorial declaration of faith among the Eastern Orthodox throughout the world. Such icons have taken on their own sense of holiness over the millennia of Christian worship and have become objects of worship and devotion in and of themselves.

The Eastern Orthodox Church is organized into four patriarchates, named for the bishops of the four major Roman cities who, in the early days of the church, were called "patriarchs." These were the bishops of Alexandria in Egypt, Antioch (now in Syria), Constantinople (now in Turkey), and Jerusalem. These four bishops along with eleven other bishops throughout the world make up the ruling authority of the Eastern Orthodox Church today, with the patriarch of Constantinople recognized as the highest-ranking prelate of the church by all Orthodox Christians.

A Crash Course in Islam

Islam is a term that literally means both "peace" and "submission to the will of God." A Muslim is therefore "one who submits to God" and is the term used to refer to the followers of Islam. It was founded by Mohammad in the Arabian Peninsula in the seventh century c.e., and Muslims believe that it was revealed to Mohammad in the form of the text known as the Quran, taking place over twenty-three years through the angel Gabriel. Its primary message is the unity of God (*Allah*) who is unique, without equal, and the creator of the world. Muslims believe that Mohammad is the final prophet of God and understand Islam to be the latest revelation of God after Judaism and Christianity. It recognizes Abraham, Moses, Jesus, and other biblical prophets, but believes that their message was distorted and wrongly taught until divinely revealed to Mohammad in the form of the Quran. It is estimated that there are 1.3 billion Muslims in the world today.[6]

In Islam the individual worships God directly without the intercession of priests or clergy and the believer's religious duties are summed up in what are called the "Five Pillars of Islam": Belief, Worship, Almsgiving, Fasting, and Pilgrimage.

The first Pillar of Belief in Islam is for the Muslim to profess that "there is no god but God (*Allah*, ALL-luh) and Mohammad is his prophet." This phrase known as the "profession of faith" is the central statement of Islamic belief (called *Shahada*, shaw-<u>HAW</u>-duh, in Arabic) and affirms both God's oneness and the central role of the prophet Mohammad. The *Shahada* appears in daily life both as part of the call to prayer five times each day and is inscribed on flags and coins in many Muslim countries. Islamic belief is composed of six aspects:

1. Belief in the oneness of God
2. God's revelations
3. God's angels
4. God's messengers or prophets
5. The "Day of Judgment" (in which every human being whether Muslim or not will be held accountable for his or her actions and beliefs)
6. The "divine decree" (or predestination) in which God has determined every human being's fate.

The second Pillar of Islam is to worship five times each day—at dawn, noon, mid-afternoon, sunset, and nightfall. This act of worship involves special washing of the feet, prostration in the direction of Mecca (the city in Saudia Arabia that is considered the center and most sacred site of the

Moslem world), and the recitation of a special prayer that can be recited anywhere and takes only a few minutes to complete. In addition to the daily prayer ritual five times each day, all male believers are enjoined to gather at the Mosque, or place of worship, on Friday at noon to pray and to hear a sermon from a prayer leader. Worshippers are called to prayer by a *Muezzin* (Mu-ZEEN) who recites the following formula before each designated time of worship every day:

"God is great (four times)
I testify that there is no god but God (twice)
I testify that Mohammad is God's messenger/prophet (twice)
Come to prayer (twice)
Come to salvation (twice)
God is great (twice)
There is no god but God."

The third Pillar of Islam is fasting. It requires that Muslims refrain from eating food and drink and having sex and smoking from sunrise to sunset every day during the holy month of *Ramadan*, which is the ninth month of the Muslim calendar. The daily discipline of abstinence during the month of *Ramadan* teaches the Muslim gratitude for the gifts of God, reinforces a sense of worldwide community, and brings about a heightened daily awareness of God's presence in the world. Since the Muslim calendar is completely Lunar, the month of *Ramadan* can come at any time during the secular year. The end of the month of Ramadan is always marked by the celebration of a feast called in Arabic, *Id al-fitr* (id all-FITTER), or feast of breaking the fast.

The fourth Pillar of Islam is the pillar of giving alms to the poor. Muslims are enjoined to give a fixed amount of their income to charity for the poor every year in much the same way as Christians have an expectation of tithing, and Jews have an obligation to acts of loving kindness and charity.

The fifth Pillar of Islam is called the Pilgrimage or *Hajj* in Arabic. It requires every Muslim male to make a pilgrimage to the holy city of Mecca at least once during his lifetime. The annual pilgrimage takes place during the first days of the twelfth month of the Muslim calendar. Anyone who has performed this pillar and successfully made the pilgrimage to Mecca is then called a *Hajji*, a title of great reverence and respect in Islam. According to Muslim tradition, before entering Mecca the pilgrim puts on a seamless white garment and enters the central shrine known in Arabic as the *Kaaba* which Islamic tradition teaches was built by the prophet Abraham to honor God.

Mohammad lived from 570 to 632 C.E. and founded Islam in the city of Mecca until he and his followers were driven out and took refuge in Medina. His fame and success in converting followers grew until he was able to return in triumph to Mecca, and eventually by the time of his death to unite the entire Arabian Peninsula under the banner of Islam. Unlike in the West where the concept of the separation of church and state is a fundamental principle of contemporary society, Islamic law sees itself as both religious and political and draws no distinction between the two. Thus Islamic law (or *Sharia*, shaw-REE-uh, in Arabic) covers all aspects of human life and daily living and is considered the divine will of God.

The major schools of Islamic thought are called *Sunni* and *Shi'a*. The *Sunni* are the largest group within Islam and believe that the first four leaders (called *Caliphs*) following the death of Mohammad were his legitimate spiritual heirs, and that since God did not specify who the rightful heirs of Mohammad should be they ought to have been elected by the people (which was the case of the first four Caliphs).

The *Shi'a* reject the legitimacy of the first three *Caliphs* as they believe that Muslims have no right to elect their leaders whom they believe were divinely chosen by God in the form of Mohammad's son, Ali, and his descendents. They see the leader of the Islamic community not as a *Caliph* or temporary ruler, but rather as an *Imam* or spiritual leader.

Islam is the second largest religion in the world today with some 1.5 billion adherents. There are more than fifty countries in the world with a Muslim majority and it is the fastest growing religion on earth. One reason for its rapid growth is its openness to converts and the ease of conversion. A non-Muslim can convert to Islam simply by declaring himself or herself to be a Muslim. A person's declaration of faith is considered enough to demonstrate sincerity of conversion without the need for any outside corroboration. The country with the largest Muslim population is Indonesia, followed by Pakistan, and then Bangladesh. Muslim's revere the Quran as their sacred text and believe that it is only sacred in the original Arabic as revealed to Mohammad. Therefore it is common for many Muslims to memorize at least part of the Quran in Arabic, especially those sections necessary to participate in daily prayer.

A Crash Course in Buddhism

Buddhism is a religious tradition that revolves around the life and teachings of Siddhartha Gautama who was born into luxury as a prince of the Sakya tribe in Nepal in around the year 566 B.C.E. According to Buddhist teachings, at age twenty-nine he first encountered the reality of suffering in the world and was so devastated by what he saw that he undertook a six-year spiritual and physical journey in an attempt at understanding the meaning of life and suffering. Siddhartha Gautama became the "Buddha" or "The Enlightened One," while sitting under a Bodhi tree in meditation, and then spent the rest of his life teaching others the meaning of life that he had understood in that transformational moment of meditation.

For the next two hundred years, Buddhism was taught from teacher to disciple as an oral tradition handed down by some five hundred monks who had learned the wisdom of the Buddha while he was still alive and teaching. Eventually as time passed and the teachings of the Buddha spread across Asia and other parts of the world, there were philosophical splits within Buddhism and many diverse schools of Buddhist thought emerged claiming to authentically reflect the teachings of Buddhism.

Regardless of their differences, there are certain fundamental teachings and beliefs that are common to all Buddhist teachings. The first of these are called "The Four Noble Truths":

1. Life is suffering
2. Suffering is due to attachment
3. Attachment can be overcome
4. There is a path for accomplishing this goal.

Overcoming attachment is called "Nirvana" and refers to letting go of hatred, ignorance, and attachments to emotions that prevent human beings from experiencing the full acceptance of their imperfections, impermanence, and interconnectedness.

In Buddhism one is instructed to achieve Nirvana by following the Dharma, or the eightfold path to enlightenment. The eightfold path involves committing oneself to the search for wisdom and morality through the practice of meditation. The eightfold path for every individual consists of what some call the eight "rights":

1. Right view is the true understanding of the four noble truths;
2. Right aspiration is the true desire to rid oneself of attachment, ignorance, and hatred;
3. Right speech involves refraining from lying, gossiping, or hurtful talk;
4. Right action includes abstaining from killing, stealing, and careless sex;
5. Right livelihood involves making a living without hurting others and avoiding dishonesty;
6. Right effort involves exerting one's powers to control the content of our minds where bad qualities are avoided and discarded and good qualities are nurtured;

7. Right mindfulness is the ability to focus on one's body, feelings, thoughts, and consciousness so as to overcome cravings, hatred, and ignorance;
8. Right concentration is to meditate in such a way as to realize the true understanding of imperfection, impermanence, and interconnectedness.

These ideas form the essence of Buddhist teachings and can be found in all forms of Buddhism throughout the world. Buddhism is not a traditional theistic religious system that focuses on worshipping God, and so often appears to people more as a spiritual philosophy than a religion in the strict sense of the term. It is a path of personal practice and spiritual development, which is practiced by some 375 million adherents throughout the world,[7] many of whom also see themselves as members of another religious tradition as well. It teaches what it calls, "the middle way" or "middle path," which is a path of moderation, a golden mean between extremes of all kinds, religious, spiritual, and philosophical. Regardless of the particular form of Buddhism that is practiced, there is an underlying understanding that Buddhism is characterized by a philosophy of nonviolence, a lack of dogma, a tolerance of differences among peoples, and usually by the practice of some form of meditation as well.

Buddhism uses meditation to clear and focus the mind, bring spiritual and emotional clarity, and as an antidote to anxiety, negative emotions, anger, hatred, and fear. It sees meditation as the spiritual practice that leads to enlightenment and peace of mind, which are the ultimate goals of Buddhist religious practice. Buddhism is seen as a path for personal transformation through the three basic Buddhist rituals of recitation, chanting, and the making of offerings.

Recitation usually reflects the central tenets of Buddhist teachings and as with chanting are most often done in Sanskrit or Pali, the ancient original languages of Buddhism. Sanskrit mantras are chanted as a way of forming an emotional connection with the verbal expressions of enlightenment. Offerings usually consist of flowers (for beauty and impermanence), candles (as symbols of light and enlightenment), and incense to symbolize the all-pervasive nature of wisdom and truth.

Festivals are a central aspect of Buddhist religious life as the Buddha exhorted his followers to gather together regularly in large numbers to give each other support and inspiration. These festivals are designed as expressions of gratitude and devotion to the Buddha and his teachings. The most important festival of the Buddhist year is called *Wesak* (WEH-sack), which is a celebration of the Buddha's enlightenment and takes place on the full moon between May and June. Dharma Day on the full moon of July celebrates the start of Buddhism itself when the Buddha rose from his initial meditation and went to teach his former disciples the enlightenment he had just experienced. The full moon of February is a day to commemorate the death of the Buddha at age eighty in India and reflect upon the lessons of impermanence and loss; and meditations are offered in the name of family and friends who have recently died.

"Karma" is a term used within Buddhism to refer to the inevitable consequences of all thought and actions. Buddhists believe that our actions determine our own future and that the goal of life is what is called "mindful actions" that lead to "mindful consequences." Buddhists generally believe that the consequences of our thoughts and actions will come to fruition either in this life or in a future rebirth and that often we can trace situations that exist in our current lives back to actions or thoughts that we expressed in lives past.

The primary texts of Buddhist thought are called *Sutras*, which are written records of the teachings of Buddha as written down by his disciples following his death. They are studied and used as the basis of meditations and study by Buddhists as part of the path to enlightenment and right living.

SEEING DIFFERENCES AS GIFTS

Each of us humans exists in as a unique, one-of-a-kind occurrence in the history of the universe. There will never be anyone else with your particular combination of genes and chromosomes, your particular social background, your life experiences, your habits, your dreams, your thoughts, your likes and dislikes, your unique mixture of nurture and nature. That is why your task in life is ultimately to be the *you* that you can, for you are the only one who will ever have that opportunity and that challenge. Since each of us is unique, no two people have the same needs and desires, interests, and world outlook, religious beliefs, or spiritual longings. That is why every relationship is a kind of dance between two unique people, a constant give and take, a perpetual negotiation between your needs and the needs of your partner on a hundred different levels and issues.

Every couple must work out a multitude of small differences each day as they share their lives; and those in interfaith and interracial relationships might find it particularly challenging to negotiate their religious and spiritual needs plus those of their children. Yet this is exactly what is being done in millions of homes throughout the world every day as couples foster family harmony, peace, a sense of mutual respect, and a commitment to nurturing the emotional, physical, and spiritual well-being of each partner in the relationship and every person in the family.

One of the ways that you can help this process of creating family harmony is by understanding differences not as problems *but as gifts*. They are opportunities, not just barriers; building blocks, not merely stumbling blocks on the road to successful relationships and loving families. Every issue can become an opportunity to reinforce your love, your family support, and your willingness to go the extra mile to serve as a source of comfort, security, and stability in the midst of religious negotiations and family stresses. Ultimately, it is the successful manner in which families such as yours confront and resolve their differences that is the best indicator of human resiliency and inner strength.

Encouraging your own children to confront the differences directly between themselves and the ones they love can ultimately help them to be successful in their relationships and loving partnerships. Pretending that these differences do not exist, or that they are not really important, or that they will simply melt away if ignored is a self-deceiving and certain to bring frustration and unhappiness in the end. Frustration delayed is not frustration avoided, it is simply delayed, and like a time bomb will ultimately explode into the lives of those you love.

The challenge of interfaith life is to create harmony out of difference, mutual respect, and love in the midst of ambiguity and paradox. It is to see every difference as a gift from those in your family who are dissimilar to you. Interfaith life provides an opportunity for you to learn and grow, expanding your understanding of others and the world in which you live. Each difference that you discover and explore and help your children to explore is just another example of something that can enrich your life and add a deeper and richer dimension to your relationships—and your life.

Eleven

WHEN THINGS DON'T WORK OUT—CHALLENGES OF SEPARATION AND DIVORCE

BASIC DO'S AND DON'TS

One of the most sensitive challenges of interfaith life involves coping with divorce and the breakup of relationships. It is never easy to end a long-term relationship and it is rarely easy to go through a divorce under any circumstances. When the relationship or marriage has the added complication of being interfaith or interracial, it is even more sensitive and difficult than ever. No matter how heartfelt the promises of the past might have been, the inevitable tension, pain, sorrow, and anger that come with the disintegration of a marriage or long-term relationship inevitably creates a host of emotionally deep and complex issues for every couple. These issues are only exaggerated and made even more complicated when the relationship is interfaith, interracial, or same gender. Emotions inevitably run high, promises of the past are often tossed aside, and religion, faith, and participation in rituals and traditions can become fodder for the anger and resentment of everyone involved.

Many interfaith couples constantly live with the tensions involved in making decisions about which religious traditions their children will incorporate into their daily lives. When such interfaith couples break up, these tensions often explode into bitter custody battles and become a reflection of unresolved angers and resentments. This added dynamic of raising children in an interfaith family naturally puts additional stresses on what is, under the best of circumstances a difficult and painful situation.

When the relationship is on track and going well most couples find ways of letting disagreements and specific frustrations go unexpressed. But when couples are in the throes of divorce, the kid gloves come off and anger, frustrations, and upsets that may have been under the surface for many years inevitably get unleashed in ugly and destructive ways. As with most divorces when children are involved, it is the children themselves who suffer most.

Part of the role that grandparents can play during the process of divorce and the dissolution of an interfaith relationship is to be a voice of calm, a voice of reason, and a safe haven in the midst of the emotional storm of separation. You can provide the place where your children and grandchildren can find emotional safety and security. Although this is often challenging, especially when your natural tendency is usually to support, protect, and take the side of your own child, it is important to keep your focus on the well-being of your grandchildren and what is ultimately best for them. What is best for children when their parents get divorced is to maintain a positive and healthy relationship with both parents. Children thrive when they are able to respect, honor, and love both (or all) their parents regardless of the ultimate resolution of custody or the "official" religion in which they are being raised. That is why helping your grandchildren to see the best in both of their parents can be an important and ongoing role that grandparents can play.

So what are the basic "do's and don'ts" when separation and divorce are taking place?

1. Do your best to walk the fine line of supporting your own children while not trashing the name or reputation of their former partner or spouse. Encourage your children to avoid putting down their former partner in front of your grandchildren and remind them that the issues that broke up their relationship are and were between the two of them and not between them and their children.

2. Provide a safe haven for your grandchildren emotionally and spiritually. Allow them to be comfortable in your presence regardless of the religious choices that they make and regardless of whether or not they celebrate the same holidays as you or claim the religious identity that you would prefer. Just as your children always know how you really feel about the religious choices that they make in their own lives, so, too your grandchildren know what your values are and what your choices for them would be if it were up to you to make those choices. Being supportive of them and providing a safe emotional and spiritual place for them to visit and express their own unique religious identity will only strengthen your own moral authority and make your own religious identity that is much more attractive in the long run.

3. Remember that your grandchildren will feel torn between their parents and make sure that your grandchildren have your phone number handy and that they know that they can call you at any time day or night when they are upset or feel scared about the transition that they are living through. They need to know that when they do call you will provide a sympathetic ear and have an open heart and spirit and not have to fear that you will express negative judgments about a parent they love who isn't your own child.

4. Be direct in asking your children how you can help them to successfully cope with the difficult experience of separation or divorce. Let them know that you will be there for them and support them as they work their way through the emotional minefield that the dissolution of their relationship has created. Ask them how you can help, and then listen to what they say. If they ask for help that you are unable to give, be forthright in saying so and seek alternate ways of providing support, and help and love. If they ask for something that you are able to do, then you will know that the help you are providing is truly what they need and want.

5. Do the same with your grandchildren. Let them know that you realize how difficult a time this is in their lives and that you have faith that they will get through this as so many other children have had to do in the past. Ask them how you can help and then to the best of your ability help them in the way they wish to be helped.

Divorce and the breaking up of relationships are unfortunately so common in our era that most kids have friends and acquaintances who have had to endure similar experiences. Encourage them to seek out other kids who have lived through the breakup of their own parents and use them as a mini support group. They are the most likely friends to be sympathetic and make your grandchildren feel that they aren't alone and the only people on the planet who have ever felt the way they feel and gone through the difficult experiences with which they are faced.

ENCOURAGING HEALTHY CONFLICT RESOLUTION

Another potentially important role that grandparents are often able to play when their own children are in the process of dissolving a relationship is as a supporter of healthy conflict resolution. When someone is hurt or in the midst of severe emotional pain and loss, there is often a tendency to strike out (or strike back if one feels treated badly or unfairly by an ex-partner) with the intention of hurting the other person as much as possible. You can be a voice that is sympathetic and supportive of your children and the pain that they are enduring, while encouraging them at the same time to explore the possibility of mediation rather than confrontation.

Mediators are trained in healthy ways of resolving conflicts between couples who are getting divorced and often can not only save a significant amount of money that a confrontational legal process inevitably creates, but can provide an emotionally healthier way for couples to come to resolutions about the distribution of shared assets, property, and custody.[1] Encouraging couples to resolve their conflicts with mediation is ultimately a gift not only to them but to their children (your grandchildren) as well as it can greatly reduce public expressions of outright hostility, and the pain and emotional suffering that court battles create in the lives of children.

Dragging children into court in the midst of a divorce battle is one of the worst things that anyone can do to someone they love. When a child is forced by a judge to give his or her opinion about custody and choose with which parent he or she would prefer to live it is inevitably a no-win situation for the child. No child should ever be put in this position since every child has a deep emotional need to maintain the love and acceptance of both (or all) of his or her parents. That is why no one wants to be forced into a position where they have to say something in public that could and most likely will be interpreted by the other parent as a betrayal.

Since one of the most devastating experiences that any child can have is to feel abandoned by a parent, forcing the child to go before a judge and give an opinion about something as emotionally charged as custody is almost guaranteed to create a deep-seated anxiety and fear. This is not fair either to the child or the parent. It is a recipe for relationship disaster between everyone involved. This is the primary reason why encouraging your children to find a nonconfrontational way to resolve conflict without resorting to legal battles and custody fights is a crucial role that you as your grandchild's advocate can play with your own children.

THE IMPORTANCE OF YOUR CHILD GETTING LEGAL ADVICE AND COUNSEL

The flipside of rushing headlong into an ugly legal battle is a situation where one parent is so afraid of putting his or her child in a difficult position that the parent avoids getting any legal advice at all and decides to make the divorce or separation work on his or her own. This is often due to a well-intentioned desire to avoid legal conflict and create as smooth and painless a transition for the child as possible on the part of one of the parents. Even though your child's intentions may be noble, it is usually a very bad idea to initiate action and make decisions that have long lasting impacts on your life without proper legal advice.

One of the problems that such well-intentioned individuals often find they have unwittingly created is that decisions that one makes even for the best of reasons and with the best of intentions can end up as setting unintended legal precedents. These precedents can come back to haunt the parent who has made them should the "voluntary" agreement fall apart and the ultimate resolution end up being decided by the legal system.

Such situations often occur when one person makes a decision regarding whether to stay in a previously shared house or be the one to move out, or when one creates ad hoc custody agreements with a child's other parent that relies totally upon both parties to continue to voluntarily agree. The minute one party gets upset or changes his or her mind or gives in to the urge to take control or be vindictive, the other party is suddenly at a tremendous disadvantage and may have created a legal hole out of which it is impossible to climb.

That is why even as you do your best to encourage your children to re-solve conflicts with their former partners through mediation, it is important to make sure that they seek out legal advice before they do anything that might create a "fact on the ground" that an opposing lawyer could easily use against them should the resolution of their disagreements end up in court.

One woman, after being married to her husband for six years and with a three-year-old child, came to realize that she had gotten married for all the wrong reasons, had never truly loved this man, and no longer wanted to be married to him. She tried to figure out how to leave him in the least disruptive and painful way both for him and for her young son and so one day she simply moved out of their beautiful home into a small studio apartment nearby. She never really told him that she didn't love him and had known that it was a mistake to marry him in the first place, but instead tried to ease the blow of her leaving by telling him that she was just not the marrying type. To show her good faith to her husband she never even spoke to an attorney but simply assumed she would ultimately ease into an agreeable arrangement with him.

In trying to leave her marriage with the least possible disruption for her young child she kept the same routine as she had while living in her home, being with her child every day, acting in exactly the same way as a mother that she had before except instead of sleeping in her previous home she would return at night after she put her child to bed to the tiny studio apartment down the road when she was "temporarily" living.

Later, much to her deep regret, when her husband eventually took her to court and sued her for custody, she discovered that the decision she made to move out of her home created a legal precedent that established *him* as the primary physical custodian of her child and when she wanted to then have joint physical custody she was no longer able to do so. Had she gone to an attorney in the first place, she undoubtedly would have been informed of the potential legal consequences of the decisions she was contemplating and would have acting accordingly.

When relationships are falling apart it is often the absolute worst time for anyone to be making significant decisions that will have a long-term impact on their lives. That is why it is always best for everyone involved to seek out professional advice from counselors, therapists, and attorneys. As a caring parent you will be doing a great service to your own children and grandchildren by encouraging them to seek out such advice before they act.

A PLACE TO ALWAYS CALL HOME

Most of the situations that individuals encounter when they go through a divorce or dissolution of a marriage or loving relationship are the same whether they are in a same faith or interfaith, heterosexual or same gender relationship. Regardless of the type of relationship you are in, the pain and grief that accompanies the loss of a loving partnership is the same. The need to adjust to a new life as a single person, the difficulties and challenges of learning to share custody and suddenly be without your children, the fears and anxieties that such a new life inevitably evokes are the same for everyone regardless of religion, race, culture, or gender.

It is important to remember that when your children suddenly find themselves emotionally adrift and caught up in the stress and trauma of a broken relationship, what they often feel they need the most is simply a sympathetic ear and an encouraging heart. They need someone to whom they can turn to share their fears and frustrations, their worries, and their grief. Yet, sometimes just having a sympathetic ear is not enough. Sometimes your children will literally need a safe haven to which they can flee where they can actually live for a while during a difficult transitional stage of their lives. This is particularly true when you discover that your children have been involved in abusive relationships. They may be in need of physical shelter and physical protection as well.

Beyond issues involving relationships that are physically or emotionally abusive, there are many situations in which adult children (particularly women) have suddenly found themselves forced to leave the home in which they have been living with little means of support and in need on short notice of somewhere else in which to live. Naturally, it is often their own parents who step in to rescue them and offer them a roof over their heads and a safe and nurturing place in which to regroup and refocus their lives. This is why knowing that there is a place where your children can always call home is sometimes not merely a metaphor but at times an actual life-saving physical reality.

All parents want their children's lives to be successful and filled with love and personal fulfillment. We want our children to grow up to be self-sufficient and able to create loving relationships with partners who respect them and with whom they can share their lives. We desire life's path for our children to be smooth and sunny and that they will grow up, get an education, find their life partners, and create a home and family of their own. That is why when things go terribly wrong and our children suddenly find themselves needing to move back in with us, it is inevitably a difficult and emotionally stressful transition for everyone.

Even though we expect our role as parents to be that of helping our children to successfully transition from single to married, sometimes the most important role we play is exactly the opposite. Sadly, there are times when our primary role as parents is to help our children learn to successfully negotiate the transition from married to single and not the other way around. Sometimes we can fulfill that role by simply being there when they need us and providing a safety net for them both emotionally and physically. When we are lucky it often becomes our role once again to provide a solid and stable emotional foundation from which they can create a loving relationship with a new partner and move on to the next stage of their lives.

WHAT ARE THE APPROPRIATE WAYS TO SUPPORT YOUR CHILD?

When all is said and done many parents are unsure as to which are the most appropriate ways to support their children. They want to make sure that they understand how to be supportive without being intrusive and overbearing at the same time. Any parent who asks this question in the first place already has enough sensitivity to the possibility of overstepping their appropriate parental bounds that they probably don't need any advice from me or anyone else. It is usually those who never even think of this as an issue who are in need of having their level of sensitivity raised regarding the emotional impact that they as parents continue to have on their adult children.

As we have discussed in detail in previous chapters, children always desire the approval of their parents regardless of their age. This is why it is probably inevitable when relationships dissolve for those involved to feel that they have disappointed their parents and let them down. In fact, many children avoid admitting to their parents that they are having difficulties in their intimate relationships exactly because they are more concerned about disappointing their parents then they are about getting their support and the opportunity to feel their love and encouragement. In spite of the pain of loss and the despair and loneliness that people often feel in the midst of a difficult separation, parental acceptance and approval is such a powerful need that for some the potential negatives of telling them seem to outweigh the potential positives of getting their help or support.

Ultimately no one can hide the dissolution and breaking up of a primary relationship forever so eventually the truth always comes out into the open. When that reality finally asserts itself there are many people beyond the immediate couple who are obviously affected in significant ways. Parents, siblings, nephews, nieces, even close friends all are impacted by the tensions that may exist between the couple and the decisions that are made regarding custody, celebrations of life cycle moments, visitations, living arrangements, and a hundred other decisions that the divorcing couple must make.

Given that so many people are affected by these decisions and that your desire as a parent is to be appropriately supportive of your own children, it is often helpful to think through your own comfort level of support in advance. More and more people are writing "prenuptial" agreements with and for each other before they get married or formally join their lives with one another so that they know what to expect from each other should the relationship end. Similarly, it may make sense for parents and grandparents whose lives will also be affected by potential breakups to formally think through for themselves in advance the level of involvement and support in all its forms that they will be willing to provide should the situation ever arise.

The best time to think about difficult decisions is before you ever have to make them. Issues of health and well-being, financial considerations regarding inheritance and distribution of wealth and physical assets are in some ways no different from questions regarding the distribution of all the various potential resources that you might make available to your children in a time of need.

Should your children end up leaving their life partners for whatever reason, are you (and your own spouse or life partner) willing to support your own children financially? Are you willing to take them into your home to live? If so for how long and under what circumstances? Do you have conditions and criteria by which you will make decisions regarding how much support you are willing to give your children both financially and emotionally and for how long? Are you willing to give them money to help pay their rent or mortgage when and if their income suddenly drops because of a separation or divorce?

If you suspect that there are issues in your child's marriage, working through these questions is exactly what couples need to do together *before* they are ever faced with actually having to make such difficult decisions. You can give yourself a tremendous gift by being willing to bring up situations and challenges such as these with your own spouse or life partner. It is true about discussing death and dying, assigning medical power of attorney to another and communicating clearly your own desires regarding end of life issues in case you are unable to speak or make decisions for yourself, and it is true of any deep emotional issue with which you will be faced that will affect both you and your partner, including the divorce of your child.

There is no one "right answer" to the question of what is the appropriate way to support your children and grandchildren when such difficult situations arise. There are many "right answers" depending on the specific circumstances, relationships, and people involved. The answers that work for you and your life partner may be very different from the answers that someone else may choose in exactly the same circumstance. Even when situations are the same from one couple to the next, the people involved are not. Every one of us is a unique one-of-a-kind and thus every relationship is unique as well. All we can do is the best we can do to make decisions that work for us. All we can do is the best we can do to be supportive of our children in whatever ways we are comfortable. This varies from person to person and family to family.

Some parents are thrilled to have their adult children move back in with them during times of stress and upset. Others turn their spare bedrooms into offices and playrooms for themselves the minute their kids move out of the house and cannot imagine ever having them move back. For some the "appropriate" way to show support for their children is to stay out of the way altogether and for others it is to get as involved as possible in the daily emotional and physical struggles that their children are experiencing. One isn't necessarily "right" and the other "wrong." They simply reflect different attitudes, different kinds of relationships between parents and children, and different outlooks about the world and your role in it.

If providing your children with the financial resources to hire a lawyer, pay the rent, or take a vacation with their children is what you need to do to feel that you are being supportive of your children, then by all means provide these resources to your children. If getting them into therapy or a twelve-step program is the kind of support that you believe they need, then find them the therapist and help them identify a program for them. Whatever will help create and continue to nurture the best ongoing relationship with your own children really is the right path for you to follow regardless of the advice that any other professional might offer. Here as with many other parenting issues with which we all deal, I follow "Rabbi Reuben's Rule." Rabbi Reuben's Rule is simply, "Whatever works, works." If it works for you and provides your children with support that they appreciate and need, then by all means do whatever it is that works. If it does not work to strengthen your parent–child relationship, if it is not what your children are asking for in the way of support, then choose another way of providing that support that does work.

GIVING SUPPORT WITHOUT "TAKING SIDES"

Now that you have explored finding the best ways to give emotional, financial, and spiritual support for your children when things do not work out in their relationships, you need to look at downside of appearing to be "taking sides" in marital and custody disputes. It is every parent's natural tendency to stand up for their children to support and defend them whenever they are under attack or suffering. But when your children are in the midst of the divorce or dissolution of their relationship and there are children (your grandchildren) involved, openly and publicly being seen as "taking sides" can have a devastating impact on your long term relationship with your grandchildren.

"I just couldn't believe how unfair my grandfather was to my dad," one teenager disclosed. "My parents were in the middle of getting a divorce, everything was falling apart, I wasn't sure where I was going to end up, and I was worried, scared and really in need of something solid I could lean on. Instead, when I talked to my grandfather on the phone and started telling him how crazy everything felt, all he did was slam my dad and start telling me what a bad person he was and how everything was his fault, and on and on until I wanted to scream. I was so mad at him that I basically stopped talking to him at all for the next two years. He just took my mom's side in everything, so I knew there was nothing to talk about after that."

This is certainly not the result that this particular grandparent intended to happen and having his grandson stop talking with him and essentially shut down their relationship for years was devastating to him. What's worse is that the grandfather never really understood what was going on and why his grandson was so angry with him. He had simply been venting that first day in the midst of his own fears for his daughter's future and his feelings of frustration at not being able to protect her from the pain she was feeling and genuinely had no idea that this one conversation had colored his relationship with his grandson forever.

It is one thing for everyone to assume that a parent's natural instinct will be to support his or her child when they are in the midst of a fight. It is quite another thing to act in such a way as to demonstrate that one-sidedness in public with grandchildren, mutual friends, and others whose vested interest is to be neutral and appear not to be taking sides at all. Your grandchildren have a desperate need to be loved by both parents and often an equally desperate need to do whatever is necessary not to be seen as betraying either of their parents so that neither parent will abandon them. In such a case, "taking sides" is clearly out of the question and as in the rules of war where friends of my enemy are also my enemy, as soon as you are publicly perceived as being totally one-sided in supporting one parent you become the "enemy" of the other parent.

So how do you give all the support without appearing to be totally one-sided and without alienating your grandchildren? You do it by maintaining the best relationship you can with your grandchildren's other parent as well. You need to talk openly with your own children and tell them that even as you will do whatever you can to support them as they go through this difficult time, you also want to make sure that you keep the best relationship you can with your grandchildren and that you believe the best way to do that is to walk the delicate balance of supporting one without trashing and blaming the other.

There is an ancient saying that it is better to remain silent and allow people to assume that you are wise than to speak your mind and demonstrate that you are not. That is certainly good advice when it comes to deciding whether or not to blame one parent over the other and discuss your negative judgments and feelings with your grandchildren. There is simply nothing to be gained from saying too much and everything to be gained from saying too little.

Frankly, anyone who has a mature understanding of the dynamics of relationships as they come undone will understand that you have natural loyalties to one parent over the other. Anyone who has ever been in a similar circumstance will also understand the delicate position in which you find yourself and your competing desires both to rail against your child's former partner for the pain that he or she has caused and to be a loving and supportive force in your grandchildren's lives. These desires are often mutually exclusive and most of the time you can't have both. If you are publicly voicing your disapproval of one of your grandchildren's parents you are most likely to alienate them from you and not from that parent.

What is in the best interests of your grandchildren at this difficult time in their lives is to find some stability in the midst of the tremendous instability that their parents' breakup represents. They need someone they can count on and a place that is emotionally safe in which they can escape from the tensions, anger and, upsets that their own home now represents. The only way they will see you and your home in this light is if you can demonstrate to them that you are able to support your own child while at the same time not be seen as "taking sides" and continuing to maintain a cordial and positive relationship with their other parent. It is a big challenge but the pay off in terms of your relationship with your grandchildren is worth it.

REMEMBERING THAT GRANDCHILDREN STILL NEED BOTH PARENTS IN THEIR LIVES

The bottom line is remembering that the best thing for your grandchildren is to have both parents as present as possible in their lives. It does not really matter who is "right" and who is "wrong" in a divorce dispute. As far as the children are concerned both parents are wrong. All children want their parents to stay together whether they are happy in their relationship or not. Parental happiness is not a child's concern and should not be a priority in their lives at all. In fact, most young children cannot articulate if their parents are happy or unhappy in their relationship or their lives as long as they continue to function as a family unit and the children continue to be taken care of and provided with the things they need and want.

Often parents reveal that the reason they are getting divorced is so that their children will see a better and healthier adult and parent role model than the one they are currently demonstrating. They believe that living in an unhappy marriage or relationship is teaching their children to accept less than fulfillment and joy in their own lives and that it will be much better for their children to live in homes without strife than to continue to live together as one family just for the sake of appearances when there is hostility in the home and a lack of love between parents.

This may be true in the long run, and it certainly is understandable from the point of view of the individual who no longer is willing to live in a loveless relationship, but most children would much rather have their parents stay together for *their* sake even if the parents are not happy, even if there is tension in their home, and even if their parents no longer feel that they are in love with one another. Most kids simply do not want their family to break up for any reason whatsoever. It is natural for them to care more about how such a breakup will affect them rather than worry about their parents' feelings and not want to have their lives permanently disrupted.

Keeping this in mind can help you as the grandparent to give your grandchildren an open ear, a shoulder to cry on, and a safe place in which to express their upset and share their fears and insecurities about the future. If you want to create a surrogate safe home for your grandchildren you need to make it OK for them to talk about their anger toward your own child as well, give them the space not to talk about the situation at all when they are with you.

Unless they are in an abusive relationship with one of their parents, children do need to have both (or all) of their parents as present in their lives as possible. You can play a role as their advocate with each of their parents and any other professional with whom they might interact whether lawyers, therapists, counselors, or school personnel. Make sure that they know you believe that they ought to spend as much time as possible with both of their parents as well. Let them hear you saying positive things about both parents and offering to be their advocate with either parent whenever they need a supportive voice. This will letting them know that you believe that they need to have both parents in their lives and that you are on their side and will be there for them whenever and whatever they might need.

It is never easy to watch as your child's life is in the midst of trauma and pain. It is never easy to watch as your grandchildren experience the fear of dislocation and the breaking up of their home and fundamental sense of security in their lives. The point of this chapter has been to let you know that although the situation is not of your choosing, you can still have an important and powerful role in helping to bring healing, hope, and faith in the future to your children and grandchildren at one of the most sensitive and crucial times of their lives.

When things do not work out in interfaith relationships, there are obviously added stresses, additional issues that need to be worked out, and particular concerns that arise beyond those of a same faith relationship. How will the children continue to be raised? If they have been raised in one religion primarily up till now, will the parent who has another religious tradition continue to bring the children to church or synagogue or any other religious setting that isn't their own? What kind of religious celebrations will now be in their multiple homes that will be different from what they have experienced in the past?

With all of these issues and with whatever challenges might occur as your children and their former life partners work through these difficult decisions, grandparents can play a crucial role. You can become a symbol of stability and consistency in the midst of the instability of the breakup. You can help provide a surrogate source of religious grounding at a time when there is a natural tendency to lose faith in oneself, in the power of love, and in God as a positive and loving force in your children and grandchildren's lives. You can be the safe harbor in the midst of the storm of divorce and dissolution for everyone involved. The challenges are significant but the opportunities for making a profound positive difference in the lives of your children and grandchildren will be worth the effort.

Love is the most important value in life and that no matter how much material wealth and success we might enjoy, our lives are ultimately meaningful only to the degree that we fill them with loving relationships. That can be your opportunity and your gift. You can be a beacon of love, a light in the darkness, a source of hope and faith in a time of disillusionment. You can be a source of joy, love, and inspiration to your family simply by being there when they need you and opening your arms and heart to the fact life can continue to have value and meaning every single day regardless of turbulence and tough times.

AFTERWORD: YOUR CHILD'S INTERMARRIAGE—CRISIS OR OPPORTUNITY?

YOUR CHILD'S RELATIONSHIP AS AN OPPORTUNITY TO DISCOVER WHAT REALLY MATTERS MOST IN *YOUR* LIFE

One of the gifts that you are given when your children marry someone who is different from you and who grew up differently from the way you did is the gift of opening your eyes to the blessing of diversity. Blessings come in many forms and often those forms are not at all what we anticipated or expected. One such gift is the blessing of recognizing that there is more than one way to live, more than one way to see the world, more than one way to experience life, more than one way to think about the important values and questions of life.

When we live surrounded by people just like us, who think like us, and worship like us, and have the same interests and world view that we do, we never have the opportunity to grow beyond our own small existence. Coming into intimate contact with people who are different, whether of a different race, a different religion, or a different sexual orientation gives us the opportunity to expand our horizons and experience life in a way that we would otherwise never have had the opportunity to experience. It allows us to realize that differences can be gifts, that diversity can be a blessing, that suspending our own biases, prejudices, and judgments long enough to see the world through someone else's eyes can function like a breath of fresh air on a smoggy day, giving us an entirely new and clearer point of view.

Your child's relationship with someone who is not the same as you actually gives you the opportunity to discover your own values and realize the things that matter most in life. The challenge is to open your mind and your heart and to decide that if there are enough good qualities in your children's partners for them to love, it must be worth the emotional investment for you to discover those qualities as well. When you do open yourself to seeing the world in a different way, usually what you discover is that the things that matter most in life are not *things* at all, but the loving relationships with family and friends that give your life its true meaning and purpose.

When your child intermarries, you are given an opportunity. You can use the occasion to learn and grow as a human being, to make your relationship with your own child deeper and more beautiful, or you can choose to grow bitter and angry, distant and unforgiving, tossing away that which is most precious about life itself. That is the opportunity and that is the gift. It is up to you to seize that opportunity and use the skills and information shared throughout this book to help you build the very best, most spectacular relationships you can with the ones you love.

WHERE TO GO FOR MORE HELP

We live in a remarkable age in which the number of resources that are available to interfaith, interracial, and same gender couples and their families are greater than ever. From books to magazines, support groups to Web sites, it is easier than ever to find information about how others successfully deal with the entire range of issues, challenges, and opportunities that such relationships present. Most books, articles, and Internet resources are written for the couples themselves who are in these challenging relationships and not their parents, which is why I have written this book. Regardless of whether you are in such a relationship yourself or the parents of someone who is, the best source of information today for just about any need can be found on the Internet.

Here are just some of the many resources that you can find that provide useful information, material, and support groups for people of every religion, race, and gender who are part of an interfaith, interracial, or same gender family:

1. www.interfaithresources.com brings together a wide range of books and materials that support universal spiritual ideals.

2. Dovetail Institute for Interfaith Family Resources, www.dovetailinstitute. org, is a resource for intermarriage, interfaith family life, and raising children interfaith.

3. www.interfaithfamily.com provides helpful, welcoming articles about interfaith families exploring Jewish life.

4. www.interfaithcalendar.org provides information on the primary sacred times of world religions.

5. www.skylightpaths.com is a publisher of many books that cater to interfaith families and interfaith education.

6. Creating interfaith community, NAIN, the North American Interfaith Network www.nain.org

7. www.pluralism.org is a project of Harvard University in Boston which explores emerging trends in interfaith life.

8. www.interfaithcommunity.org is a fifty-year-old interfaith network that publishes a journal and sponsors programs on interfaith marriage, families, and community.

9. www.beliefnet.com covers all aspects of religion and spirituality including interfaith relationships.

10. www.interchurchfamilies.org has articles on interfaith families and the challenges and opportunities they face.

11. www.tworoadsonepath.com is a Web site to help intermarried couples find the common goals of what is good and true between them.

12. www.mcmarraige.org/uk is a Web site designed as a Muslim/Christian support group with a wide variety of resources.

13. www.interfaithweddings.com is a resource for interfaith weddings and to understand the symbolism of various ceremonies.

14. www.religioustolerance.org is a Web site that explores interfaith, interracial, and same gender relationships.

15. www.interracialdatingcentral.com is a blog about intermarriages of all kinds and the issues that emerge from each.

16. www.mixedfolks.com is a Web site celebrating diversity of all kinds with extensive resources.

17. www.multiracial.com is a Web site of multiracial activism.

18. www.half-jewish.net is a Web site for adult children and other descendants of Jews intermarried to people of other faiths and cultures.

19. www.joi.org the Jewish Outreach Institute provides materials and support groups for people involved with interfaith and interracial marriages.

20. www.interracial.voice.com has books and articles on interracial relationships.

21. *The Interracial Family Circle* communicates information, ideas, and concerns to all who support a family of more than one race. IFC, P.O. Box 53290, Washington, D.C., 20009.

22. *Pareveh, The Alliance for the Adult Children of Jewish-Gentile Intermarriage* is an organization that provides information and support to adults who have grown up in Jewish/non-Jewish interfaith families. 3628 Windom Place, N.W., Washington, D.C., 20008.

23. www.pflag.org is a resource for parents, families, and friends of lesbians and gays with local chapters throughout the world and resources through their Web site.

A FINAL WORD

When all is said and done, perhaps the most important message of this book is this: There are some differences that you cannot love away, but you can always show love anyway. Your job as a parent is not to pass judgment on your children's relationships or how they are raising their children. Your job is to love your children, to love your grandchildren, to demonstrate love and acceptance and support by what you say and what you do, and how you continue to welcome them into your heart and your life.

Someone once said that having a child is choosing to have your heart run around outside your body for the rest of your life. Whenever my wife says goodbye to our daughter, she hugs her and tells her she loves her, and then adds, "Take care of my heart." That is what being a parent is really all about. The challenge of parenting is knowing that, ultimately, your adult children are out of your control, living lives of their own design, creating their own path, forming the foundation of their own future. Your choice is to watch from the sidelines as the parade passes by or seize the opportunity to jump into line and march along to the drumbeat of the music they are creating.

The purpose of this book has been to help you as you journey along this path of self-discovery and to share with you the benefit of my personal experiences working with and counseling intermarried families. Intermarried family life has its own set of challenges and opportunities, with triumphs and tragedies, celebrations, and heartache. The more you can open your heart and spirit to embrace differences and diversity, perceiving them as gifts and opportunities, the closer your relationships will be with your children and grandchildren, as well as the life partner and extended families of your children as well.

You do not get to make your children's choices for them. You can only choose how *you* will act when their choices are already made. What you do and what you say each time you are confronted with a new challenge will not only define the quality of your relationship with your children and grandchildren, in many ways it will end up defining who you are in your own eyes as well.

That is why my goal has always been to help you have the most loving, caring, nurturing, supportive relationship you can with the people you love.

My final advice is this: Follow your heart and always remember that the most important things in life are not *things*, they are the people you are privileged to cherish each day. Hold them close and give them the gift of your love regardless of the choices that they make along life's journey, for the journey itself is ultimately all that we've got to share.

NOTES

CHAPTER ONE: WHERE IT ALL STARTS—UNDERSTANDING INTERFAITH DATING

1. From www.adherents.com, a collection of over 43,000 adherent statistics and religious geography citations, updated at the time of this book's printing.

2. James Baldwin, *Notes of a Native Son* (New York: Doubleday Books, 1963).

CHAPTER FOUR: UNDERSTANDING THE ROLE OF YOUR OWN VALUES AND BELIEFS

1. Beware that written correspondence can often convey unintended opinions or attitudes that cannot be controlled by tone of voice or inflection or even body language the way one can in a face-to-face conversation, making it often less effective than one anticipates. That said, it is better to communicate at all, than not to attempt to express one's feelings.

2. Viktor Frankl, *Man's Search for Meaning* (Boston: Beacon Press, 2006).

CHAPTER SEVEN: UNDERSTANDING THE CHALLENGES OF INTERFAITH LIFE

1. A Mezuzah is a small scroll in a case that contains a passage from the Bible that includes the commandment to "write them [commandments] on the doorposts of your house."

CHAPTER TEN: THE MORE WE KNOW THE LESS WE FEAR

1. Statistics derived from www.adherents.com, a collection of over 43,000 adherent statistics and religious geography citations, updated at the time of this book's printing.
2. Ibid.
3. Ibid.
4. Ibid.
5. Ibid.
6. Ibid.
7. Ibid.

CHAPTER ELEVEN: WHEN THINGS DON'T WORK
OUT—CHALLENGES OF SEPARATION AND DIVORCE

1. Every state has its own divorce laws. You can check sites such as these to get information on divorce mediators. Always check credentials and references before hiring anyone, and do not fail to get legal advice before making any decisions! http://www.mediate.com/divorcemediators/ or http://www.divorcenet.com/states/

INDEX

About the Author

STEVEN CARR REUBEN was ordained as a rabbi in 1976. He is the author of numerous books, including *But How Will You Raise the Children? A Guide to Interfaith Marriage, Raising Jewish Children in a Contemporary World, Making Interfaith Marriage Work, Raising Ethical Children*, and *Children of Character—Leading Your Children to Ethical Choices in Everyday Life*. In addition, he contributes to a wide variety of publications as an author and composer. He serves as Senior Rabbi of Kehillat Israel Reconstructionist Congregation in Pacific Palisades and is past president of the Board of Rabbis of Southern California.